Mike Phillips'
The Art Of Detailing

Proper Techniques, Tips and Tricks to Achieve a Show Car Shine

Written by: Mike Phillips

Autogeek.net

www.Autogeek.net
A Division of Palm Beach Motoring Accessories

ISBN   978-0-615-54046-7

Printed and bound in the U.S.A.

Printed by:

Commercial Printers, Inc.
Fort Lauderdale, FL
877-423-8492 ext 235

Acknowledgements

We are grateful to all of you that contributed to the development of this manual, provided technical information and/or certain pictures and illustrations.

Important

Term, conditions, features, service offerings, prices, and hours referenced in this manual are subject to change without notice. We at Palm Beach Motoring Accessories, Inc. are committed to bringing you great printed and online services through Autogeek.net and AutogeekOnline.net. Occasionally, we may decide to update our online services and change our service offerings, so please check www.Autogeek.net for the latest information, including pricing and availability, on our products and services.

Palm Beach Motoring Accessories, Inc.
7744 SW Jack James Road
Stuart, FL 34997

www.autogeek.net
www.autogeekonline.net
www.palmbeachmotoring.net

1-800-869-3011

I wrote this book to help people better understand how to polish their car's paint. Specifically, how to use what we generically refer to as a dual action (DA) polisher to achieve a show car quality finish, the kind of finish that looks deep and wet, as though it were just painted. The DA polisher is the easiest polisher to learn how to use and master. It provides an easier way to transition from doing all your paint polishing work the old-fashioned way (by hand) to machine polishing, which always produces better results, more efficiently.

For me, polishing paint is the fun part. Swapping out engines, replacing brakes, even simple tune-ups and oil changes are the dirty routine things. While important and necessary, these aren't what most people consider fun and are better described as just plain old knuckle-busting work.

On the other hand, spending a Saturday afternoon washing and waxing your pride and joy is a time to relax and unwind on the weekend, while performing preventative maintenance and having fun. The key to having fun is getting good results. This is where knowledge comes into the equation. You see, modern clearcoat paints tend to be hard, thin and delicate in that they are easily dulled and scratched. For these reasons, it's important to have a little knowledge about the paint you're working on, the products you're using and most importantly, the process. The paint polishing process is that in which you are actually using the DA polisher to remove defects like swirls and scratches to take a diamond in the rough and turn it into a glistening gemstone.

This is where the magic happens. Perfecting your technique, with help from the information contained inside this how-to book and reinforced by interaction on the AutogeekOnline.net discussion forum, will ensure you get professional results the first time and every time. The members of our discussion forum and I are always available as a resource to see you through to success in your garage. You can even take what you learn from this how-to book and start a detailing business, earning money either part time, or if you wish, full time.

When it comes to washing and waxing your car, there is nothing more disappointing than to wipe off the final application of wax, only to

Introduction

reveal a finish that only looks marginally better than before you started. This how-to book will ensure this never happens to you.

Different strokes for different folks

Some of you may look at your car merely as a means of transportation. You are mostly interested in learning how to best protect your investment. Some of you may look at your car as an extension of your personality; you see it as an escape from the daily grind of living in a complicated world. You have a passion for polishing paint and you take it very seriously.

You want to know everything you can about the products and process you're using and how to get the best results possible from your time, money, and efforts. The term "second best" is not in your vocabulary.

Polishing paint is an art form

To achieve a flawless finish, you need to know a lot more than what the directions on the label of a can or bottle of

wax can tell you. Like the line "wax-on, wax-off" from the movie *The Karate Kid*, there's more to it than simply wiping wax on and off.

You need to combine knowledge and experience, as well as the right products and tools with the human elements of care and passion. You need to genuinely care about what you're doing and have a passion for the craft. When all these things come together, polishing paint becomes an art form as you truly create a work of art.

Information is the true secret to a show car finish

I believe you will find the information in this how-to book to be very different from anything else you have ever read in any other book, magazine article or even on any websites related to the topic of car detailing.

Over the years, I've helped thousands of people with their different paint polishing projects. While demonstrating at car shows or teaching classes, I'd explain how paint works, how polishing products

work and the different types of procedures that go with them. Afterwards, I would always be asked the same question that usually goes like this:

Hey Mike, is any of this information written down anywhere?
Until now, the answer was always "no".

Most of the information shared in this book is from my own experiences, gained from polishing just about every type of surface under the sun, in every imaginable condition.

Some of the information shared in this book comes from people I have met over the years including painters, detailers, do-it-yourselfers and the hundreds of thousands of friends I've made on detailing discussion forums and who have attended my detailing classes.

I'm confident that after reading this book, you will be ready to tackle any detailing project that comes your way.

Let the polishing begin!
Mike Phillips

Index

Early painting technology

◉ Paint History

Karl Benz, of Mercedes-Benz, was awarded the first patent for what we call the automobile in 1885. However, it wasn't until Henry Ford introduced the Model T in 1908 that the general public began the transition from riding a horse to driving a car.

It was a decade later before enough people had purchased a car for it to become established as the new mode of transportation. If we use the general year of 1910, only 2 years after the Model T was introduced, and fast forward to today (as I write this, it's the year 2011), in general terms, we've only been driving cars for approximately 100 years out of the entire known history of human existence. In context, we've only been driving cars for a very short time.

From this...

To this...

Car Paint Overview

To this...

For the largest portion of this 100 year history of the car, most of this time our cars had single stage paints. It's only been since the 1980s that car manufacturers starting switching over to the modern basecoat/clearcoat paints.

When cars were first introduced in the late 1800s and early 1900s, it was a new industry and as such, there were no specific manufacturers of car paints (because cars didn't exist).

Car manufacturers borrowed coatings from the furniture industry. This would include shellac, varnish and lacquer paints. Early cars used a lot of wood, so these coatings would prevent the wood from rotting and the steel from rusting. As the car manufacturing industry grew, paint companies introduced paints specifically for the needs of auto manufacturing assembly lines (high production output) and for the specific needs of vehicles themselves. This would include characteristics to both protect the surface from deterioration and to provide a beautiful finish.

🔴🔴 Basecoat/Clearcoat Paint Technology

Most cars manufactured from the 1990s through today have what's called a basecoat/clearcoat paint system. The top coat is a clear layer of paint which provides gloss and durability to the basecoat layer, which is the pigmented layer of paint under the clear layer that you and I see as the actual color of the paint.

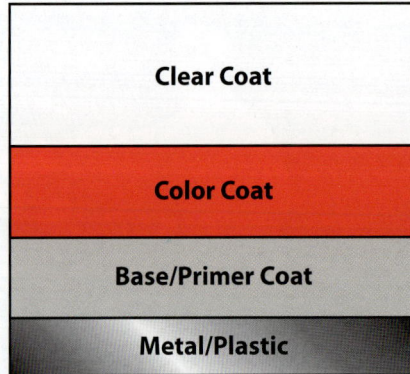

🔴🔴 Not A Miracle Coating

Some people think the clear layer is some kind of miracle coating that doesn't need to be routinely polished or waxed. That's simply not true. The top clear layer of paint is just that - it's paint with no pigment, but it's still paint.

🔴🔴 Not An Invisible Force Field

The clear layer of paint is not an invisible force field that repels everything and anything that comes near it. Clearcoat paints still need to be maintained just like old fashioned single stage paints. They need to be washed, clayed, polished and protected on a regular schedule to maintain a showroom new appearance.

🔴🔴 Paint Is Thin

The factory paint on new cars, trucks and SUVs is thin. How thin? Generally speaking, the top coat layer, the layer you can polish and wax, averages around 2 mils thick. Let me help you to understand just how thin this is by using a simple Post-it Note.

In the picture to the right, I'm measuring a test shim that comes with this tool to ensure accuracy. The tool is ready to use out of the box and does not need to be calibrated. But, if you want to calibrate it just to make sure, it's real simple. Click the two side buttons three times at the same time

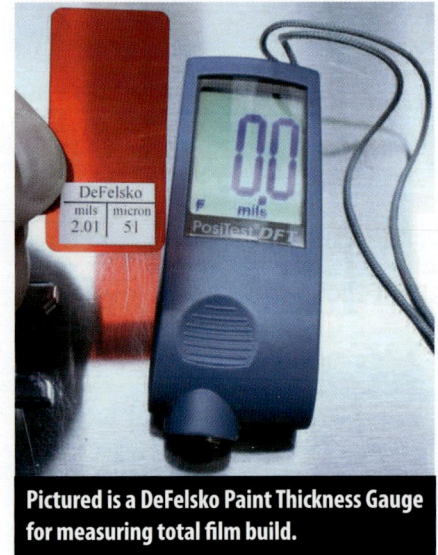

Pictured is a DeFelsko Paint Thickness Gauge for measuring total film build.

and it will automatically zero out.

After you do this recalibration, you'll want to test the measuring accuracy and you do this using a control or object with a known measurement. This is what the test shims are for.

There are a lot of paint thickness gauges on the market and they range greatly in price. But like any quality tool, you get what you pay for. This is called a 3% gauge, which means it's very accurate. Most gauges are 5% gauges and while the difference between 3% and 5% may seem minimal, when you're working on a coating that's already thin to start

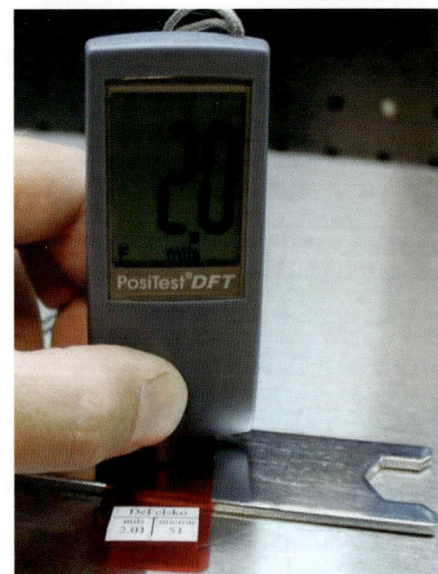

with, accuracy is of the utmost importance.

What you see (pictured on page 6) is a reading of 2.0 mils after I recalibrated the gauge. After recalibrating it, I measured a test shim that measures 2.01 mils from the factory. The 1 in the 2.01 stands for one ten thousandth of a millimeter. This test gauge, like most test gauges, doesn't read to the ten thousandth of a millimeter measurement. My point is this paint thickness gauge is calibrated and incredibly accurate. Here, I'm measuring a standard Post-it Note. The reason I'm measuring a Post-it Note is because most of you reading this will have access to one. I took 5-6 measurements and the average was 3.0 mils.

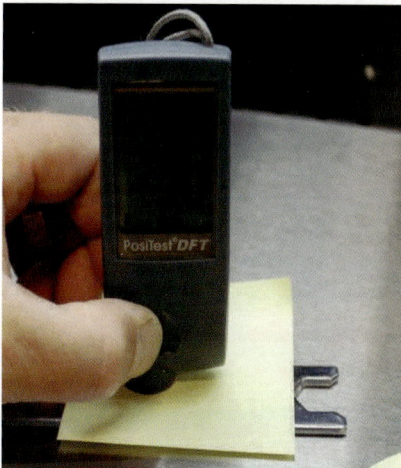

Keep in mind that the average clearcoat is approximately 2.0 mils. I'm talking just about the clear layer, not the color coat, or primer or e-coat, etc. The clear layer is the part you can work on and the coating you need to take care of in order to maintain your finish over the service life of the car.

The next time you have a Post-it Note, feel it between your fingers and understand that the thickness of paper that you're feeling is thicker than the average clear layer of paint on a modern car, truck or SUV. In other words, paint is thin!

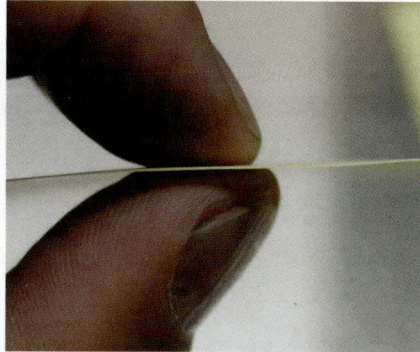

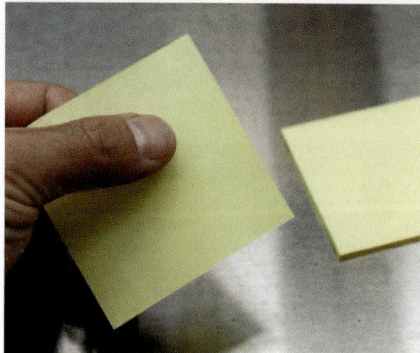

With this is mind, there's not a lot of room to make mistakes. Hopefully, understanding how thin your car's paint is will drive home the importance of obtaining knowledge before working on your paint. Understanding how thin your car's clearcoat finish is also drives home the points made in this article:

📖 *Use the least aggressive product to get the job done*

Paint Is Hard

Compared to paints from just a few decades ago, modern basecoat/clearcoat paints tend to be harder than traditional single stage paints. It's this hardness factor that makes paint more difficult to work on anytime you or I go out into our garage to polish paint.

All my detailing classes start with a Power Point presentation in which knowledge is obtained before progressing towards hands-on training. You would never go to a heart surgeon who has never been

to medical school, would you? In the same way, before you go out and start working on your car's hard and precious, thin paint, it's a good idea to learn a little bit about modern paint technology.

Difficult To Work By Hand

From the time of the Model T to the cars of the 1970s, it was easy to work on your car by hand and get pretty good results with no problems because the paints were softer and easier to polish.

All you have to do to see why machine polishing is a trend that cannot be stopped is to go out into your garage with a modern compound or polish and try to remove swirls by hand and leave a better looking finish than when you started.

As most people find out how much work this is and how frustrating it can be, the next step in the natural progression is to consider using a polisher.

The Practical Differences Between Single Stage Paints And Clearcoat Paints

I've worked on thousands of cars with single stage paints and have conducted many extreme makeovers in which the project car had single stage paint. Below, I'll outline some of the practical differences between single stage paints and modern clearcoat paints.

Clearcoat paints were introduced to production cars in the USA starting in the early 1980s. Since that time, technology has continually improved to create automotive paint systems that will last a long time as well as provide a beautiful finish with great gloss, clarity and shine.

The oldest factory clearcoat finish I've

Car Paint Overview

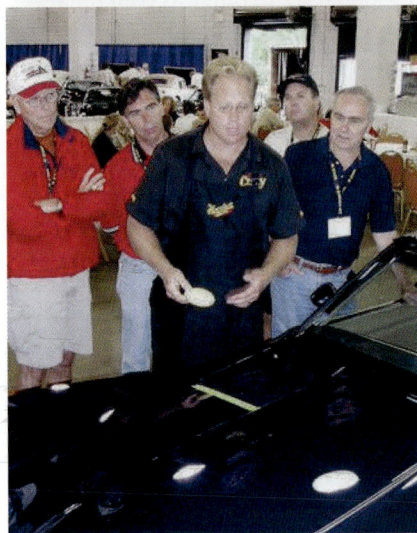

ever worked on was an all original 1980 Corvette when I was the guest speaker for the 2007 National Corvette Restoration Society at their National Convention in Boston, Massachusetts.

At their national convention, I gave a presentation on machine polishing paint. Afterwards, the owner of an all original 1980 Corvette (the owner purchased this Corvette new and has never had the car repainted) asked me to show him how to remove swirls. Since the owner had not yet progressed to machine polishing, I first demonstrated how to remove swirls by hand. Afterwards, I

demonstrated how to remove swirls using the Porter Cable DA polisher.

The clear used on this 1980 Corvette was soft and it was incredibly easy to remove swirls and scratches by hand or machine. Anyone with detailing experience that has worked on the clearcoat paint systems being used on new Corvettes knows that the current paint technology being used is very hard. This just demonstrates that since the introduction of modern clearcoat paint systems in the early 1980s, paint technology is continually changing and improving.

The next oldest original factory-sprayed basecoat/clearcoat finish I've buffed out is this 1982 Corvette, which is still in very good condition with no signs of clearcoat failure. The point is I've been teaching machine polishing classes since 1988 and had the opportunity to work on paint systems from the 1920s to a brand new 2012 Mercedes-Benz CLS63 AMG. I've seen the changes in paint technology first-hand as both

a detailer and an instructor for the craft of detailing cars and one of the primary changes I've seen take place is the hardness factor.

The hardness factor is both a good thing and a challenge as these new high tech paints are incredibly durable as far as a coating goes, but they are also incredibly hard to work on by hand.

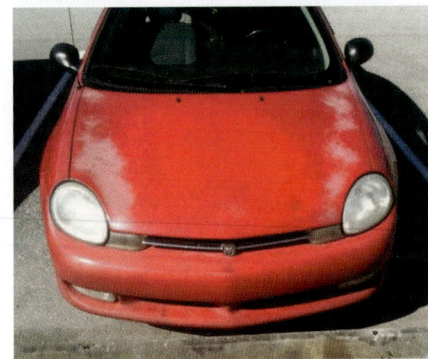

Clearcoat Failure

Since clearcoats have become the standard for automotive finishes, we now have entire generations of people that have only owned cars with basecoat/clearcoat paint systems; they have never owned, nor worked on a car that has a single stage paint system.
From time to time, a new member will join our forum and ask for help removing oxidation from their car's finish, not knowing that the problem

Mike Phillips' - The Art of Detailing

with their clearcoat is not oxidation, but is in fact clearcoat failure.

Clearcoat paints, when exposed to too much sun over time and without proper care, will deteriorate. This occurs throughout the entire matrix or thickness of the clear layer of paint, meaning you can't fix it by abrading the surface. This is called clearcoat failure and the only honest fix is to repaint the affected panels or the entire car.

Swirls - The Number One Complaint

Swirls are among the most common defects present in clearcoat finishes. Besides being ugly and unsightly, these scratches make the surface hazy and this dulls your view of the color coat under the clearcoat.

Swirls can be removed because they are topical. Like oxidation, they are in the upper surface of the layer of clear paint. All you have to do is use a compound or an abrasive polish and remove a little paint from the surface, which will act to level or flatten out the surface again, removing the swirls.

Single Stage Paints = Oxidation

Single stage paints tend to oxidize very easily. They still get swirls and scratches, but in the real world the

Before removing oxidation

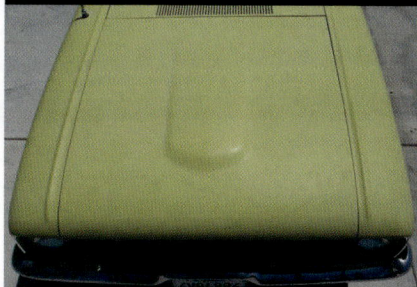

After removing oxidation

noticeable problem is the dullness and fading caused by oxidation. True oxidation is easy to remove, making restoring a show car shine is easy.

Clearcoat Paints = Swirls And Scratches

The problems with clearcoat paints are swirls and scratches, not oxidation. Clearcoats will oxidize very slowly and only if they are completely neglected. If after reading all the above you're wondering, *If single stage paints tend to be more user-friendly to work on for the average person, why do car manufacturers use basecoat/clearcoat paint systems?*

Good question!

The primary reason the Original Equipment Manufacturer (OEM) industry switched paint systems was due to new laws and regulations from the Environmental Protection Agency and other government regulatory agencies.

The new basecoat/clearcoat paint systems emit less VOCs (Volatile Organic Compounds) into the

Clearcoat finish before removing swirls

Clearcoat finish after removing swirls

air, making them safer for the environment. Another benefit this technology offers is, due to the hardness factor as well as dramatically improved resin technology, modern finishes will tend to last longer over the service life of a car as compared to the time period a single stage paint would last on new cars built before the 1980s.

Paint Hardness Or Softness - Polishable & Polishability

Most people talk about paint being either hard or soft. Better words for describing the hardness or softness of paint are polishable and polishability.

- *Polishable* - Capable of being polished
- *Polishabilty* - To the degree a surface or coating can be polished

Polishable, in the context that I use it, refers to how easy or difficult it is to remove below-surface defects from the paint.

Polishable is a range between:
- *Too Hard* - Extremely difficult to level paint in an effort to remove below-surface defects.

Car Paint Overview

- *Too Soft - So soft that just the act of wiping the paint with a clean, soft microfiber polishing towel can instill swirls and scratches.*

The best of both worlds is a paint system somewhere between these two extremes. This would be a paint system the average person can work on.

By this, I mean a paint system soft enough that defects can be removed, but hard enough to resist scratching through normal maintenance procedures while still providing long service life.

Hard Paint Or Soft paint?

When you go to work on your car in your garage, the best thing you can do is what we call a test spot. This is where you'll test the products, pads and procedures to see if they'll remove the defects and restore a show car finish. This is called your paint polishing process.

This usually means starting out with the least aggressive products you have available. If your test spots reveals that your first choice of products is not working neither effectively nor fast enough, you can always try again. For your next test spot, try substituting a more aggressive product, pad or both.

Once you determine a combination of products that will remove the defects and restore a show car shine to your expectations, then all you have to do is duplicate this process over the rest of the car. Your test spot will prove your paint polishing process works and this will give you the confidence to tackle the rest of the car.

Asking on a discussion forum whether the paint on your car is hard or soft can be a good way to get other people's opinions on the matter. If they have the same car with the same factory original paint, then their opinion can be even more valuable.

That said, the best way to find out is to go out into your garage and try a couple of products first-hand and find out for yourself how difficult or easy it is to remove defects from the paint.

You need experience

The more cars you work on, the more experience you'll gain with a wider range of paint systems. You'll soon be able to gauge if the paint on a car is hard or soft after doing few test spots. The harder the paint, the more difficult it will be to remove swirls, scratches and water spots. The softer the paint, the easier it will be.

Nothing beats first-hand experience. Your personal skill level will have a huge influence on your success or failure and can actually mislead you regarding polishability of the paint. If you're new to machine polishing, you're still honing your skills and technique, meaning removing swirls and scratches out of soft paint may be difficult.

I know the above to be true after almost two decades of teaching novice detailers how to detail cars, and more specifically, how to use a DA polisher. Technique is everything, even more important than the products and pads you're using.

In order to really know if the paint on any car is hard or soft, you must build experience.

So, get experienced!

Go out into your garage and do some testing on your paint. Dial in a process that works to your satisfaction and lock into your memory how the paint reacted, so you can draw from this the next time you're working on a different detailing project.

Paint Systems

There are about a dozen major automotive paint manufacturers in the world that supply paint systems to both the OEM and refinishing industry.

Paint systems vary

Different car manufacturers and body shops use different paint systems. These can differ and because technology is always changing, paint systems from even a single paint manufacturer can vary greatly.

Each time you work on a car, you're working on a specific paint system. Because the chemistry between paint systems can be very different, polishing characteristics can vary greatly.

Even identical models from any particular car manufacturer can have paints that are completely different (harder or softer) from year to year. Try to avoid generalization in regards to paint hardness. Instead, test each car you work on and gain experience.

Paint Type Affects Paint Hardness

Clearcoats
The hardness of a clearcoat finish is determined primarily by the type of resin used to make the paint and other factors such as catalysts, hardeners, solvents, and other additives as well as the drying or baking process used to cure the paint.

Single stage
The hardness of single stage paint is also determined primarily by the type of resin and other ingredients used to make the paint, as well as the type of pigment used to give the paint color. Different pigments can be soft or hard, altering the overall hardness of the finish.

How To Test For Single Stage Or Basecoat/ Clearcoat Paint Systems

Chances are very good that if you're working on a car less than 10 years old, you're working on a basecoat/ clearcoat finish. Even though the majority of car manufacturers since the mid-1980s come with a clearcoat finish, I still get asked how to check.

Here's a simple way to test the paint on your car to find out if it's a single stage paint or a basecoat/clearcoat finish.

Easy to see...

With a true single stage paint system, it's very apparent because you'll easily see the colored paint residue building up on the face of your buffing pads.

To test for a single stage paint system, try to find a white colored polish (if you're working on any kind of pigmented or colored paint) and a light or white colored applicator pad.

Pour some polish onto a clean applicator pad.

Use an ample amount of polish for plenty of lubrication as you're going to want to push firmly if no visible oxidation is present (as was the case

on this 1956 Pontiac Starchief). Then using firm pressure, apply the polish in an overlapping circular motion to a small section of paint.

Confirmed Single Stage Paint

As you can see, red pigment is coming off the car and onto the applicator pad, so we're working on red single stage paint. If the pad would have remained yellow with some white polish on it, this would be an indicator of a basecoat/clearcoat paint system.

◖◗ Tinted Clears

Some car manufacturers use a tinted clear for the top coat of paint over the clearcoat finish. The car has a basecoat/clearcoat finish, but the very last layer of clear paint has color added for a special effect. This can be a little misleading and make someone think they're working on a single stage paint when in fact they're not. The biggest visual indicator of a tinted clear is when you test as shown above, or when you're machine buffing the paint, you will only see a little color coming off the surface.

◖◗ How To Test For Single Stage White Paint

Testing white paint can be just a little trickier, because so many abrasive polishes are white in color. This makes it hard to see if the test results are white paint coming off, or just the color of the polish.

Tips for testing white paint
If you're testing white paint, try to use a colored polish with a dark colored

cloth (so you can confirm that you're removing white paint and not just seeing the color of the polish or the color of the cloth). Most people have old t-shirts that are blue, red or black that can be cut up for testing purposes. *Pinnacle Advanced Finishing Polish* not only works fantastic as a finishing polish, but it's also gray in color.

Interestingly, it's possible to find white single stage paints on newer vehicles manufactured in the last 20 years. Due to the ingredients used in white single stage paint, it is very hard and durable and will hold up to exposure to the elements as well as normal wear and tear without a clear layer of paint over it. It normally costs less to spray a car using a single stage paint system rather than a basecoat/clearcoat system in a production environment due to reduced costs in labor, time and materials.

Mismatched panels
I buffed out a 1956 Rolls Royce a few years ago and it had been repainted using a basecoat/clearcoat paint system. I tested on the hood and confirmed it was a basecoat/clearcoat paint system. Like I recommend in this how-to book, I started buffing on the highest point of the car and then moved downward and tackled the hood. Next up was the trunk lid. After buffing one section of the trunk lid, I discovered by the volume of white paint on the face of my buffing pad that the entire car was clearcoated except the trunk lid, which had single stage paint.

So it's completely possible to find cars like this with two types of paint that from standing distance away, can look as though they have the same type of paint on each panel, only to find out that some are mismatched.

Lesson learned
The lesson here is if you're in doubt, simply perform the aforementioned test and find out for sure. §

Washing Your Car

Washing Your Car - The Most Important Step

Washing is the most important step there is when it comes to machine polishing your car. You need the car to be surgically clean for two primary reasons:

1. To properly evaluate the surface
Whether you want to create a true show car finish or just wash and wax your car to maintain the factory finish, you need to evaluate the condition of the paint. In order to do this, it needs to be thoroughly clean and dry. When evaluating the condition of the paint, you're going to inspect it visually (in good lighting) and you're going to feel the paint with your sense of touch. For both of these steps, it's vital that the paint is completely free of contaminants.

2. To ensure all loose dirt, road grime and any abrasive particulates are removed
To make sure you don't put swirls into the paint while you're machine buffing, start by making sure there's no dirt or any abrasives particles on the car.

Two Approaches To Washing Your Car

The idea behind washing your car is to remove any built-up dirt, road grime or other loose surface contaminants from the exterior finish, trim, windows and other components.

There are two very different approaches to washing your car. The condition of your car's paint is what determines how you approach the washing process.

1. **Aggressive Approach** - Washing before a detailing session (neglected paint)

2. **Careful Approach** - Washing after a detailing session (show car finish)

Let's take a look at each approach…

Aggressive Approach - Washing Before Detailing

When washing a neglected finish, the priority is getting the car as clean as possible (not being as careful as possible). It's okay to wash a car in neglected condition a little more aggressively to get it surgically clean, because any defects you instill during the washing process will be removed during the correction steps.

Your goal is to ensure that you've removed as much loose dirt from the car as possible so that dirt particles won't enter into the claying step or any of the machine polishing procedures.

Air currents

Spinning buffing pads create air currents on the surface. It's possible for loose dirt particles to be drawn between the paint and the pad, potentially inflicting swirls and scratches throughout the entire finish. For this reason, it's vitally important to thoroughly wash and rinse the car and clean your pad often. Inspect paint that you've polished to catch any problems as soon as possible.

I can tell you from experience that if you do a stellar job of washing the car, your chances of having any problems are almost zero.

Careful Approach - Washing After A Detailing Session

If the finish on your car is in excellent condition, then you want and need to increase the level of care used while washing the car. Your priority is to avoid instilling any swirls, scratching or marring back into the paint. Anything that touches it must be clean, soft and gentle. While washing, you must focus on the task at hand and use expert technique.

Four Ways To Wash Your Car

There are four popular approaches to washing and cleaning cars. Below are descriptions of the four different approaches, followed by the products they can be used with.

1. Normal Car Wash
   A normal car wash is simply the more

1960 Ford Ranchero - Neglected, oxidized finish. This picture was taken right before I washed it in preparation for a complete multi-step machine paint polishing process.

traditional method of using a hose and bucket to wash your car. This system works well, but it also uses a lot of water and in some geographical areas, this may not be allowed.

2. Waterless Car Wash
   A waterless car wash is a high lubricity pre-mixed spray detailer used to heavily saturate a panel. The panel is then carefully wiped to remove any dirt or road grime. The key to working safely with a waterless car wash is to use plenty of clean, microfiber polishing towels. After one becomes contaminated, switch to a clean towel so you don't simply transfer dirt removed from one panel to another.

3. Rinseless Car Wash
   A rinseless car wash is a cross between a normal car wash and a waterless car wash. Like a normal car wash, you're still going to use water, but only a couple of gallons. Like a waterless wash, instead of rinsing your wash solution off, you'll work panel by panel, wiping each panel to a dry shine using microfiber drying towels like the Cobra Guzzler.

With a Rinseless Wash, you'll use dramatically less water but still be flushing the panel with plenty of high lubricity wash solution to leave

behind a scratch-free finish.

4. Spray Detailers
   Spray Detailers are for removing:
- Light Dust
- Fingerprints
- Smudges

As long as your car only has a light accumulation of dust, you can clean or wash your car using a spray detailer.

How To Use A Normal Car Wash

Tools Needed

- Car Wash Soap
- Wheel Cleaner
- Tire Cleaner
- Wash Mitt, Sponge or Brush
- Wheel Brush
- Tire Brush
- Drying Towels or Chamois
- Spray Hose
- One 5-Gallon Bucket - Optional use the Two Bucket Method
- Grit Guard Inserts

Buckets
A good wash bucket holds up to 5 gallons of car wash solution. You don't necessarily want to fill the bucket with 5 gallons of water. Instead, use 3-4 gallons of water,

Washing Your Car

1956 Ford F150 - Show Car Quality Finish. This picture was taken right after I machine polished and machine waxed the paint. To prevent re-instilling swirls and scratches into the black mirror finish this truck must be washed and dried as carefully as humanly possible using the best car washing products that can be obtained. "Best Truck" Award at 2009 Grand National Roadster Show.

Single Grit Guard Insert

Dual Grit Guard Insert - Twice the distance to keep removed dirt off your wash mitt

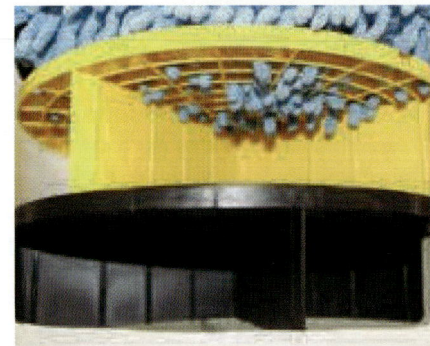

leaving some room at the top of the bucket. You want more than 1 or 2 gallons because you want an adequate volume of water to enable you to move your wash mitt, sponge or brush around to allow gathered dirt to loosen and fall off to the bottom of the bucket.

Single Bucket Wash Method
The single bucket wash method is the most common way people wash their car and it's pretty straight forward. Get a clean bucket and add about 4 gallons of water. Then, measure and add your car wash soap and mix thoroughly.

💬 *My Comment...*
I use the single bucket method to wash wheels and tires.

Two Bucket Wash Method
In this method, one bucket contains your wash solution and the second bucket contains clean rinse water. To use the two bucket method, gather some wash solution and use it to wash a single panel. Instead of placing your mitt back into the soapy water bucket, you first rinse the mitt in the clean water bucket

to remove the majority of dirt. After rinsing, squeeze a little water out and then start the process over again by dipping the mitt into the soap solution bucket.

💬 *My Comment...*
For washing the body panels of a car, I always use the two bucket method.

Grit Guard Inserts
My good friend Doug Lamb invented these back in 1989 and I've been using one ever since I was introduced to these ingenious and beneficial tools. The Grit Guard Insert is as the name implies - it is a plastic insert that fits into the bottom of a 5-gallon bucket that will trap the dirt that comes off your wash mitt. The design includes a plastic grill that dirt and other abrasive particles can fall past to the bottom of the bucket. The grill is suspended about two inches off the bottom of the bucket by four vanes. These vanes help to trap dirt particles by preventing the water at the bottom of the bucket from swirling around. This stops dirt particles from rising back above the grill where they could potentially get onto your wash mitt.

💬 *My Comment...*
Once you use a Grit Guard insert and see all the dirt it traps onto the bottom of the bucket, you'll never want to wash a car without one again.

Best Practice
Don't *scrub* your car's paint. By this,

I mean you only need to make a few passes over each square inch of a panel. This will loosen the bond any dirt or road grime has on the paint, allowing it to freely rinse off.

People watching

If you watch the average person wash their car, you'll see they don't focus on the task at hand. This leads to rubbing their wash mitt back and forth, over and over again to the same area. There's no reason to do this. If there was dirt on the surface and you did effectively loosen it, rubbing your wash mitt back and forth over and over again just grinds the dirt into the paint. This needlessly instills swirls and scratches into the paint. Focus on the task at hand and only rub your wash mitt over each section for a few passes and then move onto new territory.

Tips & Techniques

For as long as I can remember, everyone that writes about how to wash a car says the same thing, *Start washing at the top and work your way down*

Allow me to share my method…

Start at the bottom and then move to the top

Start by washing and rinsing your car's wheels and tires. When rinsing your wheels and tires, you can't avoid getting water splatter on the surrounding paint. If you still have to wash the body panels of your car, this won't matter.

You don't have to repeat any steps - this saves you time. The order in which you wash your car is relative. It doesn't matter if you start up high or down low - the goal is to get the car clean while avoiding water spots, which my approach helps to prevent. The old-fashioned approach means moving incredibly fast or continually re-wetting the car, otherwise you risk

instilling water spots into the paint.

🔆 Step By Step How-To Wash Your Car

In this order,

1. *Wash wheels and tires*
2. *Wash car body - Start at the top and work down*
3. *Dry the car body panels and glass*
4. *Dry wheels and tires - Use dedicated towels*

🚶 *1. Wash Wheels And Tires*

Personal Safety First: Wear appropriate safety gear, including safety glasses and protective gloves.

Make sure the wheel is cool to the touch and work in the shade out of direct sunlight. Never spray water on hot wheels or brakes.

1. Wash one wheel and tire at a time.

2. Spray wheels and tires first with a strong blast of water to remove any loose brake dust, dirt and road grime.

3. Spray wheel cleaner onto wheel. *Follow manufacturers recommendations for dwell time to allow cleaner to penetrate and loosen brake dust, road grime and dirt.*

4. Agitate with a wheel brush that is safe and appropriate for the type of wheel.
   - *Optional:* Use a [Daytona Speed Master Wheel Brush](#) to clean behind the wheel, hard to reach areas and intricate wheel designs.
   - *Optional:* Use a [Lug Nut Brush](#) to clean lug nuts and the barrel around the lug nuts.

5. Spray wheel with strong blast of water.

6. Spray tire with tire cleaner. *Follow manufacturers recommendations for dwell time to allow cleaner to penetrate and loosen road grime and dirt*

7. Agitate tire with a tire brush

8. Spray tire with a strong blast of water and then re-spray both wheel and tire.

9. Repeat to rest of wheels and tires.

Wheel safety

Use a wheel cleaner that's safe for your type of wheels so you don't cause damage. In order to choose the right wheel cleaner, you need to know what your wheels are either coated with or the material they're made out. If you don't know what your wheels are made out of or coated with, contact the manufacturer.

Match the right wheel cleaner to the wheel

When you work on a set of wheels, you're either working on:
- A material
- A coating
- Sometimes both

An example of working directly on a material would be working on uncoated, polished aluminum wheels. If you own uncoated, polished aluminum wheels, the entire wheel is made from aluminum. If you use the wrong wheel cleaner, you can destroy the appearance in a matter of seconds.

If you're working on a painted or clearcoated aluminum wheel, then you're not working directly on an aluminum surface but instead a clear layer of paint.

Either way, if you're working on non-coated or coated/painted wheels, you need to make sure that the wheel cleaner you're using will not harm or stain it. In some cases, it will be less expensive to simply replace a damaged wheel by purchasing a new one.

For more information see:
📖 *Identifying Wheel Type*

One wheel at a time
Only spray your wheel cleaner onto one wheel at a time. If a mistake is made by using the wrong type of wheel cleaner, you will only damage one wheel, thus preventing further damage to others.

Some people make the mistake of spraying all of their wheels at once. The wheel cleaner will be working on the other three wheels, loosening and dissolving brake dust and road grime, making it easier and faster to clean these wheels after they've finished with the first wheel.

However, if you have mistakenly purchased the wrong wheel cleaner and you sprayed all four wheels with it, by the time you realize damage is being done, it's usually too late.

2. Wash Car Body Panels

Spray the entire car with water to remove loose dirt and road grime. Saturate areas with excessive dirt on the car to soften and loosen the dirt before running a wash mitt, sponge or brush against the paint.

1. **Start with the top and work your way down**
   Start at the top and wash the roof, and if the vehicle is not too large, wash the windows, A-pillars and B-pillars. After washing a panel, immediately rinse off soap suds.

2. **Horizontal panels**
   Next, wash horizontal surfaces panel by panel and rinse each panel after washing. As you finish rinsing a panel, re-wet previously washed and rinsed sections to keep them wet and to prevent water from drying, which will prevent water spots. Also re-spray wheels and tires. This will act to continually remove any remaining wheel and tire cleaner out of cracks and crevices.

3. **Vertical panels**
   Next, wash and rinse the vertical surfaces, panel by panel using the method in step 2.

4. **Final rinse**
   After the entire car has been washed and rinsed, give it one more final rinse to ensure all loosened dirt and soap residue has been removed.

3. Dry Car Body

As soon as you're finished with the final rinse, it's time to quickly get the standing water off the car.

» **Wiping or Blotting**
To dry a panel, you can either wipe or blot it dry.

If you're working on a daily driver or getting ready to buff out the paint, wiping is sufficient. If you're doing a maintenance wash on a car with a finish in excellent to show car condition, you might consider the blotting technique with a light wipe with a spray detailer afterwards.

» **Metro MasterBlaster**
8 Horsepower
The MasterBlaster blows filtered, warm air at 58,500 feet per minute to remove water from your car's body panels and out of all the nooks and crannies. Filtered air means no blowing any dirt, dust or other particles onto your freshly washed paint. By heating the air before blowing, drying is faster and more complete. Drying your car by blowing filtered, heated high volume air reduces the potential for inflicting any toweling marks. This is definitely a must-have tool for anyone striving to maintain a show car finish.

» **Water sheeting technique -**
Optional
After rinsing with a spray nozzle, you can use what's called the water sheeting technique to remove the majority of standing water from the car. Remove the spray nozzle from the end of the hose and use a slow flow of water to flood the surface. This allows all standing water to combine with the flowing water, causing it to run off in a single sheet or collection of water.

4. Dry Wheels And Tires - Use Dedicated Towels

Dedicate specific drying towels used ONLY for wheels. There are abrasive particles that come off your brake pads and rotors which can lodge into your microfiber towels and potentially embed strongly enough that they won't wash out.

For this reason, it is a good idea to dedicate specific drying towels and store them separately from your other towels, especially any that are used on painted body panels.

Car wash soap and shampoos
In the best interest of your car, I recommend a premium brand car shampoo. The days of using dishwashing detergent to wash your car are long gone as detergent soaps are overkill for what you're trying to accomplish. Here are some features to look for in a premium quality car shampoo.

» **pH balanced** – pH is measured after the wash soap is diluted with water, not as a concentrate in the bottle. After mixing your car wash solution, you want a pH neutral rating of 7. Too high of acidity or alkalinity can break the bond of some paint protection ingredients and remove them from the paint.

» **High lubricity** – You want a car wash solution that provides lubricity as this makes the surface slippery, allowing dirt and grime to glide off the surface.

» **Long lasting suds** – Suds are bubbles at their core, which can help to cushion the contact between dirt and paint to reduce wash-induced scratching. Suds are also a visual indicator as to where you've already washed and also where you need to rinse in order to flush loosened dirt off the car.

» **Avoid detergents**
Avoid using detergent products like dish washing soap, especially if you're working on any paint in excellent condition. While detergent washes work really well for cleaning and stripping your car's finish clean, they are overkill for the task at hand.

» **Exception**
If you're working on a car that has been neglected, some will argue that using a detergent wash won't hurt anything and will in fact help to strip off any previously applied wax or paint sealant, thus preparing the paint for claying and correction work.

I would agree that any damage done by a detergent wash will be of little long term effect as long as you continue with the steps of claying, cleaning, polishing and sealing. If you choose to use a detergent soap for the initial, pre-restoration wash, then after the finish is restored, switch back to only using non-detergent car wash shampoos.

☞ *Mike's Mixing Tip...*

- Always follow the manufacturer's directions for diluting car wash concentrate with water. The manufacturer knows their product best and has done their homework before writing any directions for correct dilution levels of car wash soap to water.

☞ *Mike's Method...*

- I always use a 5-gallon bucket filled with about 4 gallons of water. I add the water first, measure and pour in the car wash, and then mix it thoroughly with my hand. This method creates a thoroughly mixed solution of car wash soap and water. After you mix the soap and water together, you can blast the solution with a strong spray of water to create mountains of suds.

☞ *The Caveman Method Of Mixing Your Car Wash*

- The caveman method is to add your car wash soap to the bucket and then add the water. The problem with this method is that the blast of water hitting the concentrated car wash soap creates a bucket filled and overflowing with suds, but hardly any water. This wastes product and time and you don't have any soapy water solution to dip your wash mitt into.

Links: Car Washes and Shampoos

- Wolfgang Auto Bathe
- Pinnacle Bodywork Shampoo
- Pinnacle XMT Gel Shampoo & Conditioner
- Detailer's Pro Series Xtreme Foam
- Formula Auto Shampoo
- Muc-Off Ubershine Car Shampoo
- Eco Touch Waterless Car Wash Concentrate
- Prima Mistique Car Wash
- Prima Hydro Wash Shampoo
- Sonax Gloss Shampoo Concentrate
- Dodo Juice Sour Power Gloss Enhancing Shampoo
- Dodo Juice Basics of Bling Wax-Safe Shampoo
- Dodo Juice Supernatural Shampoo
- Sonus Gloss Shampoo
- P21S Bodywork Conditioning Shampoo
- Poorboy's World Super Slick & Suds Concentrated Car Wash
- Poorboy's Super Slick & Wax Car Shampoo
- Griot's Garage Car Wash
- Four Star Auto Wash Shampoo
- Mothers California Gold Car Wash
- Meguiar's Ultimate Wash & Wax
- Meguiar's Shampoo Plus

- 🖥 *Meguiar's #62 Carwash Shampoo & Conditioner*
- 🖥 *Meguiar's Gold Class Shampoo & Conditioner*
- 🖥 *Meguiar's NXT Car Wash*
- 🖥 *Wurth Car Shampoo*
- 🖥 *1Z Einszett Perls Shampoo Premium Car Wash*
- 🖥 *Optimum Car Wash*
- 🖥 *P21S Total Auto Wash*
- 🖥 *Ultima Paint Guard Wash*
- 🖥 *CarPro Iron X Soap Gel*

👀 6 Reasons To Use A Waterless Wash, A Rinseless Wash Or A Spray Detailer

Now that we've talked about the traditional car wash, let's take a look at some of your other options.

In a perfect world, everyone would have access to free flowing water, warm temperatures, and no restrictions on when and where they can wash their car. However, we don't live in a perfect world, so here are 6 reasons to use an alternative car wash method.

1. Areas with government enforced water restrictions

There are many cities and even entire countries with government enforced water restrictions. In these places, it's against laws and/or regulations to wash your car with a free flowing source of water.

2. Geographical areas of drought

In some places, there may be no official restrictions against water use, but the geographical area itself is experiencing severe drought. This prevents people from using a free flowing source of water to wash their vehicles.

3. People who live in apartments

If you live in an apartment, a condo or a townhouse, there may be no place to wash your car with a free flowing source of clean water or there may be rules against it that you have agreed to comply with.

4. Washing in cold winter months

In cold weather, extreme low temperatures can make washing a car with a free flowing source of water dangerous and difficult at best.

5. Mobile detailers

Rinseless washing enables mobile detailers to wash cars without having to depend upon a water source or the extra hassle of transporting hundreds of gallons of water. Besides that, some areas require mobile detailers to contain and capture their run-off water. This is an added expense which can be difficult and time consuming.

6. Anytime you're traveling

If you are doing any long distance traveling, you may not have access to a free flowing source of water. Using a waterless wash, rinseless wash or spray detailer enables you to get your car clean.

👀 How To Use A Waterless Wash

Tools needed
- Waterless wash
- Wash mitt, sponge or microfiber towel for washing
- Microfiber towels for drying

Tips & techniques
If you plan on using the Waterless Wash approach, here are two tips to help you.

1. Wash often

Clean your car often. Removing light amounts of accumulated dirt and road grime is much faster, easier and safer than putting the job off until the car is visibly dirty.

2. Maintain a good coat of wax, paint sealant or use a paint coating

Dirt and road grime will wipe off faster and easier if you wax your car often, because a coating of wax helps prevent dirt from forming a strong bond onto the paint.

↱ Mike's Method - Step By Step How-To Use A Waterless Wash

- My method of using a waterless wash is pretty simple. Use a lot of product and only tackle a small section at a time. Use premium quality microfiber towels with a fluffy nap, not a flat weave, so any dirt on the surface can bury into the fluffy nap.

✦ How-To Step By Step

1. Start at the top and work your way down

2. Manageable work area

Set your spray nozzle for a wide fan spray and saturate an area of about 18" by 18". If your car is only lightly dirty, spray down a larger section of about 24" by 24", or even an entire panel as long as you have the ability to remove the product before it dries. The goal is to keep your work area manageable. The dirtier the car, the smaller the section you should wipe clean while using more microfiber towels.

↱ My Favorite Tool

- 🖥 *The Double Action Kwazar Mercury Pro+ 1 Liter Spray Bottle*

- The Kwazar spray bottle sprays product both when you pull the squeeze lever AND when you release it. This double-action sprayer lays a lot of product down faster, in less time, and with half the energy required by a normal spray head. Since the goal is to lay down plenty of waterless wash, the Kwazar spray bottle is the perfect choice. You can get these bottles in both 17 and 33 ounce sizes - for waterless washes, I prefer the 33 ounce bottle.

Flat Weave Microfiber

Fluffy Nap Microfiber

» **Have plenty of microfiber towels**
A large collection of clean, premium quality microfiber towels is ideal when using a waterless wash.

» **Work clean**
Because it's important to use a clean microfiber towel, dedicate a clean, accessible area for storage. It doesn't do any good to maintain a collection of clean microfiber towels if you set them down on a dirty surface.

» **Use good wiping techniques**
After wiping one or two sections, re-fold your microfiber towel to a clean, dry side. After using all 8 sides of your microfiber towel, switch to a clean, dry microfiber towel.

For more information see,

📖 *How to correctly fold and use a Microfiber Towel*

Links: Waterless car washes

🖥 *Detailer's Pro Series Waterless Auto Wash*
🖥 *Detailer's Pro Series Waterless Auto Wash Concentrate*
🖥 *Eco Touch Waterless Car Wash Ready To Use*
🖥 *Poorboy's World Spray & Wipe Waterless Wash*
🖥 *Griot's Garage Waterless Spray-On Car Wash*
🖥 *Ultima Waterless Wash Plus+*
🖥 *Ultima Waterless Wash Plus+ Concentrate*
🖥 *Optimum No Rinse Wash & Shine*

🔴 How To Use A Rinseless Wash

- **Measuring your rinseless wash concentrate**
Most rinseless car washes on the market are mixed at 1 ounce per 2 gallons of water.

🖥 *Detailer's Pride Rinseless Wash & Gloss*
🖥 *Optimum No Rinse Wash & Shine*

- **Fast, easy way to measure 2 gallons of water**
If you have a 5-gallon bucket like the ones that come in all Autogeek's car wash kits, here's a fast, simple way to measure two gallons of water.

Take any standard 12 inch ruler

Place a ruler into the Autogeek 5 gallon bucket until the end is against the bottom and make a mark at 6 inches.

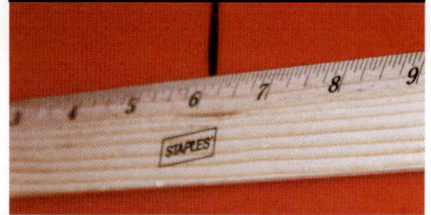

Now every time you want to add 2 gallons of water, all you have to do is fill the bucket to the mark.

and fill the bucket until the water level reaches the 6 inch mark on the ruler. This will be approximately two gallons of water. If you plan on using a rinseless car wash often, you can even use a permanent marker to mark the inside of the bucket for fast reference when adding water.

- **KISS = Keep It Simple Simon**
Little techniques like this save time by making frequent procedures easy to repeat over and over again without having to measure or think about them.

🚶 *Using A Grit Guard Insert In The Rinseless Wash Bucket*

If you want to use a Grit Guard insert with either the one or two bucket

Washing Your Car

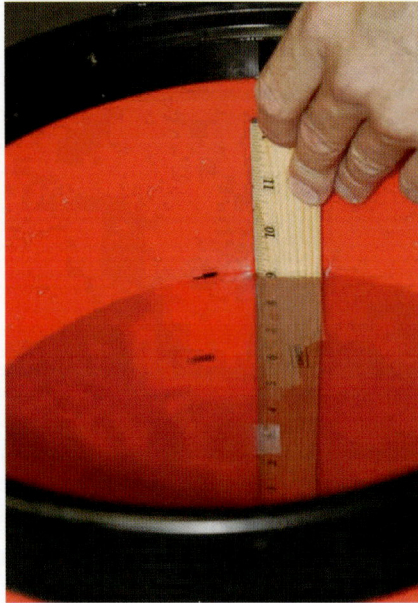

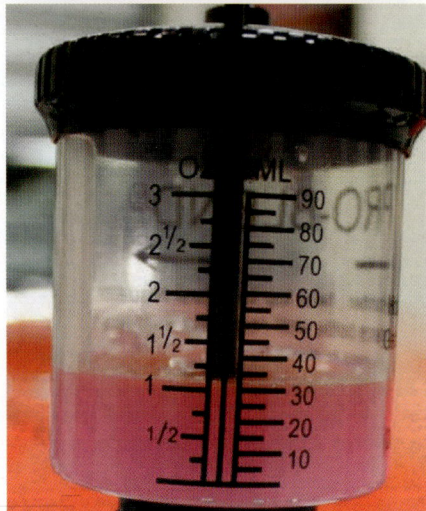

rinseless wash, check out these two articles,

- 📖 *How to use a Pro Blend Bottle Proportioner*
- 📖 *How dirty is too dirty to safely use a rinseless wash?*

⚐ Step-by-Step How To Wash Your Car With A Rinseless Wash

Start at the top and work your way down

If you start washing the lower panels and move towards the roof, when you wash the roof, you'll likely have cleaning solution running down and re-wetting a dry panel. This means that you will have to dry the panel again or possibly wash and dry the panel a second time.

Wash one panel or section at a time

If you try to wash too large of an area before drying, the cleaning solution can dry onto the panel.

Two factors that determine how large of a panel or section of a panel you tackle at one time,

- **Size of the panel**
  If you have a small panel to wash, such as the hood of a Mini Cooper, then it's small enough that you can wash the entire panel and dry it before the cleaning solution can dry. If, however, you're washing a vehicle with a large hood or other large panels, then you might find it easier to break it up into separate sections or halves and wash and dry one a section at a time.

  The goal is to wet the panel, loosen any dirt or road grime and then wipe or blot the panel or section dry. Again, if a panel is too large, you could risk having your cleaning solution dry before you have a chance to wipe or blot the panel or section of panel dry.

- **Temperature and air flow**
  On warm or hot days, or in areas

where there's a strong wind, these two factors can cause your cleaning solution to dry faster than in lower temperatures and no-wind environments. Take this into consideration when deciding how large of a panel or section of a panel to tackle at one time.

Dividing your car into sections

Here's how I divide a car when washing with a rinseless car wash. I start at the top, but add a twist which goes like this:

- » **Roof**
- » **Side glass** - One side of the car at a time
- » **Horizontal panels** - The hood and trunk lid
- » **Vertical panels, upper portions only** - The upper portions tend to be cleaner than the lower portions
- » **Front bumpers and grills**
- » **Rear bumpers and rear vertical panels** - Found on SUVs and some passenger cars or for example, the tailgates on trucks. Keep in mind that air currents swirl around the rear of cars, trucks and SUVs as you're driving at highway speeds, sometimes depositing an oily road film onto these rear, vertical panels.
- » **Vertical panels, lower portions** - Lower portions of the vertical panels are washed last, as these are the dirtiest sections of the car.
- » **Lastly, the wheels & tires** - For the wheels and tires you may choose to use a brush instead of a wash mitt. Admittedly, washing the wheels, tires and things like grills is harder to do without a brush and source of free flowing water, so improvise and do the best you can.

For drying off wheels and tires see:
- 📖 *The 4 minimum categories of wiping towels*

Use a gentle touch

When using a rinseless car wash, the idea is to carefully move your wash

method, add an extra gallon of water and an extra 1/2 to 1 ounce of rinseless wash concentrate to make up for the portion of water covered and protected by the Grit Guard insert.

To measure an extra gallon of water when using a Grit Guard insert, measure from the bottom of the bucket to about the 9" mark and then add water until it reaches this mark. This will give you approximately 3 gallons of water with the protection of the Grit Guard insert, so you'll want to add an extra 1 1/2 to 2 ounces of rinseless wash concentrate.

For more information on using a

mitt over the surface only enough to loosen the grip any dirt or road grime has on the paint and then STOP.

It's pretty common to see people washing their cars without thinking about what they're doing and pushing their wash mitt over the same section of paint for dozens of strokes. In reality, one or two passes would have been sufficient. Focus on the task at hand and only make as many gentle passes as you deem necessary to loosen and dirt or road grime.

1. **Place wash mitt into your rinse water bucket**

2. **First things first - dry the paint**
   The first thing you want to do after washing a panel or section is to either wipe or blot it dry.

3. **Rinse your wash mitt and re-gather fresh cleaning solution**
   After you wipe the panel dry and you're ready to wash another panel, that's when you'll clean your wash mitt or sponge by scrubbing it against the Grit Guard insert (this acts to extract dirt particles from your mitt or sponge) and then wring out the excess water before gathering fresh cleaning solution.

4. **Repeat the above process as you work your way around the car.**

⚐ *How-To Use A Rinseless Wash To Clean Wheels And Tires*

Wheels and tires tend to be dirtier than the body panels on your car and this is why you want to wash them last. Brake dust can contain small metal particles that can instill swirls and scratches, so always wash the wheels and tires last when using a rinseless wash.

1. Dip a wheel brush, microfiber towel or wash mitt into your remaining solution of rinseless wash and use this to clean your wheels and tires. Wash one wheel and tire at a time. Immediately after washing, wipe dry using microfiber or terry cloth towels that you have dedicated specifically for wheels and tires.

2. When washing wheels and tires using a rinseless wash, instead of using your high quality wash mitts and/or sponges that you use for paintwork, consider using ones that are dedicated for wheels and tires.

- 💻 *Detailers Pro Series Rinseless Wash & Gloss*
- 💻 *Optimum No Rinse Wash & Shine*
- 💻 *Professional 5 Gallon Wash Bucket*
- 💻 *Pro Blend Bottle Proportioner*
- 💻 *Dual Bucket Dolly*
- 📖 *Car Wash Tools*

📷 How To Use A Spray Detailer To Wash Your Car

The primary difference between using a spray detailer to maintain a finish or to wash a car is the amount of spray detailer you use. If you're in a situation where the best option to clean your car is to use a spray detailer, use the product heavy or wet.

For more information see:
- 📖 *How to use a spray detailer to maintain your car*

📷 Identifying Wheel Type

Before you can choose the right wheel cleaner to safely clean your wheels, you first need to determine what your car's wheels are either made out of or coated with.

Wheels come in 5 general categories

- Factory Painted
- Uncoated Metal
- Combination of Coated and Uncoated

- Chrome
- Anodized

Factory Painted Wheels
Coated wheels have a layer of paint, but it's not the same as car paint. It is usually a much harder and corrosion resistant type of paint. Many new cars come with factory painted wheels.

» **How to check**
If your car has painted wheels, chances are they have a clearcoat finish, although it's possible they could have a pigmented finish. To test, rub a light paint cleaner onto a small section of the wheel using a soft piece of cloth like a piece of t-shirt and then turn the applicator over. If your wheel is clearcoated, you shouldn't see any color change on the t-shirt. If the wheel is painted with a pigmented paint, you'll see the color of the wheel coming off and onto the cloth.

Machined aluminum wheels with a clearcoat finish can be deceiving as they can look like uncoated, polished aluminum wheels when in fact there is a clear layer of paint over the metal surface.

Uncoated metal wheels
Uncoated usually means aluminum or magnesium wheels. This means the exterior surface is bare metal and as such will oxidize and stain over time.

» **How to check**
You can check to see if your wheel is uncoated aluminum or magnesium by rubbing a little metal polish onto the wheel with a white cloth like a piece of t-shirt. If it's uncoated aluminum or magnesium, your cloth will turn a dark grayish black color.

Magnesium wheel
Uncoated, magnesium tends to turn a dark gray if not constantly maintained or if an acid wheel cleaner is used on it.

Combination of coated and uncoated
Some modular or component wheels can be assembled using separate pieces to form the complete wheel and for decorative purposes, not all portions of the wheel have the same type of finish.

» **How to check**
Because there are so many wheel companies and such a great variety of wheel types and fashions, if you have a modular wheel there are two things you can do.

1. **Safe approach**
Use a wheel cleaner that's safe for uncoated polished aluminum.

Why? Because uncoated polished aluminum is probably the most susceptible to dulling or staining by strong cleaning agents. Wheel cleaners formulated for uncoated aluminum are very safe and therefore generally safe for any type of wheel.

2. **Manufacturer's recommended approach**
Contact the manufacturer of your brand of wheel and get their specific instructions for how to wash and maintain their wheels and their official recommendations for wheel cleaners.

Chrome wheels
The good news about chrome wheels is that when kept clean from dirt build-up, chrome coatings are incredibly corrosion resistant. It's only when dirt, road grime and brake

dust are allowed to build-up on the chrome coating and attract and hold moisture that over time, the chrome will deteriorate and in extreme cases to the point where the layer of chrome will peel and flake off the wheel.

Since chrome is corrosion resistant, you can use strong wheel cleaners including wheel cleaners that use acid to dissolve and remove brake dust.

» **How to check**
Real chrome has a mirror-like, reflective shine and is fairly easy to identify just by close examination. Rubbing a clearcoat safe paint cleaner should show no black or dark gray color on your cloth like you see when removing oxidation from uncoated aluminum wheels. Chrome is an electroplated layer of the element chromium; it is, in simple terms, grown onto the underlying metal substrate through an electroplating process. Because it is a type of metal, if you tap lightly on it with something metal, you will hear the sound of metal against metal.

Anodized Wheels
A process called anodizing is used by some wheel manufacturers to create a corrosion and oxidation resistant finish on aluminum wheels. Anodizing is not a coating "on" the aluminum; it is a process in which the surface is changed through an electrochemical process

by which aluminum is converted into aluminum oxide. The aluminum oxide finish increases corrosion and wear resistance and can be tinted with dyes to a variety of colors. If you use the wrong wheel cleaner on anodized aluminum, it's possible to dull or stain the finish. The only way to undo the damage is to de-anodize the component, remove the stained portion of aluminum, and then re-anodize. The time, labor and expense is usually costlier than simply replacing with a new wheel.

» **How to check**
In the early days of anodizing, you could usually see that the original aluminum finish was not polished but a brushed or matte finish. As anodizing technology has been improved, appearance quality has been increased to provide better gloss and shine in finished parts. Typically, the component will not impart color when rubbed on with some type of paint or metal polish. To be safe, check with the manufacturer of the wheel or check with a local custom wheel store as they should be able to determine if your wheel is anodized or not.

Wheel Cleaners

- Pinnacle Clearcoat Safe Wheel Cleaner
- Wolfgang Tire & Wheel Cleaner
- Sonax Full Effect Wheel Cleaner
- P21S Wheel Cleaners
- Griot's Chrome Wheel Cleaner
- Mothers Foaming All Wheel & Tire Cleaner
- Mothers Polished Aluminum Wheel Cleaner
- Mothers Wheel Mist Chrome/Wire Pro Strength Cleaner
- Meguiar's Hot Wheels Aluminum Wheel Cleaner
- Detailer's Pro Series
- Griot's Garage Wheel Cleaner

- Griot's Garage Heavy Duty Wheel Cleaner
- Duragloss All Wheel Cleaner
- Dodo Juice Mellow Yellow Wheel Cleaner
- Dodo Juice Supernatural Wheel Cleaner
- Four Star Ultimate Wheel Cleaner Gel
- Muc-Off Frequent Use Wheel Cleaner
- Meguiars Hot Wheels Aluminum Wheel Cleaner
- Meguiar's Wheel Brightener
- Poorboy's World Spray and Rinse Wheel Cleaner
- 1Z Einszett Wheel Cleaner
- S100 Wheel Cleaner
- 3M Tire and Wheel Cleaner
- Amazing Roll Off

Big picture
If you don't know what the wheels on your car are made from or coated with, before purchasing a wheel cleaner, contact the wheel manufacturer or wheel store where you purchased your wheels, or contact the dealership where you purchased your car and find out to avoid making a costly mistake.

💬 Car Wash Tools

- Wash mitts
- Wash sponges
- Wash brushes
- Chamois and drying towels
- Buckets, dollies and car wash systems
- Grit Guard inserts
- Spray nozzles
- Brass quick connectors

💬 My comment…
Quality tools help you to work more efficiently. In this chapter, you'll find tools I use and recommend.

There are two things to know about wash mitts, sponges and brushes.

1. **Use the best quality wash mitts, sponges and brushes you can obtain**
Always use premium quality products that are soft and gentle to the paint, whether you choose a mitt, sponge, or brush. To judge the softness and gentleness of any tool, first let it soak in your wash solution for 10 to 20 minutes. Water has a softening effect and this must be taken into account. For example, a boar's hair brush should be allowed to soak for 20 to 30 minutes to allow water to soften the individual hairs. A natural sea sponge feels softer and is more gentle after it soaks in water; this is totally different than how it feels when it's right out of the package and still dry.

2. **Periodically switch to new wash mitts, sponges and brushes**
Anytime your wash mitt, sponge, or brush appears worn, delegate it to work that doesn't include washing the major body panels. It's better to substitute a brand new wash mitt, sponge, or brush for carefully washing delicate, scratch-sensitive clearcoat paint than it is to try to squeeze every last use from your current wash mitt.

What's our time worth?
Simply think about how much time it takes to do a complete detail job to your car's finish. This includes washing, claying, removing swirls and scratches, polishing and sealing with wax or a paint sealant. I think you'll agree with me that the time and energy required to do the job right far out weigh the cost of a new wash mitt.

🚶 Wash Mitts, Sponges & Brushes

💬 My comment…
Below, I try to show as best as I can the relative size of the various mitts, sponges and brushes by including a

standard 12" ruler in the photos and to also hold the different tools in my hand for perspective.

All the washing tools at *Autogeek. net* are top quality and best-in-class for their category. They all work exceptionally well and when it comes to which one is best, that really comes down to personal preference. The best way to find out which one is best is to test out a few different types until you find the one that's best for you and your car's unique shape and size.

If you already have a wash mitt, sponge or brush that you like, then use that. If you're looking for a new replacement, then consider the below tools and maybe test out 2-3 that interest you the most and then stick with the one that works best for you.

Autogeek's Sheepskin Wash Mitt

Offers a one and a half inch thick pile made from the best all natural wool imported from Australia. This wash mitt provides a separate place for your fingers and thumb to help you wash the car and even mold the wash mitt around the various components on the car like contoured edges, rear view mirrors, spoilers, grills, antennas

💻 *Autogeek's Sheepskin Wash Mitt*

The real deal

This is a shot (shown bottom left) of the inside of the mitt to show that this is real lambswool. This is how you can tell a fake or synthetic wash mitt from the real deal.

CarPro Wool Wash Mitt

Made from 100% Merino wool, which is a premium wool prized for its softness and length. This mitt has a mesh pocket on the back to slide over your hand while washing your car.

💻 *CarPro Wool Wash Mitt*

CarPro 2Fingers Mini Wool Wash Mitt

This is a miniature version of the full-size CarPro Wool Wash Mitt specifically for washing hard to reach areas like under door handles, under wings and spoilers, around rear view mirrors and under and around luggage and ski racks.

💻 *CarPro 2Fingers Mini Wool Wash Mitt*

Optimum Opti-Mitt 8 Inch Foam Wash Mitt

This is like two wash mitts in one. The gray foam is the primary car washing foam. It's very soft and porous, with plenty of space for dirt to be soaked up by the pad, rather than rubbed into the paint. The yellow side provides a gentle scrubbing surface for removing bugs, tar, and other

built-up contaminants. When used with Optimum No Rinse or Optimum Car Wash, this mitt helps prevent wash-induced swirls by effectively moving dirt off the paint.

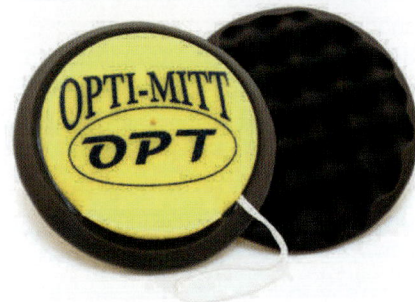

💻 *Optimum Opti-Mitt 8 Inch Foam Wash Mitt*

Dodo Juice Supernatural Wash Mitt "Wookie's Fist"

This is called the Wookie's Fist and it's probably the largest, fluffiest, furriest wool wash mitt you've ever seen. The wool used to make this wash mitt comes from the Merino sheep and is regarded as one of the finest, softest wools available from any sheep. Because of its large size, it is capable of holding lots of soapy water.

While this is a very luxurious natural lambswool wash mitt, due to its long fiber strands, the manufacturer, Dodo Juice, actually recommends

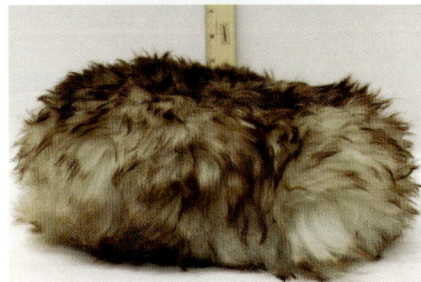

you brush it after it's dried with a pet brush to restore the fluffiness. From my personal experience, this is an accurate recommendation.

🖥️ *Dodo Juice Supernatural Wash Mitt "Wookie's Fist"*

Cobra Microfiber-Chenille Wash Mitt

This wash mitt always catches everyone's eye because it looks so strange. The word chenille is actually a French word meaning caterpillar, only these caterpillar-looking things are actually thin microfibers woven into plump caterpillar-like strands that are both absorbent and non-abrasive. This design gently removes dirt and road grime off clearcoat finishes and then releases any collected dirt easily when rubbed against the Grit Guard insert.

🖥️ *Cobra Microfiber-Chenille Wash Mitt - 3 pack*

Mothers Genuine Lambswool Wash Mitt

Natural soft lambswool becomes very

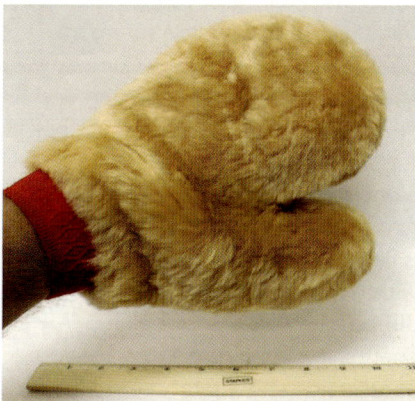

silky and gentle when it becomes wet. The natural fibers pull dirt away from the finish and then release trapped dirt when rubbed against the Grit Guard insert.

🖥️ *Mothers Genuine Lambswool Wash Mitt*

Cobra Bone

This is a thick, porous foam pad in the shape of a bone, covered with tiny, super plush microfibers. What makes this microfiber unique is that the fibers themselves are open-ended, not shaped into a loop. This creates millions of tiny microfiber fingers that gently clean delicate clearcoat finishes. The pile is deep enough to enable loosened dirt to migrate into the fibers instead of being dragged against the paint. Because these fibers are open-ended, dirt is easily released when rinsed rather than being trapped inside the loops of fibers.

🖥️ *The Cobra Bone*

Cobra Cotton Chenille

Made using a very specific type of cotton that is non-abrasive, this wash

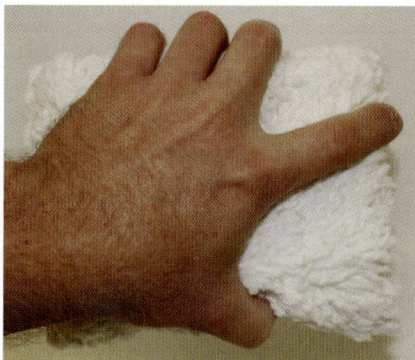

pad is super soft and absorbent. It also attracts dirt onto itself when used to wash your car, but when you place it into a bucket of rinse water, it releases dirt quickly and easily. This self-cleaning characteristic is further enhanced when you use a Grit Guard insert.

🖥️ *The Cobra Cotton Chenille Wash Pad*

Natural Sea Sponge

This sponge holds tons of car wash solution that is easily released with a light squeeze as you're washing a panel, drenching the paint with lubricating and cleaning suds. After it becomes saturated with water, it is very soft and pliable with plenty of cushion to shape to the panels of your vehicle.

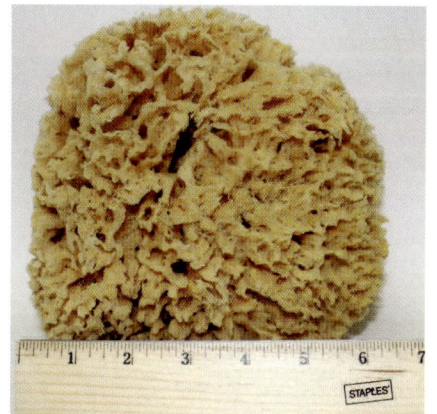

🖥️ *Large Natural Sea Sponge*

Lake Country Foam Car Wash Sponge

The working face of this sponge

is cross-cut into 1/4 inch cubed or slotted tabs. These cubed tabs help to channel dirt and grime away from the paint. The softness of the foam, coupled with its porous design allows it to hold and release plenty of solution. This keeps the surface lubricated, but when you rub it against the Grit Guard insert inside your fresh water bucket, these cubed fingers will open up to release any removed dirt so that it will fall past the insert and become trapped on the bottom of your bucket.

💻 *Lake Country Foam Car Wash Sponge aka Big Blue Cube*

ULTI-MIT Wash Mitt & ULTI-MIT Scrubber Wheel Mitt by Lake Country

The Ulti-Mit wash sponge also incorporates ¼ inch cubed or slotted tabs which are cross-cut across the working face of the sponge. The foam is very soft and gentle and actually becomes softer when it becomes wet. It holds plenty of solution to lubricate the surface as you're

washing each panel. Dirt is guided into the channels between the slotted cubes and then released into the rinse water when the mitt is rubbed against a Grit Guard insert.

💻 *ULTI-MIT Wash Mitt & ULTI-MIT Scrubber Wheel Mitt by Lake Country*

Meguiars Microfiber Wash Mitt

This mitt is made of quality microfiber that is both absorbent and ultra soft. The dense microfiber loops remove dirt particles from the paint and trap them within the fluffy pile. Dirt is lifted away from the paint where it cannot mar or swirl the finish.

💻 *Meguiars Microfiber Wash Mitt*

Carrand Microfiber Max Premium Wash Sponge

Five sides of this sponge are covered in luxurious, plush microfiber fingers to safely wash your car's clearcoat finish, while the other side is covered with polymesh netting to gently remove dried bugs and other stubborn contaminants. There's even a built-in pocket on the polymesh netting side to enable you to comfortably hold the sponge without the fear or risk of potentially dropping

it onto the ground.

💻 *Carrand Microfiber MAX Premium Wash Sponge*

Carrand Microfiber MAX Total Clean All Over Wash Mitt

This is four wash mitts in one! One side is microfiber chenille with strands that are are 30% longer than most microfiber chenille wash mitts, providing even more dirt lifting and removing power.

The other side offers plush, deep-pile microfiber that lifts and carries dirt away from your car's finish. On both edges, you'll find polymesh netting to get under and remove bugs and other stubborn contaminants. To top it off, there's a waterproof lining inside the mitt to keep your hands clean and dry and away from the wash solution with an elastic cuff.

💻 *Carrand Microfiber MAX Total Clean All Over Wash Mitt*

SchMITT Multi-Purpose Foam Mitts

This is a sponge-type wash mitt which uses the same foam used in manufacturing the ultra soft foam buffing pads by The Edge Company. The foam itself is incredibly soft and gentle to automotive clearcoats, while the soft foam cell structure holds plenty of solution. The SchMITT offers two designs for the working face; one is flat while the other is convoluted with hills and valleys so it won't trap dirt particles against the paint. There's an opening slot to place your hand inside and a safety cord to prevent accidental dropping of the mitt onto the ground.

🖥 The SchMITT Multi-purpose Foam Mitts

🚶 Bucket Dollies And Accessories

Bucket dollies

To make washing your car easier, you can use dollies with wheels, allowing you to roll your bucket(s) as you work around the car. This prevents you from walking back and forth to the wash bucket and also dripping your wash solution all over the ground instead of using it to wash the body panels.

🖥 Double dolly

The Two Bucket Dolly makes it easy to move your Two Bucket Wash System

around the car. There's also a locking mechanism to lock the wheels so the dolly can't roll away.

Diamond Plate Dolly Connector

Connects two Grit Guard Single Bucket Dollies together to form a two bucket dolly system.

🖥 Diamond Plate Dolly Connector

Grit Guard Inserts

The Grit Guard Insert is a plastic insert that fits into the bottom of a 5-gallon bucket that will trap the dirt that comes off your wash mitt on the bottom of the bucket. The design includes a plastic grill that dirt and other abrasive particles can fall past to the bottom of the bucket. The grill is suspended off the bottom of the bucket by 4 vanes which also prevent the water at the bottom from swirling around, which prevents the trapped dirt from rising above the grill.

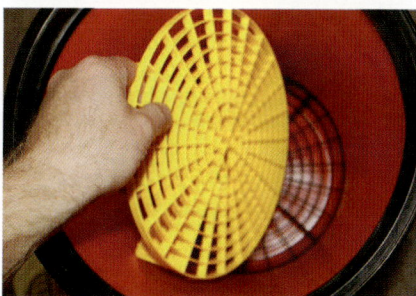

Once you use a Grit Guard Insert and see all the dirt it traps onto the bottom of the bucket, you'll never want to wash a car without one again. They fit into all the Autogeek 5-gallon buckets and most other conventional 5-gallon buckets.

🖥 Grit Guard Inserts

🚶 Spray Nozzles & Connectivity Tools

Connectors enable you to switch between tools quickly and easily. Shut-off valves enable you to turn the water off at the end of the hose instead of walking back to the spigot. This can be a huge time saver.

🖥 Fire Hose Nozzle
🖥 Solid Brass Water Jet Nozzle
🖥 Brass Hose Connectors & Shut-Off Valves

🚶 Brushes

🖥 Daytona Speed Master Wheel Brush
🖥 Daytona Speed Master Jr. Wheel Brush
🖥 All Montana's Original Boar's Hair Brushes
🖥 Muc-Off 5x Brush Set

Washing Your Car

🏃 Misc Wheel Tools

🏃 Microfiber Drying Towels And Chamois

Drying the paint without scratching is the goal and you can do this as long as you're using drying towels and chamois that are soft and gentle.

🗨 **Tip:** *Instead of wiping water off, try blotting. By blotting off the water, you will not be physically rubbing the towel or chamois against the paint. This is also known as the least evasive method of drying a car.*

There are all kinds of high quality drying chamois and microfiber towels available. Like choosing a wash mitt, sometimes you need to test a product out in person to find the perfect match for your preferences. Below is a selection from the Autogeek store. To

see everything that's available, click the link below.

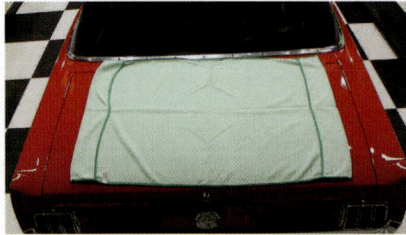

Cobra Guzzler Waffle Weave Drying Towels
These drying towels get their name because they simply guzzle up water. They make removing the water from your car's finish fast and easy.

Cobra Guzzler Heavy Duty Waffle Weave Drying Towel - Inner Foam Core
This has an inner open cell foam core and works great for the blotting technique.

Mother's Microfiber Drying Towels
The Mothers Ultra Soft Drying Towel has an open cell foam core which

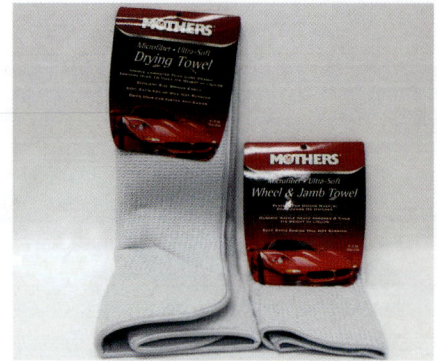

acts like a sponge to soak up water. It's also easy to wring out so you can continue working your way around the car, gently wiping water off or using the blotting technique.

The Wheel & Jamb Towel is a high quality waffle weave microfiber towel that dries and cleans the dirtiest parts of your vehicle, such as the wheels, grill and door jambs.

Give this towel its own special place in the garage marked wheels only, because once it's used on them, it should never touch the paint again. Even after you've washed the wheels, some lingering brake dust can stick to the towel and be transferred to other parts of your vehicle. By designating Mothers Wheel & Jamb Towel for the work-horse parts of your vehicle, you can prevent cross-contamination.

The Meguiar's Water Magnet uses the popular waffle weave design to safely remove water from your car's finish.

- Water Sprite Plus® Chamois 4 sq. Feet

- P21S Drying Towel

Cleaning Microfiber Towels

All the microfiber drying towels Autogeek offers can be machine washed in your washing machine and then dried on the low heat setting of your dryer. It's best to use a dedicated microfiber washing solution specifically formulated for removing car care products from microfiber materials.

- Detailer's Pro Series Microfiber Cleaner
- Pinnacle Micro Rejuvenator Microfiber Detergent Concentrate
- Micro-Restore Microfiber Detergent Concentrate
- Sonus Der Wunder Microfiber and Pad Wasche

Traditional Leather Chamois

Genuine chamois are 100% natural leather and tanned using cod oil, which gives it the softness and its leather smell. If you like the smell and feel of real leather, you won't be happy with a synthetic. The Prince of Wales Chamois come in sizes of 2.5, 3.5, and 4.5 square feet of superb, high end leather. The 4.5 version is obviously the most popular for its size, sufficient for any job. Chamois are meant to be used without cleaning solutions or chemicals. If you use it for polishing and drying only and care for it correctly, your chamois may outlast you.

- Prince of Wales Chamois - 2.5 square feet
- Prince of Wales Chamois - 3.5 square feet
- Prince of Wales Chamois - 4.5 square feet
- Jumbo Wales Chamois - 6 square feet

- Griot's Garage Chamois Cleaner
- Chamois/Towel Wringer

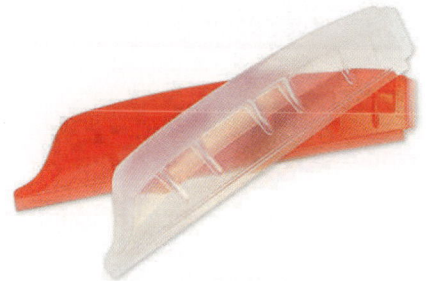

- The Original California Jelly Blade

- Metro Vac N'Blo® Portable Vacuum

Miscellaneous Washing Tools

- Foam Guns - Use with Water Hose
- Foam Cannon - Use with Pressure Washer
- Tornador Air Foam HP

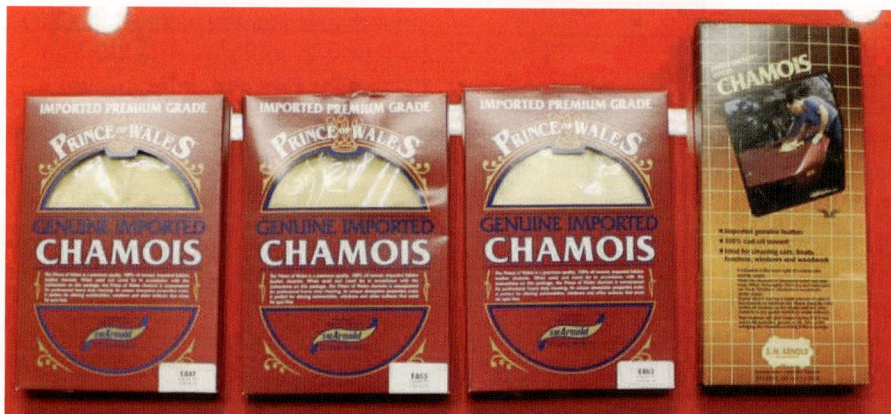

Visual And Physical Inspection

Inspecting your car's paint

Now that your car is clean and dry, you need to inspect the paint to determine what may be wrong. The results from your inspection will then guide you to which specific product you'll need to reach your goal.

There are two ways to inspect your car's finish. One is with your sense of touch and other is visually.

Paint Condition Categories

As you inspect your car's paint, try to fit it into one of these 11 categories. Most paint will fall into one of the first five groups.

1. Show Car Quality
2. Excellent Condition
3. Good Condition
4. Mildly Neglected
5. Severely Neglected
6. Horrendous Swirls - Caused by the misuse of a rotary buffer
7. Extreme Oxidation
8. Extreme Orange Peel
9. Unstable
10. Clearcoat Failure
11. Past the Point of No Return

Two categories of paint defects

- Above-Surface Bonded Contaminants
- Below-Surface Defects

Paint defects can be placed into one of two categories. It's important to understand the two different types, because removing them requires different approaches. Let's take a look at the two different categories and how to inspect for paint defects.

Above-Surface Bonded Contaminants - Inspecting Using Your Sense Of Touch

Using your clean hands, you can feel the above-surface bonded contaminants that you usually cannot see.

Types of above-surface Contaminants

Anytime your car is exposed to the environment, it is exposed to any and all the contaminants in the air and there are lots of them. These include:

- Overspray paint
- Tree sap mist
- Industrial fallout
- Airborne pollution
- Jet fuel exhaust
- Automobile and truck exhaust
- Brake dust
- Air blown dirt and dust

It's hard to see above-surface bonded contaminants because the particles are small. Your sense of touch, however, can easily feel the contaminants because it gives the paint a rough, textured or pebbled feeling. In worst case scenarios, it can actually feel gritty or grainy.

If you really want to feel what's going on at the surface level of your car's paint, then use the baggie test when inspecting it for above-surface bonded contaminants.

If working on a customer's car, let them also do the baggie test with you. The average car owner doesn't know how to test for above-surface bonded contaminants and doing so will reveal the true condition of the paint.

Afterwards, letting them feel the smooth and slippery paint will solidify their trust in your expertise. This can help you to retain their business and potentially lead to referrals via word-of-mouth advertising.

> **The Baggie Test**
> Simply place your hand inside a clean sandwich baggie and then feel the horizontal surfaces like the hood, roof and trunk lid. The thin film of plastic acts to intensify the surface texture created by

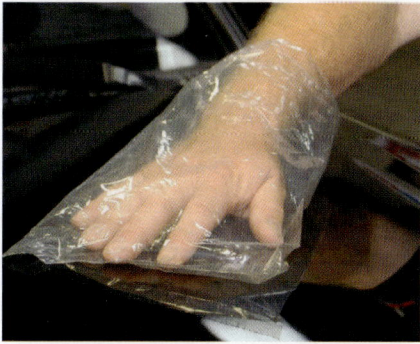

contaminants bonded to the paint, making it more dramatic to your sense of touch.

Whichever way you want to inspect the paint, whether using just your hands or the baggie test, it's important to first wash and dry the car; this will prevent you from rubbing surface dirt over the paint.

What to do if your car's paint feels rough
This is an indicator that you need to use detailing clay to safely remove the above-surface bonded contaminants.

🔵 Below-Surface Defects - Inspecting Your Paint Visually

After washing the car to remove loose dirt and then claying the paint to remove above-surface bonded contaminants, the next thing you want to do is inspect your car's paint for what we call "below-surface defects".

Below-surface paint defects describe any kind of defect that is "in" the paint or below the surface level.

Types of below-surface paint defects

- Water spots or water etchings (craters in the paint)
- Scratches and swirls
- Straight-line scratches
- Cobweb or spiderweb swirls
- Rotary buffer swirls, buffer trails or holograms
- Oxidation
- Sub-surface stains

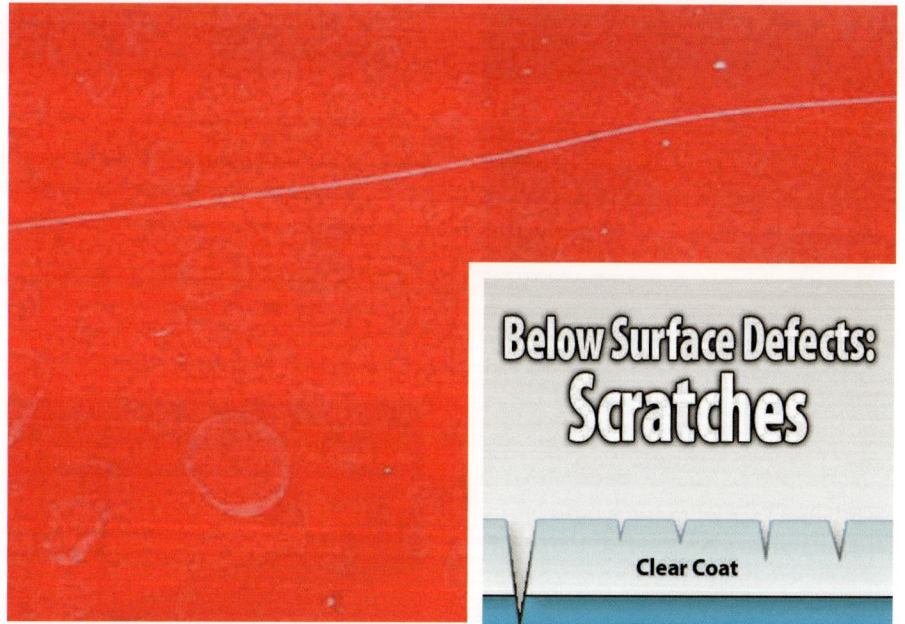

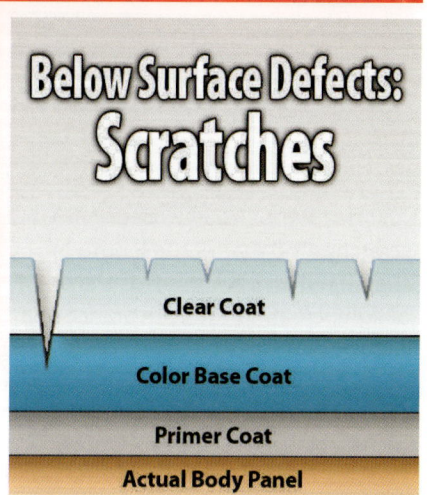

It's important to know whether the defects are on the surface or in the paint. Which type of defects you're trying to remove will determine how you remove them and which products you'll use.

- » **Question:** Which type of defect do you remove first?

- » **Answer:** Remove the above-surface bonded contaminants first and then go after the below-surface paint defects.

Why?
The above-surface bonded contaminants are on the top of the paint and should be removed first. Once they are out of the way, you can tackle everything that's below the surface.

Let's look at the different types of Below-Surface Paint Defects

🔵 Scratches

Most of us think of scratches as defects that are in straight-lines, like these.

Straightline scratch

Below Surface Defects: Scratches

Clear Coat

Color Base Coat

Primer Coat

Actual Body Panel

Scratches in fender caused by a shopping cart rubbing against the paint

🔵 Cobweb (Spiderweb) Swirls

The terms cobweb and spiderweb swirls come from the appearance of swirls in the paint which can look like a spider's cobweb. The swirls have a circular or radial pattern to them when the paint is highlighted with a strong focused point of bright light, such as the reflection of the sun or a *Brinkmann Swirl Finder Light*.

The scratches are not actually in circular patterns but are randomly inflicted throughout the entire finish. When you place a strong point of light on the surface, the edges of the scratches (no matter the length or shape) reflect back towards the point of light, creating the appearance of a circular pattern.

You can easily prove this to be the case by simply moving your body position in a way that moves the point of light around to a different place on a body panel.

As you move positions and thus move where the light is shining onto the paint, it appears that wherever you place the point of light, there appears to be a circular or cobweb pattern of scratches.

Cobweb scratches are instilled through normal wear and tear, improper washing and drying techniques, and use of worn-out wash mitts, sponges, brushes and drying towels or chamois. Automatic, hand, and even charity car washes will also contribute to the cobweb effect.

Cobwebs swirls are not the same as rotary buffer swirls
The cobweb swirl pattern is a different pattern than what you see with rotary buffer swirls. Rotary buffer swirls are not instilled randomly over time; they are instilled by a known source, usually in one detailing session.

» **How to remove**
The only way to remove cobweb or spiderweb swirls is to use a

compound or polish to abrade and the paint.

For more information see:
📖 *How to Remove Swirls and Scratches: The Major Correction Step*

👀 Rotary Buffer Swirls (Holograms or Buffer Trails)

Here you can see the rotary buffer was moved up and down the side of the door.

These are circular scratches caused by a rotary buffer, usually by the individual fibers that make up a wool cutting or polishing pad. The abrasives used in most compounds and polishes can also inflict swirls into a car's finish. Any time you're using a wool buffing pad and a compound or polish, you now have two things potentially inflicting swirls into the paint.

Foam pads can also inflict rotary buffer swirls into paint depending upon the aggressiveness of the foam formula and the product and tool used.

It is the direct drive rotating action of a rotary buffer that instills the circular pattern of scratches into paint, usually in some type of zig-zag pattern that mimics that in which it was moved over the paint by the technician.

It's possible to use a rotary buffer and

Below Surface Defects: Swirl Marks

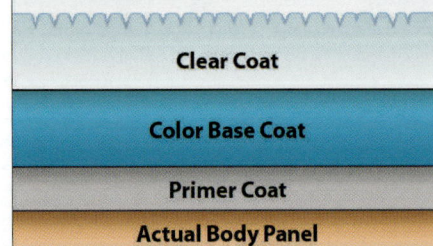

Clear Coat

Color Base Coat

Primer Coat

Actual Body Panel

Note how the swirls in the paint closest to the windshield have an almost floating or 3D effect; this is where the term hologram comes from in the context of talking about swirls caused by the misuse of a rotary buffer.

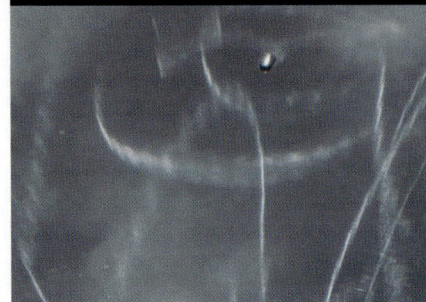

Here's the same hood under florescent lights. In this picture you can see the rotary buffer has left a pattern of trails which mimic how the rotary buffer was moved back and forth from the front of the hood towards the windshield.

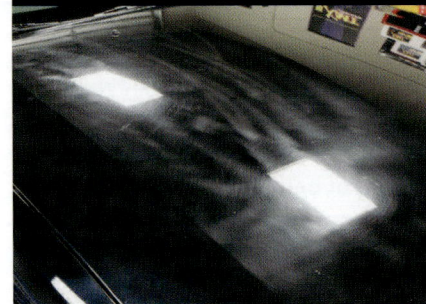

not instill swirls if the operator has a high skill level and uses quality pads and products. If swirls are instilled, a true professional will perform a follow-up procedure to remove them using less aggressive pads and products. For information on swirl removal, refer to this chapter:

   📖 *How to Remove Swirls and Scratches: The Major Correction Step*

🔵 Water Spots

Before you can remove water spots, you have to figure out which type you are dealing with.

⬧ *Three Types of Water Spots - Type I, Type II and Type III*

- **Type I Water Spots**
  Mineral deposits on the surface

- **Type II Water Spots**
  Craters in the paint

- **Type III Water Spots**
  Stains in the paint

Below Surface Defects: Water Spots

Clear Coat

Color Base Coat

Primer Coat

Actual Body Panel

Type I Water Spots
These are mineral deposits, or what people commonly call hard water spots. They can be the remains of minerals suspended in city water or well water that are left behind after the water evaporates from the finish. This can happen if hard water is allowed to dry on paint, whether it is from sprinkler water, acid rain, or other water sources.

  » **How To Remove**
    Type I Water Spots can usually be

removed by washing or wiping the paint clean using a normal car wash, rinseless wash, waterless wash or spray detailer.

There are also specialty products just for this including,

📖 *Duragloss 505 Water Spot Remover*

Type II Water Spots
These are actual etchings or craters in paint, caused by something corrosive in a water source landing on the finish without being removed before etching occured.

  » **How to remove**
    You must remove enough paint to level the surface with the lowest depths of the craters you're trying to remove. The best and safest way to do this is by machine, but it can also be done by hand.

For more information:

   📖 *How to Machine Polish Paint to a High Gloss: The Polishing or Minor Correction Step*
   📖 *How to Remove Swirls and Scratches: The Major Correction Step*

Type I and Type II Water Spots
In some cases, a water spot can be both a Type I and a Type II. This means there are mineral deposits sitting on top of the surface and the water could be corrosive enough to also etch the paint, leaving a crater where the spot formed.

  » **How to remove**
    Type I Water Spots can be washed or wiped from the paint, but if an imprint remains, you'll need to

Type II Water Spot - Crater Etching
If you look closely, you can see that the inner edges of the perimeter of the spot are angled downward. This is not a spot on the paint, it's a crater or etching.

Established Type I and II Water Spots
These water spots look like they're established water spots. In other words, every time it rains or a sprinkler goes off, the water pools in the same place giving any corrosive substances repeated opportunity to etch into the paint.

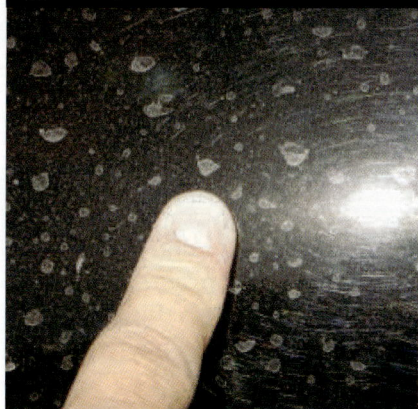

use a compound or polish to level the upper surface to the lowest depths of the imprints or craters left behind.

For more information:

   📖 *How to Machine Polish Paint to a High Gloss: The Polishing or Minor Correction Step*
   📖 *How to Remove Swirls and Scratches: The Major Correction Step*

Type III Water Spots
These are spots that look dull and faded and are found primarily on single stage paints. They are usually found after a water source pools on

Visual And Physical Inspection

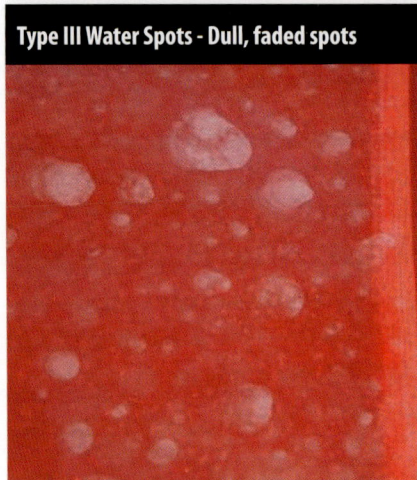

Oxidation Before

Oxidation After

Type III Water Spots - Dull, faded spots

the paint and is allowed to dwell on the surface.

Modern clearcoat paints tend to be harder and impermeable, so liquids don't penetrate easily. Therefore, stain spots tend to be topical, only affecting the very upper surface and are easier and safer to remove with a compound or polish.

Older single stage paints tend to be soft and permeable. It's common for liquids to penetrate into the paint and stain below the surface. Removing stains out of single stage paints can be risky because in order to remove the stains, you have to abrade the paint. If the stains penetrated too deep, then you risk removing too much paint in an effort to remove them completely.

> » **How to remove**
> You'll need to use a compound or polish and abrade the surface until you see the stained portion of the paint has been removed.

For more information:
- *How to Machine Polish Paint to a High Gloss: The Polishing or Minor Correction Step*
- *How to Remove Swirls and Scratches: The Major Correction Step*

Oxidation

Oxidation is the loss of at least one electron when two or more substances interact. When your car's paint is exposed to oxygen and moisture, the oxygen molecules interact with the paint resin, causing free radicals to be eliminated.

Simple Explanation
A free radical is an organic molecule that is unstable, or lacking an even number of electrons. These free radicals attach to electrons from other molecules, in this case referring to the oxygen molecules in the air or present in moisture/water. It is this process of losing electrons that eventually causes paint to appear dull, whitish, or chalky looking.

Oxidation is more common to old-school single stage paints, but it can and will happen to basecoat/clearcoat finishes if the paint is neglected long enough and exposed to outdoor climates for great lengths of time.

- *Dodge Neon Extreme Makeover with Dodo Juice Need for Speed*

> » **How to remove**
> Oxidation can be removed by

abrading the surface with some type of abrasive compound and/ or polish, which will remove the oxidized paint and expose a fresh layer of non-oxidized paint underneath. After the oxidized paint is removed, it's a good idea to use a finishing polish and then seal the paint with a wax or paint sealant.

For more information:
- *How to Remove Swirls and Scratches: The Major Correction Step*

RIDS = Random Isolated Deeper Scratches

This type of scratch comes from normal wear and tear. RIDS are like tracers in that they are deeper scratches that show up after the shallow scratches have been removed through a machine or hand buffing process, usually with a compound or paint cleaner. After the shallow swirls

After removing thousands of shallow swirls and scratches, this single, random, isolated deeper scratch remained in the paint on a 2011 Corvette.

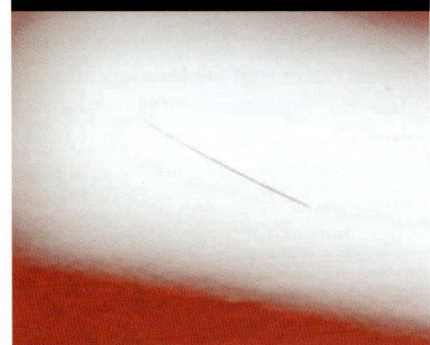

and scratches have been removed, any deeper scratches that remain will now show up like a sore thumb to your eyes because there are no longer thousands of lighter, more shallow scratches camouflaging them.

Tracers

Tracers are deeper scratches left by the hand sanding process, usually in straight lines because most people move their hand in a back and forth motion when wet sanding. Tracers show up after the paint is compounded and all shallow scratches have been removed. Remaining in the paint are the deeper sanding marks and these are called tracers.

Tracers are usually difficult to remove because they are deeper and removing them means either re-sanding or re-compounding to level the surface. The problem with re-sanding is that you could remove one group of tracers, only to leave behind a new set of tracers, making this a catch-22 situation. This is why it's so important to use the highest quality finishing papers you can obtain.

This paint was sanded by hand and then the sanding marks were removed, but a few tracers remained.

Pigtails

When an abrasive particle gets trapped between the paint and the face of your oscillating sanding disc, it abrades the paint in a curly pattern

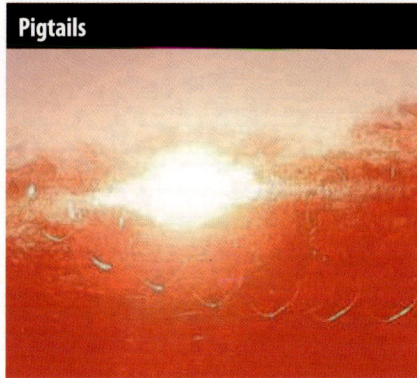

Pigtails

that represents a pigtail, hence the name.

> » **How to remove**
> Removing tracers and pigtails can be a little tricky. The safest way is to re-sand using a very fine grit finishing paper or foam backed finishing disc in the #2000 to #3000 range. You can use the Feathersanding Technique by hand using the techniques shared below.

📖 *RIDS and Feathersanding - A Highly Specialized Technique by Mike Phillips*

💬 My personal favorite way to remove RIDS, tracers and pigtails is by using the Griot's Garage 3" Mini DA polisher with a #3000 Meguiar's Unigrit Finishing Disc.

The small 3" Griot's Garage Mini Polisher works great for a spot dampsander. After sanding the affected area, simply use a compound or a medium polish with the appropriate pad. Remember, if you're working on a daily driver, it's usually a good idea to only improve a deeper defect than it is to try to completely remove it due to the risk of removing too much paint.

- 💻 *Griot's Garage 3" Mini Polisher*
- 💻 *Meguiars Unigrit 3 Inch Foam Interface Pad*
- 💻 *Meguiars Unigrit 3000 3 Inch Finishing Discs, 15 per box*

Machine sanding paint to remove below-surface defects is an advanced skill and caution should be used.

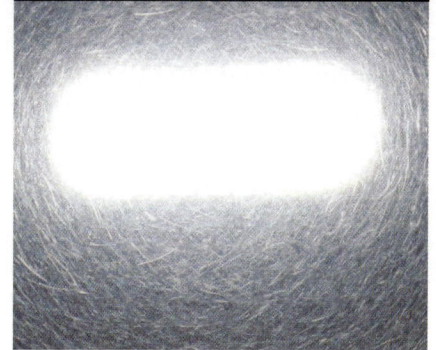

Extreme Micromarring - This micromarring was created using too aggressive of a compound with a DA Polisher

Micromarring - Tick-Marks - DA Haze

These three terms describe a scratch pattern caused by the oscillating and rotating action from compounding using a DA polisher.

Unlike cobweb swirls or rotary buffer swirls, the scratch pattern instilled by a dual action polisher is made up of millions of tiny scratches. Some are curved or circular, but some are straight, like a small tick mark.

Tick marks are a sign that either the paint is easily scratched or the pad and compound or polish you're using are too aggressive to finish without leaving marring. In most cases, tick marks can be removed by re-polishing with a different pad and product combination.

> » **How to remove micromarring**
> Micromarring is removed by re-polishing the area using a finer polish.

For more information:
📖 *How to Machine Polish Paint to a High Gloss - The Polishing or Minor Correction Step*

◐ Paint Transfer

This occurs when the paint from one object is transferred to another, usually the result of some kind of accident.

» **How to remove paint transfer**
Paint transfer is easier to remove by hand because you can exert a lot of force with a few finger tips to abrade the offending paint from your car's paint. Then, after removing the paint transfer, finish with some machine polishing to perfect the paint. For more information on removing paint transfer, see my forum article.

🖵 *How To Remove Paint Transfer*

◐ Chemical Stains

Chemical stains are more common with older single stage paints since they tend to be more porous, allowing liquids penetrate easily into the paint. It's much more difficult to chemically stain clearcoats because they are impermeable. Chances are that if some type of liquid chemical makes contact with your car's paint, it will attack and etch the very top surface of the clearcoat but not seep into the paint and stain it.

» **How to remove stains**
To remove stains, you need to abrade the surface with some type of compound or polish until you remove enough paint to level the very upper surface with the lowest depths of the stain or etching.

For more information:
📖 *How to Remove Swirls and Scratches: The Major Correction Step*

1. Show Car Quality

Paint in this condition is as perfect as it can be in any lighting condition. The only defects you should see are fingerprints, smudges or light dust on what otherwise appears to be a flawless show car finish.

The finish on a car in this category can hold up to close scrutiny under bright lights by the most discerning eyes.

The paint in this category has been put through a series of machine polishing procedures to maximize DOI (distinction of image), gloss, clarity, depth, reflection, richness of color, shine and even slickness.

If needed, the paint has been sanded, cut and buffed to remove orange peel and any other surface texture to create a 100% flat surface to maximize DOI.

RIDS have been removed to the extent that it is safe to do so without compromising the top coat. Paint is meticulously cared for on an as-needed basis to ensure that it is always display-ready.

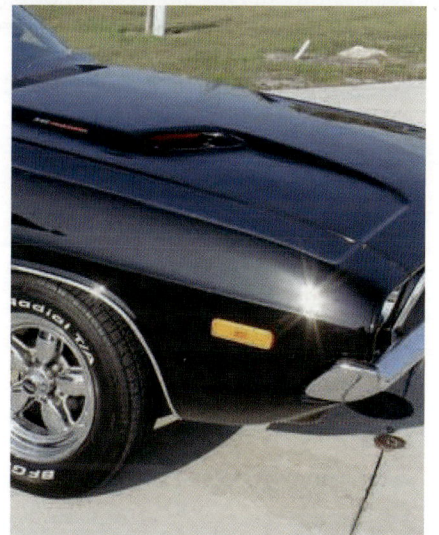

2. Excellent Condition

Paint in this category looks factory new or better. The paint looks like it has been professionally machine polished and sealed with a wax, paint sealant or coating and is regularly maintained.

When viewed in bright sunlight, the paint looks excellent. There are few or no visible swirls or scratches, or so few that there are not enough of them to require machine polishing.

Paint Condition Categories

3. Good Condition
Light Swirls, Scratches, Water Spots And Oxidation.

When viewed in bright sunlight, the paint should look pretty good overall, with the exception that it has light or shallow looking cobweb swirls and scratches throughout the paint. Any water spot problems should be shallow imprint type stains common to Type I Water Spots, certainly not deep craters like Type II or Type III where the paint is physically stained. Paint in this condition would require one or two polishing steps before a finishing wax could be applied to bring the quality to Excellent or Show Car Quality.

4. Mildly Neglected

Normal day-in, day-out wear and tear and minimal appearance maintenance outside of the occasional car wash. Paint in this condition has medium to light swirls, scratches, water spots and oxidation.

5. Severely Neglected

Paint in this condition has deep swirls, scratches, water spots and oxidation. Paint in this condition has normal day-in, day-out wear and tear plus no real regular maintenance. Vehicles in this category are rarely washed on a regular basis and when they are washed, they are washed improperly or taken through an automatic car wash.

- **Cobweb swirls and scratches**
  Paint that is severely neglected, when viewed in bright, overhead sunlight, will show many swirls and scratches with an overall hazy appearance.

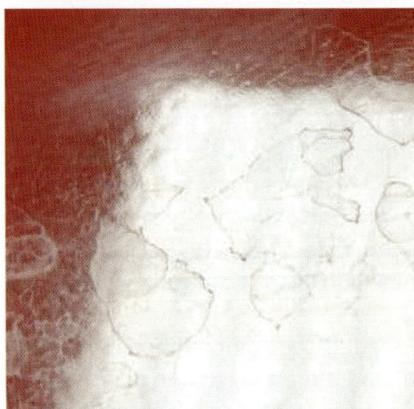

- **Water spots**
  Paint that is in the severely neglected category can have Type I, Type II and Type III water spots on all horizontal panels and even the vertical panels if caused by a sprinkler or some type of water spray.

- **Severe oxidation**
  Paint in this category has oxidized to the point where the surface has a uniform dull appearance to the horizontal surfaces, and to some extent, the vertical panels. Clearcoats do oxidize, but usually slower than single stage paints and don't normally get the whitish, chalky appearance with a rough texture common to old, neglected single stage lacquers and enamels.

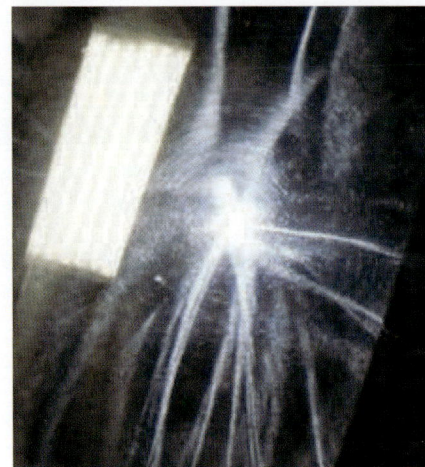

6. Horrendous Swirls - Caused By The Misuse Of A Rotary Buffer

This category is primarily for cars that have been improperly polished using a rotary buffer, leaving the finish inflicted with rotary buffer swirls, also known as holograms or buffer trails. The severity of the swirls can range from shallow to deep, depending upon the pad and product used with the rotary buffer as well as technique, or lack thereof.

7. Extreme Oxidation

Paint in this category is primarily associated with traditional single stage lacquer and enamel paints and normally found cars built before 1980. Extremely oxidized paint has deteriorated to the point that it has a chalky, whitish appearance.

Mike Phillips' - The Art of Detailing

Before removing oxidation

After removing oxidation

Paint in this category is typically antique or original. Extreme oxidation can be corrected by carefully removing the dead, oxidized paint and rejuvenating the remaining paint with polishing oils. After polishing, the color is restored and remains even when exposed to sunlight. If the color fades away, this is an indicator that the paint has become unstable.

8. Extreme Orange Peel

Paint in this category is primarily aftermarket. It doesn't normally include factory orange peel on a brand new car or truck. Due to how thin the top coat is on a factory paint job, there's a certain amount of risk you have to accept if you choose to remove the factory orange peel. Repaints will tend to have enough material that the problem can be safely corrected via sanding and buffing.

9. Unstable

This category is for older, single stage paints that have been exposed to the sun for a long enough period of time that the pigments have become unstable. Even if you remove the oxidation and saturate the paint with some type of polishing oils, any original color that is restored is only a temporary fix. Therefore, when the paint is exposed to the sun or after a few days pass, the color fades back to where it was before you started.

10. Clearcoat Failure

Clearcoat failure is the point in which the top clear layer of paint has either de-laminated from the basecoat and is peeling off or has deteriorated to the point in which it's turning a whitish color. Full blown deterioration

occurs when it has turned white and is flaking off and the car looks like it has a severe rash.

11. Past The Point Of No Return

Paint in this condition falls into one of the above categories, but it is so far gone that nothing you pour out of a bottle or scoop out of a can from any company will fix it.

What's Your Goal?

Which products do you need?
After you wash and dry your car and inspect the paint both visually and with your sense of touch, it's time figure out which products you'll need to detail it.

Your goal will determine your products and steps to follow

- *Do you want to create a true show car finish?*
- *Do you want to simply wash and wax your car?*

Simply washing and waxing your car is pretty straight forward. If you want to create a true show car finish, however, depending upon the condition of the paint, this could take a few hours or several days. The biggest time issue with creating a show car finish is what we call the major correction step. In this step, you'll be removing below-surface defects like swirls and scratches.

In order to remove below-surface defects, you need to use some type of abrasive product to gently and in a controlled manner remove a little paint from the surface until the upper surface is level with the lowest depths of the defects you're trying to remove.

The fastest way to remove swirls and scratches is by machine. Even if you work by machine, it can still take hours because modern clearcoat paints tend to be harder than traditional single stage paints.

◧ The 1-Step Approach

If you only want perform one step after washing and drying, but your paint is neglected, then you want to use a one-step cleaner wax.

1. Wash and Dry

2. Inspect - Inspect the paint both with your sense of touch and visually.

3. Clay Paint - Remove above-surface bonded contaminants using detailing clay.

4. Apply Cleaner Wax

As you can see, even a one step approach includes more than a single step as you have to wash and dry to remove loose dirt, and if your inspection reveals a rough feeling texture to the horizontal surfaces of the paint, then it's best to use clay before applying any kind of wax. A cleaner wax will remove some above-surface bonded contaminants, but claying is the most effective way to remove all of them.

A cleaner wax will clean, polish and protect in one step:

» **Clean** - Cleaning undoes the damage done to the paint caused by neglecting regular maintenance and normal wear and tear.

» **Polish** - Polishing will restore smoothness and clarity.

» **Protect** - Protection ingredients are left behind on the surface to protect the paint and lock in the shine created by the cleaning and polishing ingredients.

A one step approach does cut out two extra steps, but you're not going to remove any of the deeper below-surface defects like swirls, scratches and water spots. Cleaner waxes vary in that some are non-abrasive and rely on chemical cleaners, while others contain abrasives which will remove swirls and scratches. For show car results, you're going to want to perform a multiple-step process using a dedicated compound and polish, not rely on a cleaner wax to tackle all the below surface paint defects.

For more information:
📖 *How To Apply Cleaner Waxes*

◧ The Multi-Step Approach

If your goal is to create a like-new or show car finish and the paint needs to be clayed and/or have swirls, scratches and water spots removed, you'll need to do multiple steps to reach your goal.

How many steps you'll need to do will depend upon the condition of your car's paint. The worse the condition, the more steps you'll need to restore it to a like-new or show car quality.

A multiple step process is usually as follows:

1. **Wash and Dry.**

2. **Inspect** - Inspect the paint both with your sense of touch and visually.

3. **Clay Paint** - Remove above-surface bonded contaminants using detailing clay.

4. **Major Correction Step** - Use a compound or a swirl remover to remove swirls, scratches, oxidation, staining and water spot etchings.

5. **Polishing or Minor Correction Step** - Use a fine or less aggressive finishing polish to follow-up the more aggressive correction step to further refine any remaining shallow defects and maximize gloss, clarity and smoothness of the finish.

6. **Jewelling Step** - In this optional step, you will repeat the last step using your finest or least aggressive finishing polish and a soft foam finishing pad.

7. **Sealing or Protection Step** - Since you have already removed the defects and polished the paint to a high gloss, using a cleaner wax would be working backwards in the process. At this point, you would use either a finishing wax, a paint sealant or coating that offers no cleaning, just pure protection.

Detailing clay is a relatively new product on the market relative to most other car care products. It was introduced to the car detailing world sometime in the early 1990s and relative to the history of the car which dates back to the late 1880s, it's only been around for a short time.

In that short time, it's become very popular and actually a staple in the professional detailing industry. Clay enables you to remove above-surface bonded contaminants without using a rubbing compound or sanding the paint.

This key feature is invaluable when it comes to restoring and/or maintaining a high gloss finish because gloss comes from smoothness.

Any car that is daily driven is subject to a build-up of contaminants on the horizontal or flat panels, so claying is usually an important step for any detailing project. Most detailers use detailing clay as a normal procedure for every car they wash and wax - it's that important.

◉ Claying - What, Where, Why & When

» **What is detailing clay?**
Detailing clay is type of synthetic or man-made clay with a special type of abrasive in it.

» **What does detailing clay do?**
Clay has the ability to remove contaminants that are bonded to your car's paint and won't come off when washing or wiping your car clean. In simple terms, it works to abrade anything sticking to the paint above the surface level. It then glides over the surface of the paint - it does not sand or abrade the paint itself.

» **Where?**
Any smooth surface, including glossy paint, glass, hard plastic, chrome, stainless steel, and gel coat.

» **Why use detailing clay?**
By removing any contaminants from the paint, your choice of wax or sealant can more easily bond or adhere, thus it can last and protect longer.

» **When to use detailing clay**
Anytime you discover a rough or textured feel to your car's paint. It's a good practice to feel your car's paint after you wash and dry the vehicle to inspect for above-surface bonded contaminants. How often you need to clay depends upon what's in the air where you park your car. Normally, you would clay the paint after washing and drying and before any other paint-related procedure.

» **How to use detailing clay**
Knead the clay into a round patty, like a pancake. It should be large enough to cover the palm of your hand or at least your 4 fingers. Spray a clay lubricant onto the clay patty and onto a section of paint and then rub the clay over

Mist clay lubricant onto paint, then onto face of detailing clay and then rub clay over a section of a body panel until contaminants are removed.

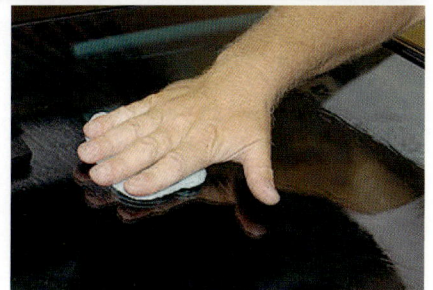

Claying Overview

the paint until it glides effortlessly. Wipe off the residue on this section of paint and move onto a new section, overlapping into the previous section.

4 Benefits Of Claying Your Car's Paint

Let's take a look at the four primary benefits to using detailing clay.

- Claying safely removes above-surface bonded contaminants
- Claying enables your choice of wax or paint sealant to better bond or adhere to the paint
- Claying restores a silky-smooth, clean surface
- Claying makes polishing easier, more effective and safer

1. **Claying safely removes above-surface bonded contaminants**
   If your car is parked outside for any length of time, then any dirt or airborne contaminants that land on the paint will tend to bond if they are not removed in a timely manner. Once bonded, some of them won't come off from normal washing. This is where detailing clay comes into the picture.

Before detailing clay became popular, people would use coarse rubbing compounds to remove above-surface bonded contaminants and while these types of products would work, they would also

- Instill scratches into the paint
- Remove perfectly good paint

These are two things you don't want to do to your car's precious and thin layer of paint.

2. **Claying enables your choice of wax or paint sealant to better bond or adhere to the paint**
   Restoring a clean surface maximizes the bond between the paint and a wax or sealant.

The paint on the 1949 Chevrolet Sedan Delivery is incredibly glossy and the results started with claying the paint to remove above-surface bonded contaminants.

One of the most common questions I am asked is, *"How long will brand X Car Wax last?"*

The correct answer is, *"It depends upon how well the surface is prepared to accept the wax".*

You see, a good chemist will create a car wax or sealant formulation to bond or adhere to car paint, not a layer of dirt.

When contaminants build up on the surface, they create a layer or film of gunk. The protection ingredients cannot reach the paint until this layer of contaminants is removed.

If above-surface, airborne contaminants are on the paint when a wax or paint sealant is applied, it will not last very long because it won't be able to bond very well.

3. **Claying paint restores a silky-smooth, clean surface**
   A build-up of contaminants on your car's finish creates an irregular surface or texture that feels rough or bumpy to the touch. This uneven, bumpy surface reduces gloss. Claying your car's paint will remove the contaminants, restoring a smooth, high gloss surface.

Fresh clay used on the hood of a 1973 Lincoln Continental that sits outside 24 hours a day, 7 days a week

4. **Claying paint makes polishing easier, more effective and safer**
   By removing any above-surface bonded contaminants, you enable your polish and pad to immediately work on the paint with nothing in the way.

A smoother surface allows your pad to move over the surface easier, with less potential for hopping or grabbing.

You reduce the potential for accidental marring during the buffing process, since there are no contaminants that can come loose and become trapped between the pad and the paint.

🔴 How To Clay Your Car

Detailing clay can be purchased by a number of suppliers. In this example, I'm using Pinnacle Ultra Poly Clay, which is available as a *single 4 ounce clay bar* or *two 4 ounce clay bars*.

Four ounces is approximately 114 grams, which is very healthy chunk of clay that you can easily break into two pieces. Use one piece and save the rest for another project.

1. Remove the cellophane wrapper

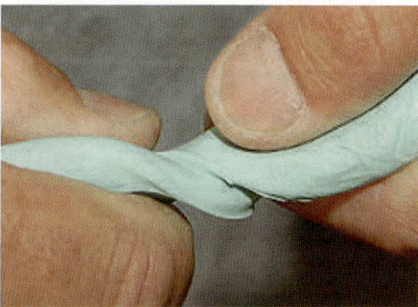

2. Tear the clay bar into two pieces

You can store your clay in the plastic container it comes or a sealable sandwich baggie.

3. Knead the clay into a flat patty like a small pancake. A round patty of about 4 1/2 to 5 inches in diameter works well for most people.

4. When you're ready to start claying, mist your clay lubricant onto the face of the clay patty. In this example, we're using *Pinnacle Clay Lubricant*.

5. Next, spray the section you're going to clay. This is usually a section

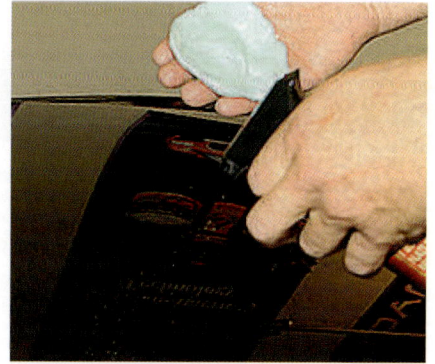

of approximately 16 to 20 square inches. You don't want to work on too large of an area at one time because you want to be thorough with your claying passes, so stick with a manageable section.

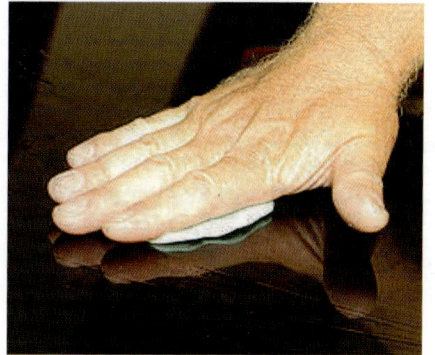

6. Begin moving the clay patty over the paint. Most people, including myself, use a simple back and forth motion, working the clay in straight lines over the paint. You can move your hand in straight lines or circles or a combination of both if you'd like. Because detailing clay is non-abrasive (except for aggressive grades), as long as everything is clean, it doesn't matter which way you move your hand because you shouldn't be instilling scratches into the paint.

In some cases, you will feel the clay try to drag as you move it over the surface. As the clay removes the bonded contaminants, you'll notice a decrease in drag and the clay will begin to glide effortlessly over the paint. This is an indicator that this section of paint is now clean and smooth.

Claying Overview

After you're finished claying a section, wipe the excess residue from the surface before moving on to new territory. This means having an ample supply of clean microfiber towels on hand and a clean and accessible area to store them.

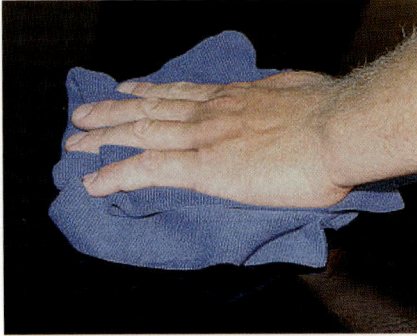

7. After you wipe the section clean and dry, check the surface with your hand to ensure it is in fact smooth and glassy feeling. If it is, try to remember how long you clayed the section or approximately how many strokes you used and then lock this into your memory and duplicate this to each new section you clay. Keep in mind that some bonded contaminants are more stubborn than others and may take more effort to remove or a more aggressive clay formula.

8. After claying each section, turn your clay patty over and inspect for contaminants.

If contaminants are discovered, remove any large dirt particles and then fold your clay in half and re-knead it to expose a fresh surface.

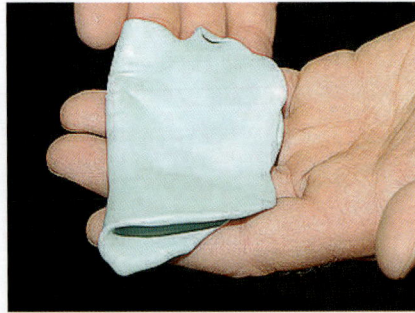

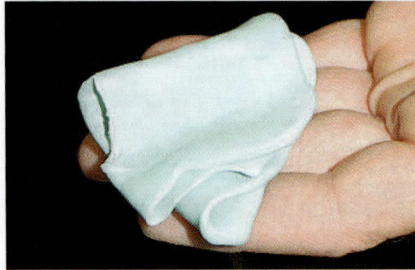

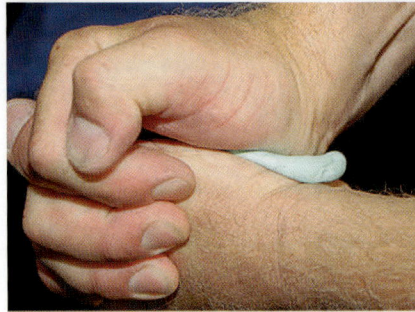

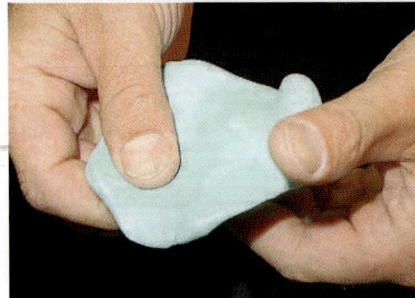

Now that I have the clay patty started, I will hold the small, thick patty between my fingers and thumbs and begin methodically kneading it to again create a round patty about 4 1/2 to 5 inches in diameter.

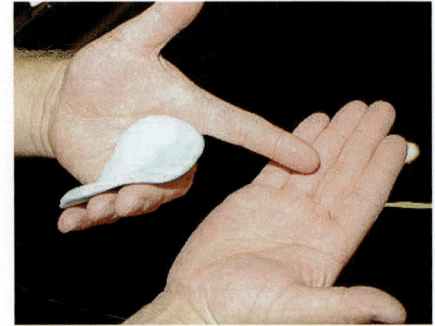

You want it to fit across the distance of your hand with your fingers next to one another, with your fingertips extending past the edge of the patty.

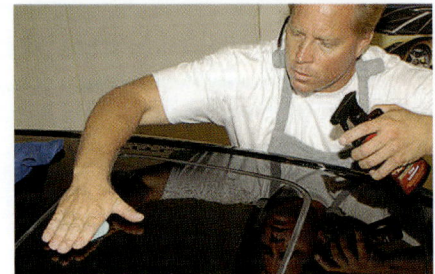

9. Repeat the above until you've clayed all the contaminated panels, wiping the clay lube residue off after claying each section.

💬 Here's why you should place the clay in your hand with your fingertips extended past the edge of the clay patty. If you position the clay like

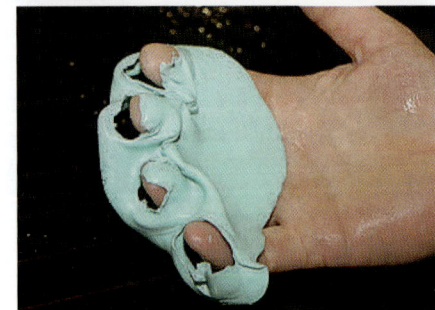

Mike Phillips' - The Art of Detailing

this, you'll apply equal pressure over the entire surface of the face of your fingers without really thinking about it. This will help to place equal pressure over the surface of the clay patty. You can use the patty until you decide to stop, fold the clay over and re-knead it. In other words, you're in control. If you place your fingertips inside and on top of the clay patty, you tend to exert more pressure on your fingertips and you'll push holes through the clay patty. You now have to stop, fold the clay and re-knead it whether you were ready or not. Now, the clay is in control. It's just a little tip, but I like to be in control of each process; you can try this technique and then make up your own mind.

If the car you're working on has any kind of vinyl graphics, stickers or pinstripes, avoid claying over them as you can easily cause the edges to lift. Once the edges of any graphic have lifted, it's never going to lay flat against the surface again and usually will lift more and more. This also applies when working with paint care products.

Important
Claying your car's paint will tend to remove any previously applied wax or paint sealant. After you finish claying the paint, at a minimum, you'll want to apply a fresh coat of wax or a paint sealant.

If you don't re-apply a layer of protection, your car's paint will be exposed to the elements and subject to deterioration.

◉ Frequently Asked Questions About Detailing Clay

» **What is detailing clay?**
From the website for the United States Patent and Trademark Office, detailing clay is a plastic flexible grinding stone.

» **How long does clay last?**
How long a piece of clay will last is completely determined by the amount of contaminants that have built-up on the paint of your car.

» **How much clay do I need?**
You only need to use about 50 grams of clay to form a clay patty large enough to clay your car's paint. Clay normally comes in 50, 100 or 200 gram bars or chunks of clay. If you have one of the larger versions, simply break it into smaller pieces and store the unused clay for a future detailing project.

Example: *Wolfgang Elastic Poly Clay bar* is a hefty 200 gram bar of detailing clay that can easily be broken up into four 50-gram clay bars, or even 2-3 larger bars depending upon your personal preference. Form one chunk into a clay patty and store the other pieces for a future detailing session.

» **Will claying remove swirls and scratches?**
No. Claying only removes above-surface bonded contaminants and does not remove below-surface defects like swirls and scratches and Type II Water Spot Etchings.

Average Paint Condition After Washing

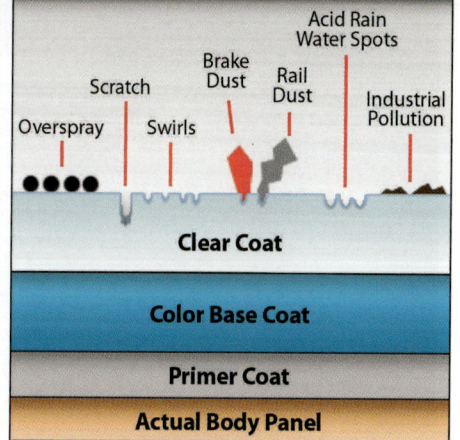

After Claying the Paint Surface

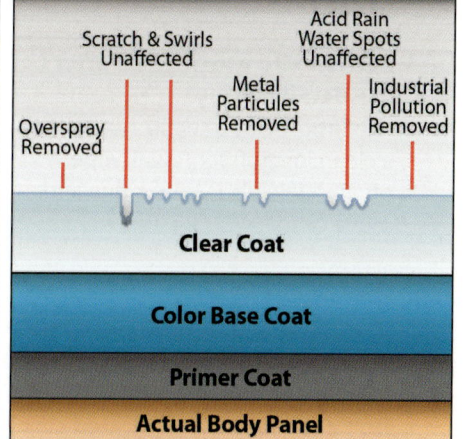

» **How often do I need to clay my car's paint?**
As often as needed as dictated by the results from your hands-on inspection.

For more information:
📖 *The Baggie Test*

» **Do I use detailing clay before or after polishing?**
First, remove the defects sitting on top of the surface (above-surface bonded contaminants). Then, remove the defects that are in the paint (below surface defects).

• **Above-surface bonded contaminant** = Tree sap, overspray paint, industrial fallout, rail dust, industrial fallout and airborne pollution.

Claying Overview

- **Below-Surface Defects** = Swirls, Scratches, Type II Water Spots and Bird Dropping Etchings

» **Do I need to wash my car after I use detailing clay?**
No. Simply clay a section and using a clean, microfiber towel, wipe off any clay lubricant residue and move onto a new section.

Read Full Article here:
💻 *Do I need to wash my car after I use detailing clay*

» **Do I need to use a dedicated clay lubricant or can I just use soapy water?**
The goal of claying your car is to remove above-surface bonded contaminants safely, to do this you want and need to use a lubricant on the surface of the paint so the clay will glide over the paint while it's abrading off the contaminants. Soapy water doesn't wipe off to reveal a "just detailed look". In fact, it usually looks streaky and this will worry people who are inexperienced. Of course, any follow-up steps like polishing and/or waxing will remove any smears or streaks, but again, inexperienced detailers tend to panic at the appearance of anything other than clean, shiny paint as they don't have the experience to understand the next steps will fix the problem.

💬 My recommendation…
I recommend using a clay lube that is matched to the clay you use or a clay lube from a reputable company.

» **Will using detailing clay remove previously applied wax?**
Yes. To what degree detailing clay will remove previously applied coats of wax or sealant is a great question. However, there is no simple definitive answer because there are too many variables involved, such as:
- Type of clay - level of aggressiveness or non-aggressiveness
- How many passes made over each square inch of paint
- Downward pressure used by the person using the clay
- Amount of lubricant used
- Skill level of person doing the claying
- Type of protection ingredients bonded to the surface

» **I bought a new car; do I still need to clay the paint?**
Most people think that because the car they bought is brand new, it shouldn't need anything. However, from the time the car rolled off the assembly line and out of the manufacturing plant, it's been exposed to the air and any and all contaminants in the air.

This would include:
- Shipping by truck, train, ship
- Sitting parked in an unloading area
- Sitting parked at a VPC or Vehicle Processing Center
- Sitting parked outside at a dealership lot

Whether or not you need to clay your new vehicle can only be determined by the results of a hands-on inspection. For more information, refer back to the section covering *Visual Inspection*.

» **Are there different types of clay?**
Generally speaking, there are 3 different grades of clay:
- Ultra Fine Grade
- Fine or Medium Grade
- Aggressive Grade

There may other niche grades, but the above grades are the industry norm. The aggressive grades of detailing clay can be quite abrasive as they are intended to remove things like overspray paint, which can be very difficult. It's possible for aggressive clays to mar the paint during the claying process - this is called clay haze, which is another term for clay-induced scratching.

Keep in mind that the majority of the market that uses the aggressive clay is going to follow this with some type of machine compounding or polishing procedure.

» **Which type of clay should I use?**
For most people working on their daily drivers, the Ultra Fine, Fine and Medium grades are normally considered safe for use by just about anyone and can be used for all general claying purposes.

People that regularly wash and wax their cars will tend to stick with the Ultra Fine clays, because that's all that's needed to maintain a clean, smooth surface.

Pinnacle Ultra Poly Clay is an ultra fine clay and a good choice for frequent claying.

» **If I drop my clay on the ground, can I keep using it?**
No. Detailing clay tends to be tacky and any sharp, abrasive particles on the ground will stick to it. Some of these particles will be invisible. If you attempt to use clay that has been dropped onto the ground, you risk instilling deeper scratches that will be difficult and time consuming to remove.

Cut your losses, discard the dropped clay and get some new or unused clay to finish the claying process. This is another good reason to cut larger clay bars up into smaller chunks.

» **Do you clay single stage paint the same way you clay a clearcoat finish?**
This depends on whether or not the single stage paint is oxidized.

If you're working on severely oxidized single stage paint, then it's a good idea to use a compound or a paint cleaner to remove the dead, oxidized paint. Otherwise, as you're claying, the dead, oxidized paint will load up onto

your detailing clay.

The follow-up question I get to my answer on claying oxidized paint usually goes like this,

"If I use a compound or paint cleaner to remove the dead, oxidized paint, can't I skip the claying step? Won't the compound remove the above-surface bonded contaminants?"

The answer is,
"If you remove the dead, oxidized paint using an aggressive compound and wool cutting pad with a rotary buffer, then YES, you will likely remove any and all above-surface bonded contaminants".

If you apply the compound any other way, like with a foam pad instead of a wool cutting pad, and any other tool besides a rotary buffer, then here's what I know from personal experience.

In the past, when I've removed heavy oxidation by hand or with a DA style polisher and then went back and clayed the cleaned paint, when I turned the clay over to inspect it, I've found above-surface bonded contaminants that were left even after compounding.

Foam pads tend to just glide over the contaminants, while a wool cutting pad will actually cut them off the paint. This has to do with both the type of material (foam vs wool fibers), and the drive action of the tool, with the rotary buffer being the most aggressive tool.

That leads me to this statement:
"Claying is the most effective way to remove above-surface bonded contaminants".

The DA Polisher

DA polishers Overview

All five of the below tools are of the same type. They are all single head, random orbital polishers that use a free floating spindle assembly for a drive mechanism.

🖥 Porter Cable 7424XP

- 4.5 AMP
- 500 Watt Motor
- 5 pounds
- 3 Year Limited Warranty
- 1 Year Free Service

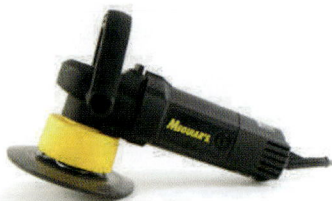

🖥 Meguiar's G110v2

- 4.2 AMP
- 430 Watt Motor
- 5 pounds
- 1 Year Limited Warranty

🖥 Griot's Garage Random Orbital polisher

- 7.0 AMP
- 850 Watt Motor
- 5.5 pounds
- Griot's Lifetime Warranty

🖥 Griot's Garage 3" Mini polisher

- 2.0 AMP
- 240 Watt Motor
- Griot's Lifetime Warranty

🖥 Shurhold Dual Action polisher

- 4.2 Amps
- 500 Watt Motor
- 5 pounds
- 1 Year Limited Warranty

The Basics

- Lightweight, compact in size and easy to hold while buffing.

- Very easy to learn how to use and master like a professional.

- Always enable you to create better results faster on clearcoat paints as compared to working by hand.

- Variable speed polishers - you can pick and set the speed setting from a very low speed of 1 to a very high speed setting of 6 for removing swirls and scratches.

- Offers more than enough power to remove swirls and scratches out of your car's clearcoat finish.

- Very versatile in that they can all be used to remove swirls, polish paint to a high gloss, and apply or remove wax or paint sealant.

- Can safely be used on cars, trucks, SUVs, boats, motorcycles, RVs, trailers and pretty much anything with paint, plastic, or gel-coat.

- Easiest tool to learn how to use if you are new to machine polishing.

- Very safe and when used correctly, they will neither instill swirls into your car's paint nor burn through it.

Safest tool to learn how to use

A lot of people are apprehensive about letting anyone work on their car's paint with a machine let alone learning to do it themselves. This is because of all the horror stories associated with machine buffers.

🗨 Here are the two common fears people have about machine polishing.

1. **Burning through the paint, also called strike-through.**
   To burn through the paint means to buff so long on a section of a car that enough paint is removed to abrade through the clear layer of paint, exposing the colored layer of paint. If by chance you're working on a single stage paint and burn through the colored coat, then you'll expose the primer.

The problem with burning through the clear layer of paint and exposing the colored layer is that the colored layer is dull or matte in appearance. No amount of buffing with any kind of polish or wax will restore a glossy appearance to the exposed color coat. When this happens, the only way to fix the problem is to have the area repainted.

The problem of burn-through is normally a problem associated with the misuse of rotary buffers, which are direct drive tools. DA polishers, on the other hand, use a free Floating Spindle Bearing Assembly, which makes this a non-issue.

2. **Swirls**

Swirls are scratches that appear to us as being in some type of circular pattern instead of straight lines. They can be the result of improper maintenance techniques as well as improper use of a rotary buffer.

For more information, see:
📖 *Paint Condition Categories*

DA Polishers Are Very Safe!

When used correctly, you can safely buff out your car's paint without burning through or instilling swirls. DA polishers are the easiest and safest polishers to learn how to use.

I have personally taught thousands of people how to successfully use DA polishers and the techniques taught in this how-to book will ensure you don't experience either of these two problems.

To show just how safe these types of tools are to use, is my son (shown right) at age 9 using a Meguiar's G110v2 Dual Action polisher to apply wax to the front of a 1966 Batmobile recreation owned by my good friend Nate Truman in Southern California.

Free Floating Spindle Bearing Assembly

The reason why DA polishers, including the Porter Cable 7424XP, Meguiar's G110v2, Griot's Garage 6" ROP and Shurhold polishers are so safe to use for beginners and pros alike is because they all use what's referred to as a free floating spindle bearing assembly.

With this drive mechanism, if you apply too much downward pressure to the face of the buffing pad or hold the tool so that more pressure is applied to just an edge of the buffing pad, it will simply stop spinning. Therefore, you cannot burn through the paint nor instill swirls. Rotary buffers are direct drive tools. With this drive mechanism, the pad will continuously rotate and there is no mechanism or design feature that will stop it. This gives the rotary buffer a lot of power for correction work, but with that power comes a certain level of risk.

It is the free floating spindle bearing assembly that takes the risk or danger out of machine polishing. This has cleared the path to introduce and enable the masses to machine polish and truly create professional, show car results without having to learn how to use a rotary buffer.

Handle Or No Handle

The topic of handles on DA polishers comes up from time to time, and in all my classes, I show how to use these tools with and without the handles. I leave it up to each person to decide which approach works best. Regardless of which approach you prefer, the handle can affect pad rotation, so check out the below information and then do some experimenting with your DA polisher and see which approach works best for you.

- **Reduced fatigue**
  Without a handle, you will have better control over the polisher and pad with less overall energy required for operation. Reducing fatigue is important because buffing out an entire car requires anywhere from an average of 4 to 12 hours, depending upon the size of the vehicle, condition of the paint and the goal for the end results.

- **Keeping the pad flat to the surface**
  When using a DA polisher, it's important to keep the pad flat to the surface. This helps to maintain pad rotation, which is essential in the defect removal process.

Without the use of a handle, even,

downward pressure can be applied over the head of the polisher. If you apply uneven pressure to the head of the polisher, you can stop the pad from rotating and at this point you will no longer be removing swirls and scratches.

- **Bail handle - Meguiar's, Griot's and Shurhold polishers**
Like using a polisher without a handle, the bail handle enables you to apply pressure directly over the head of the polisher, which helps you to keep the pad completely flat against the surface.

The drawback to a bail handle is that it extends your hand away from the head of the polisher. This can cause you to expend more energy and tire your forearm muscles controlling the polisher. It also reduces your control over the movement of the polisher.

- **Stick handle - Porter Cable**
The stick handle enables you to easily control directional movement of the polisher.

The drawback to the stick handle is that if you're not paying attention, you can easily apply too much pressure to the handle side of the polisher. This causes you to hold the pad crooked or on edge, which can and will slow down or even stop pad rotation.

- **Personal preference**
My preference is to remove any handle and simply place my hand on the head of the polisher to guide and control it. This is especially helpful when using the polisher with one hand.

Here are three popular DA polishers with their handles removed.

With the handle removed from your DA polisher, your hand fits comfortably over the plastic housing covering the head of the polisher.

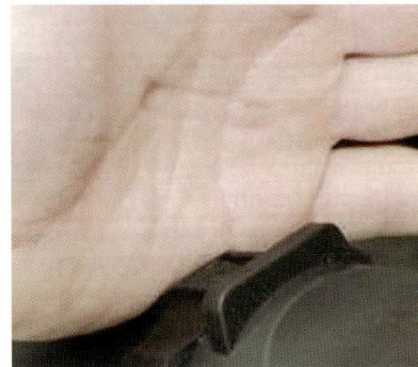

With the bail handle removed from the Meguiar's G110v2, there's a built-in tool rest. This keeps the polisher from tipping over if you place it on its back with the bail handle removed or adjusted to the extreme forward position. While this does provide a benefit, this tool rest gets pressed into your hand. This might bother some people buffing without the bail handle.

Of course, there's enough room inside the bail handle on both the Meguiar's and the Griot's polishers to place your hand on the head of the unit while leaving the bail handle in place.

With their handles removed, the Griot's and Meguiar's units have built-in, plastic locking tabs to prevent the plastic housing from sliding off. You can pry it off, but it won't slide off.

The plastic housing on the Porter Cable polisher, however, doesn't have a built-in plastic locking tab. If you remove the handle, the plastic housing can easily slide off. If you're buffing out a car and this happens, it may startle you.

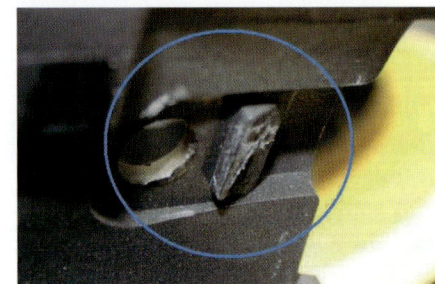

Griot's Garage = Locking Tab.

Meguiar's G110v2 = Locking Tab

Porter Cable = No Locking Tab

▣▣ How To Bolt The Plastic Cover Onto A Porter Cable 7424Xp

Above is the inside of the plastic housing off the Porter Cable polisher. As you can see, there is no plastic locking tab. For this reason, if you want to use the Porter Cable polisher without a handle, you should go to your local hardware store and pick up two metric M8 x1.25 socket cap bolts for new PCs or two 5/16" x 1/2" socket cap bolts and matching washers for older models.

Porter Cable recently switched the thread type over to metric. Below are the dates of the change from the Porter Cable website.

- **U.S. Threads**
  DATE CODE 2009-10 AND EARLIER = 5/16-18 Threads

- **Metric Threads**
  DATE CODE 2009-11 AND NEWER = M8x1.25 Threads

The date of manufacture can be found on the side of the Porter Cable 7424XP just below the model number and to the right.

I purchased the above Socket Head Cap Screws at my local Lowe's for less than $2.00 a packet. Pick up a couple of flat washers while you're there.

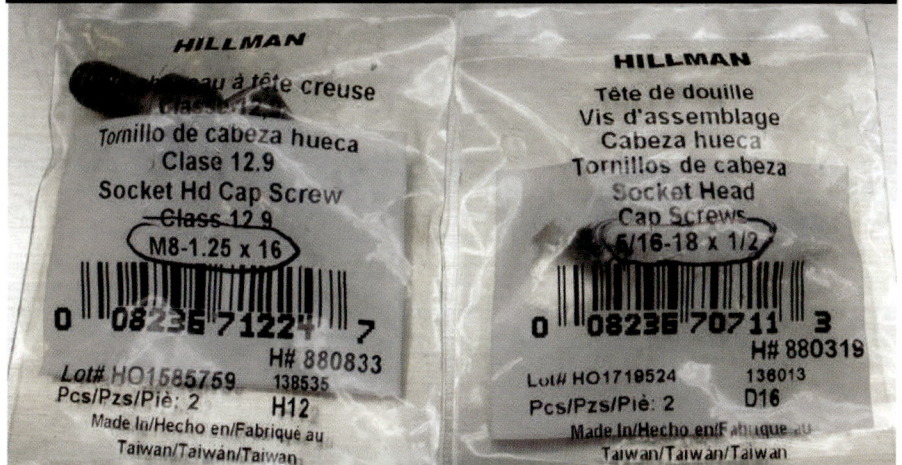

Then use an Allen Wrench to snug the bolts down on the polisher

DA Backing Plates

DA Backing plates are very important components that can have a huge effect on the performance of a DA polisher. The right backing plate will ensure your buffing pad and choice of compound or polish are being worked to their fullest potential. The wrong backing plate can negatively effect the transfer of power from the tool to the face of the buffing pad. This loss of efficiency means any job involving correction work will take longer.

Mark your backing plates
Mark your backing plate with a line like you see here. This will make it easy to see if the buffing pad is rotating versus just vibrating against the paint.

Design features of a backing plate

Here are the primary design features that make up a good backing plate.

✵ *Well Built And Reinforced*

Firm, downward pressure to the head of a DA polisher puts more stress on everything. This includes the foam used to make the foam pad, the adhesive used to attach the hook and loop to the foam pad and backing plate, the hook and loop material, the backing plate and also the tool itself. Every component of the DA buffing process is subjected to more stress and this leads to more failures of the various components.

One common component known to fail is the backing plate, because it is subjected to the oscillating action of the tool where it's attached to the free floating spindle bearing assembly.

The oscillating actions at low speeds are fairly non-violent and don't build up a lot of heat at the center of the backing plate. Bump the speed up to the 5 and 6 speed setting and the oscillating action becomes a lot more violent and powerful. With time and pressure added to this violent oscillating action, backing plate designs begin to fail in two ways,

1. The attachment of the 5/16" threaded arbor to the inner hard plate material breaks at some place and renders the backing plate unusable.

Parts of the DA Backing Plate

5/16" arbor

The spacer must be in place for proper clearance and operation of the backing plate.

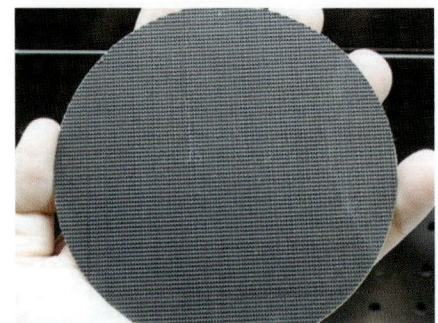

The hook portion of a hook and loop interface

2. The adhesive that holds the hook and loop material breaks down and loses its bond.

» **Not holding the pad flat**
When you hold a DA polisher at an angle so that more pressure is applied to just one edge of a buffing pad, you create more force against the arbor where it mounts into the backing plate and against the spindle where the 5/16" arbor attaches to the DA polisher. The results are more broken backing plates and DA polishers.

» **New and improved!**
Today's offerings of high quality, long lasting backing plates are well-manufactured in all aspects. This includes overall design, materials, adhesives, rivets, hook and loop and even the arbors.

Multi-Piece, One Piece And Two Piece Backing Plates

Multi-Piece
Early backing plates were made from multiple parts. The hook and loop was glued onto the backing plate itself and the backing plate was formed over some type of inner plate with a 5/16" arbor.

Molded
Next were one-piece units where all parts were molded together and generally speaking, a backing plate that is molded together will be more durable than a backing plate that is assembled out of multiple pieces.

Two piece
The other approach is for two piece backing plates that use an inner plate made of fiberglass. To this, a steel collar is riveted to attach the 5/16" arbor. A flexible molded urethane outer skin with molded-in hooks is then attached to the fiberglass plate to provide backing support to the buffing pad.

Correct Hook And Loop Design

There are different types of hook and loop designs. The most important part is that the hook on the backing plate matches the loop material on the buffing pad for best attachment strength and longevity of the hook and loop material.

KISS = Keep it Simple Simon
One simple thing you can do is to purchase backing plates and foam pads from the same manufacturer. Most of the time, this will prevent any mismatch issues as most reputable companies do their homework and ensure they are using the correct hook and loop materials for both their backing plates and their pads.

Where you can run into trouble is purchasing lesser quality and cheaper backing plates that don't belong to a line of pads. There is a difference, so invest in a quality backing plate.

Hook and loop material - three general grades of quality
Hook and loop material is available in three general grades: consumer-grade, industrial strength and mil-spec. Leading manufacturers of backing plates use industrial strength materials.

• **3 important characteristics**

1. **Pull-apart strength**
Pull-apart strength is a measure of how much force is required to separate two pieces straight apart from each other.

2. **Shear strength**
Shear strength is a measure of how much force is required to slide the opposing hook and loop pieces apart.

3. **Cycle life**
Cycle life is the measure of how many times two apposing pieces of hook and loop material can be pulled apart before the attachment strength degrades to 50% of its original value.

Hook and loop wears out
The more you use your backing plate, the faster the hook and loop will wear out. At some point, you'll want to replace a worn backing plate with a new one.

3 Types of hooks
• J-hooks
• Barb or Mushroom Hooks
• Micro-Hooks

All three styles will work and are being used in the industry.

1. **J-hooks**
J-hooks come in varying lengths. Shorter J-hooks work well, but

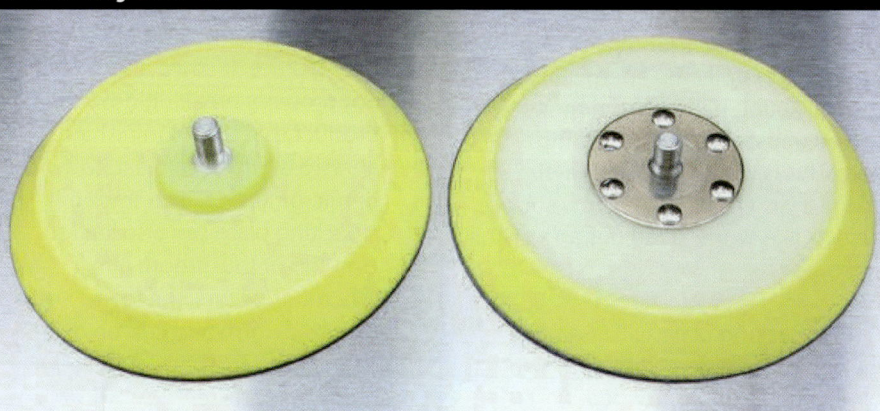

Left: Early DA Backing Plate - No attachment plate, no re-enforcement material.
Right: New reinforced backing plate design - Steel attachment plate embedded in a fiberglass reinforced rigid material.

DA Backing Plates

longer J-hooks are too long for use with DA backing plates and

buffing pads. Long J-hooks create a measurable distance or gap between the pad and the backing plate, even though the J-hook does mesh into the loop material.

This gap leads to grinding between the J-hook and loop material, which leads to friction when the tool is operated at high speeds. Over time, this friction generates excessive heat.

2. Barb or mushroom hook
Barb style hooks are not good for DA polishers as they offer high engagement, which means the two types of material form a very strong attachment to one another. This strong attachment is ideal in situations of low frequency of engaging and disengaging the hook and loop. When engaged and disengaged frequently, these hooks wear out quickly, which decreases their pull-apart strength and cycle life.

3. Micro-hooks
There are 3 different types of designs of micro-hooks, but they

all offer sufficient attachment strength and long cycle life. The short distance of the hook also helps to keep temperatures low, which helps all aspects of backing plate performance.

4. Flexible Backing Material With Tapered Edge

Early backing plates were basically hard plastic with a hook and loop interface on one side and a 5/16" arbor on the other side. New designs incorporate both rigid and flexible materials, each serving their own purpose. The centers of quality backing plates are made using a rigid fiberglass and glass cloth material to provide a strong and stable support for attaching the 5/16" arbor. Fiberglass offers superior heat resistance and can be heated to higher temperatures than plastics while retaining its shape and strength. The rigidity also works best to transfer power from the tool to the pad without absorbing or dissipating any power.

The outer edges are usually made from a flexible urethane material and are tapered. The flexibility comes from both the urethane material and its tapered edge. These are both features that help to maintain flat pad contact and provide flexability when changes in pressure occur due to curves and contours of body panels.

5. Thin Versus Thick

The thinner the backing plate, the more successfully the energy and the oscillating pattern from the tool will be transferred to the buffing pad. This is what you want anytime you're trying to remove below surface defects like swirls, scratches and water spots.

A thick backing plate will dissipate energy and interfere with the oscillating pattern provided

from the tool. This could be ideal when machine sanding and a less aggressive sanding action is needed.

Backing plates for machine polishing trend towards being thin for the important reasons listed above and also to help in flexibility of the backing plate as well as to reduce heat retention by simply reducing mass. Less material also usually means lower manufacturing cost.

6. Correct Diameter

It's important to match the correct sized backing plate to the size of the buffing pad you are using. You want this to fit as close as possible. This will ensure maximum surface area for contact between the hook and loop interface. This maximizes potential grip strength between your backing plate and your buffing pad.

- **Too big**
  If you use too large of a backing plate, there will be little to no safety margin between the edge of your buffing pad and the edge of the backing plate. This presents the potential for the backing plate to make contact with a painted surface, possibly marring the paint.

- **Too small**
  If you use too small of a backing plate, there won't be enough support to ensure even pressure over the face of the buffing pad. This can reduce the effectiveness of any mechanical abrading taking place. It could also mean not properly breaking down any product that uses diminishing abrasives, which can lead to swirls or micromarring. Too small of a backing plate can also lead to a muffin or mushroom effect. When this occurs, the foam tries to deform and curl up over and around the backing plate, reducing pad life.

Mike Phillips' - The Art of Detailing

Types of Foam Pads

There are a lot of foam pads on the market to choose from and it can be overwhelming to pick the type and style of pad if you're new to machine polishing. The truth is that as long as you're using premium quality paint care products and good technique, then all top quality pads from reputable pad companies will get the job done.

First, let's talk about the types of foam formulas used to make foam buffing pads as this is an important factor that affects how a foam buffing pad performs.

Reticulated = Open Cell

Open Cell Foam means the cell wall structure is open, leaving only the framework in place. Reticulation is created by exploding the foam, which blows out the membranes, leaving behind an open pore skeletal structure which fluids and gasses can easily pass through. Think of a window frame without the glass.

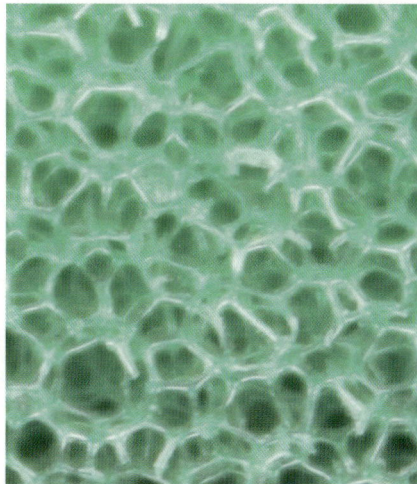

Here's a close-up of the cell wall structure of open cell foam. There are no membranes walling-off the cell structures, just a porous skeletal structure in which liquids or air can easily pass through.

Compared to closed cell foam, open cell foam is:

• more absorbent
• more porous
• less dense
• less elastic

Non-Reticulated = Closed Cell

Closed Cell Foam means the cell wall structure is closed with the membranes intact. This makes the foam non-porous, and while it's not impossible for air and liquids to flow through it, it is more difficult.

Close-up of the cell wall structure of closed cell foam. If you look closely, you can see the membranes intact and this is what makes a foam pad reticulated or closed-cell. Think of a window frame with the glass in place.

Compared to open cell foam, closed cell foam is,

• less absorbent
• less porous
• higher density
• more elastic

The Practical Difference

Open Cell Foam
With an open cell wall structure, both air and liquids can pass through the foam easily.

• **Air** - Because air can flow through

Foam And Fiber Buffing Pads

open cell foam, this aids in heat transfer. The pad will buff cooler as heat from the pad transfers to the air passing through the foam. One effect this has is that any liquids can evaporate, causing the product being used to dry up.

- **Liquids -** Because liquids can easily flow through the open cell wall structure of the foam, it is more easily penetrated by and saturated with any chemical you're applying.

Closed Cell Foam

With a closed cell foam structure, air and liquids cannot easily pass through the foam.

- **Air -** Because air cannot flow through the closed cell membranes easily, heat will tend to build up faster. This will decrease the evaporation rate of any liquids.

- **Liquids -** Because liquids cannot easily penetrate into the foam, they will be trapped on the surface of the pad and remain between the surfaces of the pad and paint. As you use closed cell pads, liquids will tend to migrate into the inside of the pad.

Closed cell foam formulas like to retain liquids, so this can make cleaning a tad more difficult and time consuming.

PPI or Pores Per Square Inch

The term PPI is often used when differentiating between types of foam pads. However, there are many other influencing factors that affect the benefits and features of a foam pad than PPI. PPI becomes an extreme generality as far as it relates to any specific comparison between types of foam. For this reason, it's better to focus on the other factors discussed more in-depth in this chapter.

Density of foam

In simple terms, density refers to how stiff or soft the foam is. The stiffer the foam, the more aggressive it will tend to be, while the softer the foam, the more gentle it will be. Foam cutting pads tend to be more dense than polishing pads, and polishing pads tend to be more dense than finishing pads.

- **Density changes with use**
  As polishing and cutting pads become saturated with liquids and warm from use, density drops off or the stiffness of the foam decreases. This reduces the mechanical ability of the foam's performance. This is why a clean, dry foam cutting pad will be more aggressive than the same pad after it's been used to buff a panel or two.

- *If you're going to rely on foam cutting pads to remove below-surface defects, a good rule of thumb is to have one pad per panel to maximize efficiency. More pads are always better. As soon as a pad becomes broken-in, or saturated with product, remove it and switch to a clean, dry pad.*

Elasticity - tensile strength

Elasticity is another way of referring to the tensile strength of foam. Tensile strength is a measurement of how far foam will stretch before it will tear.

Open cell foam pads tend to have higher tensile strengths than closed cell foam.

Example: *Hydro-Tech pads (closed cell foam) have lower tensile strength and will tear and wear more easily than CCS pads (open cell foam).*

Aggressiveness or gentleness

How aggressive or how gentle a foam pad is can be controlled and tailored to specific tasks by the addition or subtraction of different chemical agents added to the foam. Like car

wax companies, foam companies are very secretive about their formulas and this kind of information is proprietary. Reputable suppliers of foam pads will state whether a foam pad is aggressive or gentle.

Two tests you can do to gauge aggressiveness or gentleness,

- Compress a pad between your two palms. A stiff or dense pad will offer more mechanical ability than a soft or less dense pad.

- Draw your clean fingertips over a clean pad. An aggressive foam pad will have a coarse feel to it, while a non-aggressive pad will feel soft and gentle.

Foam Pad Face Design

Foam buffing pads come in a variety of different face designs in which the working face of the pad has a distinct pattern cut or formed into it. Manufacturers state that the different designs offer specific benefits to either the buffing process or the user and usually both.

Comment - When buffing with a DA polisher, as long as you're using good quality foam pads, which type is best often comes down to personal preference. More important than the choice in type of pad is the products you choose to use and your technique. If you're using great products (compounds, polishes and waxes) and perfect technique, the design of the pad is the least of your worries.

More important

Matching the correct aggressiveness or gentleness of the foam for the product and process is more important than the design of the face of the pad. Simply put, you can get great results from any of the below pads as long as you choose and use the right product and technique.

Lake Country CCS Pads - Reticulated/Open Cell Foam

Close-up of the collapsed cell structure

✦ **Lake Country CCS Pads Reticulated/Open Cell Foam**

CCS stands for Collapsed Cell Structure. This means the face of the pad has little pockets formed into the foam through a heat process in which the cells are melted and closed to make these pockets more dense and less porous. This will prevent the product you're using from penetrating inside the foam, allowing it to remain on the surface between the pad and the paint.

CCS pads help create a smoother buffing experience. Product in the pockets is released as you buff, maintaining a well lubricated surface.

Other benefits include longer buffing cycle for the product and a decrease in pad saturation. Pad saturation is a common problem with all foam pads due to the fact that foam absorbs liquids. The more wet or saturated your pad becomes with product, the more it will absorb and dissipate the energy and oscillating pattern provided by a DA polisher.

✦ **Lake Country Constant Pressure CCS Pads (referred to as CP Pads)**

These pads include a layer of soft foam as a cushioning interface between the backing plate and the actual foam formula used for the working face of the pad. The design allows the foam to flex and conform to curved body panels. These are available in both CCS and Flat pad designs.

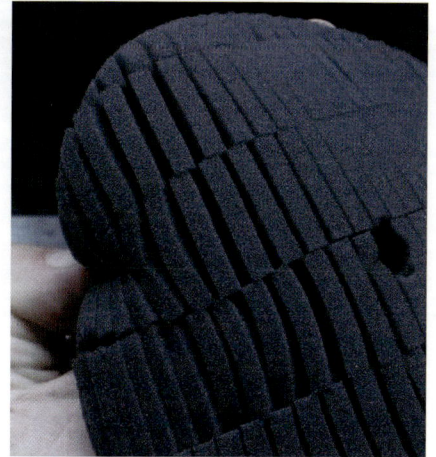

✦ **Lake Country Kompressor Pads Reticulated = Open Cell**

Slotted tabs
Kompressor pads have a slotted or tabbed face. They are cut in a criss-cross pattern to create flexible, rectangular tabs instead of a solid foam interface. The benefits include incredible flexibility which means they easily conform to curved panels.

Compressed sweet spot
These pads are arched in a way that when you place them onto your backing pate, the center compresses into itself, making the foam stiffer or more dense in this area. You still get plenty of flex for buffing curved panels, but polishing products will tend to remain in the center of the pad versus sling outwards.

Recessed back - (7" versions)
The Kompressor pads come in both 6" and 7" sizes. The 7" versions have a recessed backing that makes centering a 6" backing plate quick, easy and accurate for smooth buffing operation. It also provides a safety margin of foam surrounding the lip of the backing plate in case you accidentally run the edge of the pad into any portion of a car's painted panels. This prevents the actual backing plate from contacting and harming the paint.

Foam And Fiber Buffing Pads

Easy to clean

The slotted tabs make cleaning the pad easy as you can spread the tabs apart with your fingers to allow product residue to escape. If you use a Grit Guard Universal Pad Washer, the tabs spread apart as you push the face of the pad against the Grit Guard insert. Built-up product residue is easily removed from the face and sides of the slotted tabs.

⬩ Lake Country Hydro-Tech Kompressor Pads - Closed Cell

Same closed-cell foam formula as the Lake Country Hydro-Tech flat pads, with the Kompressor slotted design. Excellent for buffing contours and curved body panels.

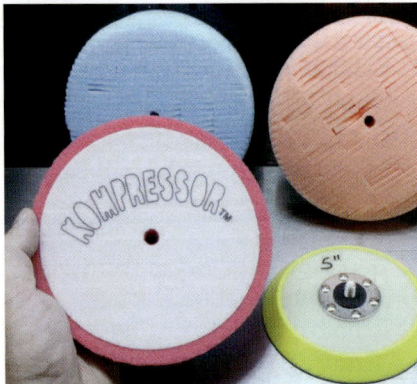

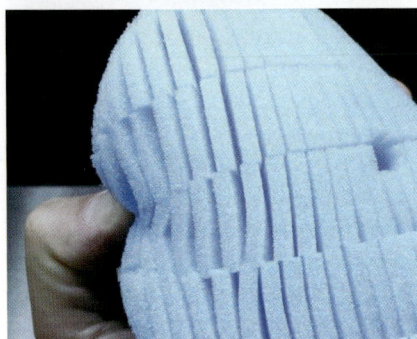

⬩ Cobra Cross Groove DA Pads Reticulated = Open Cell

Reduces surface tension

The Cross Groove name comes from the way the face of the foam pad is cut in a criss-cross pattern. This design reduces tension by reducing the total surface area of foam in contact with the paint for a smoother buffing experience.

Reduces product waste

The grooves also trap and hold product inside themselves, releasing throughout the buffing cycle.

Beveled edges

A soft curve to the edge provides gentle polishing action when buffing inside or around curves.

Reduces heat build-up

The cross-cut grooves allow air to flow through the pad as you're buffing, capturing heat and then releasing it to maintain low surface temperatures.

⬩ Flat Pads

The flat-faced foam buffing pad was introduced to the car detailing world by a man named Larry Meguiar, son of Floyd Meguiar of Finish Kare. Larry dropped the foam pad project and it was revived by Water Cotton. This first foam buffing pad was introduced to the market back in 1965, about the time the Ford Mustang was introduced and Gilligan's Island debuted.

The introduction of the foam buffing pad was a pinnacle moment for car detailing perfectionists. It enabled them to turn out a dramatically nicer looking finish than could be obtained using wool pads. Wool buffing pads are great for when you need an aggressive pad to remove below-surface defects, but when it comes time for the finishing work, foam, with its uniform surface texture will always leave a nicer finish.

Here are three companies that offer a flat-faced foam buffing pad. While the colors and sizes between the different brands will vary, they all have a few things in common.

Mike Phillips' - The Art of Detailing

- Lake country = Reticulated/Open Cell
- Meguiar's Pads = Reticulated/Open Cell
- Griot's Garage Pads = Reticulated/Open Cell

100% contact

With a flat pad design, you get maximum engagement of the foam to paint which would mean maximum efficiency when working product against the paint.

Easy to clean

Any contaminants or particulates will be on the face of the pad, not lodged into any of the subsurface sections of the pad. Inspecting the face of the pad is faster and easier.

Optimized for diminishing abrasives

Any time you're using a product that uses diminishing abrasives to correct paint, the goal is to work them until they have completely broken down. If you stop buffing before the abrasives have completely broken down, it's possible to have left swirls or micromarring in the paint as the abrasives were still actively cutting or abrading.

Lake Country Flat Pads
Reticulated = Open Cell

The 5 1/2" Lake Country Flat Pads are pretty much the simplest and easiest pads to use for people new to machine polishing. Their small size

5 1/2" Yellow Aggressive Cutting, Orange Light Cutting, White Polishing, Black Polishing, Blue Finishing and wax and sealant application

left to right: 6 1/2" Cyan, Tangerine & Crimson - 4" Spot Repair Cyan, Tangerine & Crimson

makes them perfect for modern cars with long, thin panels. They are easy to control, easy to clean, and work with any DA-approved compound, polish, paint cleaner, glaze, cleaner/wax or finishing wax.

Lake Country Hydro-Tech Pads
Non-Reticulated = Closed Cell

To use any of these on a DA polisher, you'll need either a 6 inch, 5" or 3.5" backing plate. Shown are the Lake Country Backing Plates. When you purchase backing plates and buffing pads from the same manufacturer, you can trust the hook and loop materials will match for maximum attaching strength and longevity.

Hydro-Tech Pads are a flat-faced pad, but what makes them unique is they are made using closed cell foam. They'll retain their density longer and absorb liquids more slowly.

Meguiar's 4", 6 1/2" and 7"
Soft Buff Flat Pads
Reticulated = Open Cell
Exception: W7207 Foam Cutting
Pad = Non-Reticulated = Closed Cell

All these pads from Meguiar's are flat

From this angle you can see the thickness difference between the pads, the thin pads 3rd from the left are the 5 1/2" Hydro-Tech Pads and they work great with DA polishers.

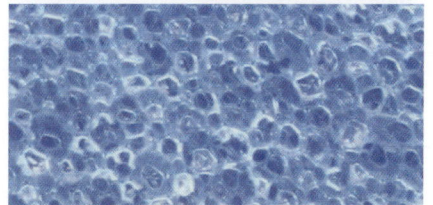

pad designs. All of the pads in the 4" and 6 1/2" group are open cell. In the 7" size group, the yellow polishing and black finishing pads are open cell while the maroon cutting pad is closed cell (the 4" and 6 1/2" maroon cutting pads are open cell).

Note: Meguiar's does not recommend using their maroon foam cutting pad with DA polishers. This is because the foam is very aggressive and it can cause micromarring to some automotive paints.

Foam And Fiber Buffing Pads

4" Soft Buff Pads - *At this time, Meguiar's does not offer a 3 1/2" backing plate, but the one from Lake Country works well.*

Griot's Garage Foam Buffing Pads Reticulated = Open Cell

Griot's offers a real simple flat pad system that will take care of most people's machine polishing needs. Use the polishing pad with either an aggressive compound or polish, or for less cut, use it with a light or ultra light polish. After the paint is corrected to your expectations, use the red wax pad to apply your choice of wax or paint sealant.

Griot's 6" Orange and Red Buffing Pads

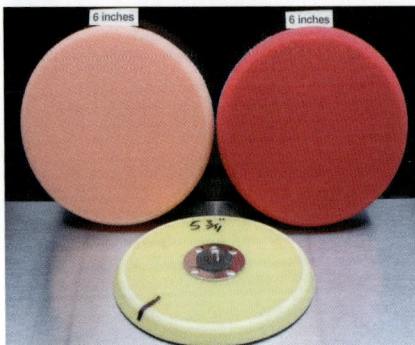

The factory 6" backing plate that comes with the tool measures in at 5 3/4". Like most 6" backing plates, the actual diameter is a little smaller to provide some safety margin around the outside of the pad while buffing.

Lake Country CCS Pad - The 6 1/2" pad is 1 1/4" thick and the 5 1/2" pad is 7/8" thin

Lake Country Flat Pad - The 6 1/2" pad is 1 1/4" thick and the 5 1/2" pad is 7/8" thin

Foam Pad Thickness and Diameter

Foam buffing pads come in a variety of thickness levels, and while traditionally foam pads have been on the thick side, the trend now is for thinner pads.

The first foam pads were made for use on rotary buffers. For this application, a thick foam pad works well as it provides plenty of cushion to conform to the curves of car body panels. Thick foam pads can also help to reduce swirls just by the fact that thick foam offers more cushion. Besides these two reasons, because a rotary buffer is a direct drive tool, by design they have more than enough power to rotate pads regardless of how thick they are.

Originally, foam pads were simply configured to attach to air powered orbital DA sanders used in body shops. Not much thought was given to the design needs of a pad for use on a DA polisher as compared to a rotary buffer, like diameter and thickness.

The first DA foam pad was introduced in the 1980s.

Thin is in
The trend today is for thinner, smaller buffing pads for use with DA polishers.

Why?
Because thinner pads rotate better than thicker pads due to less friction and rotating mass.

Surface area for different pads sizes
3.0" pad = 7.1 Square Inches
4.0" pad = 12.6 Square Inches
5.5" pad = 23.7 Square Inches
6.0" pad = 28.2 Square Inches
6.5" pad = 33.1 Square Inches
7.0" pad = 38.5 Square Inches
8.0" pad = 50.2 Square Inches

The difference between buffing with a 5 1/2" pad and a 6 1/2" pad means an increase of 9.4 square inches of foam for the DA polisher to rotate and oscillate.

If you think in terms of diameter, to go from a 5 1/2" to a 6 1/2" pad looks like a very small change of only 1", and while this is true, it's not an accurate representation of what's really taking place on the surface.

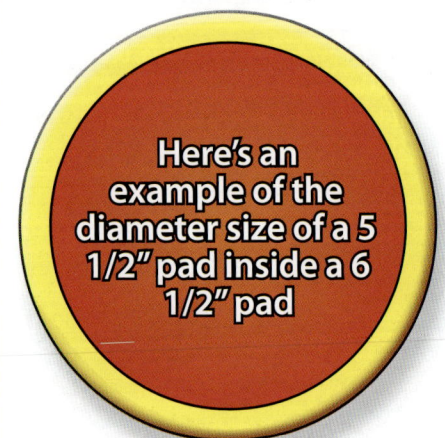

Here's an example of the diameter size of a 5 1/2" pad inside a 6 1/2" pad

Mike Phillips' - The Art of Detailing

Leverage

A larger diameter pad has a larger circumference and this gives the pad leverage over the tool's ability to rotate it. The further outward a pad extends from the center, the more power it will require to overcome the friction between the pad and the paint. For this reason, smaller diameter pads rotate more easily on DA polishers and are more effective at removing below-surface defects.

🔴 Foam Pad Attachment Systems

Hook and loop Interface

The majority of all pads are attached using a simple hook and loop material, with the loop material being used on one side of a buffing pad and the hook side being used on the backing plate.

Hooks

Loops

Center pad onto backing plate

When attaching a pad to a backing plate, the goal is to center the pad onto the backing plate as close as you can. This will reduce vibration.

Quick Change Adapter

There is another system for attaching a foam buffing pad to a DA polisher and that's using a Quick Change Adapter from "The Edge Company" with their Edge 2000 6 Inch DuraFoam Buffing pads.

DuraFoam Buffing pads are double-

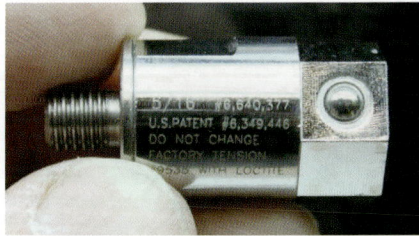

sided, so you are basically getting two pads that share an internal attachment plate - there's no need for normal hook and loop style backing plate.

Even though these pads are thicker than those that attach using a normal style backing plate, the pressure is focused on the lower half between the paint and the internal backing plate. The pads are 1 3/4" thick overall, but the portion of pad you're using is only 7/8", which is the same as all the other thin foam buffing pads.

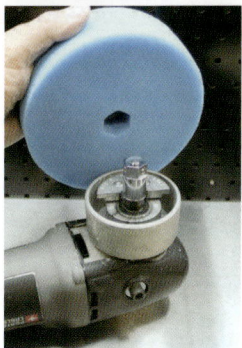

The benefit to this attachment system is that the pads are automatically self-centering. There's no need to try to eye up your pad to the backing plate and attach it so that it is perfectly centered. A perfectly centered pad will reduce vibrations, and theoretically, it would cause the least strain on the drive mechanisms of DA polishers.

Another benefit is the quick change feature. The pads snap onto the adapter and with a press of a center located button, they release from the adapter.

🔴 How To Prime And Apply Product To A Clean, Dry Pad

Priming the pad

Priming a clean, dry pad is considered the best approach for using a DA polisher. This ensures that 100% of the working surface of the pad is wet with product and working at maximum efficiency when you turn the polisher on. I originally learned of this technique from my friend Kevin Brown.

Priming the pad also ensures that you don't have any dry portion of the pad working over the paint un-lubricated.

Start with a clean, dry pad and add some fresh product to the face of the pad. Using your finger, spread the product over the pad and work it into the pores. Don't saturate the pad - use just enough product to make sure that 100% of the working face of the pad has product coverage.

Pea-sized drops of product

Circle pattern on a clean dry pad and then worked for a section pass

For some products and paint conditions, you may want more product on the surface working for you. Here's an example of dime-sized drops of product.

After working the circle of product over a section, you can see it spread the product out over the entire face of the pad without having to spread it with your finger. The pad is now equally primed with residual product.

Any extra product can be taken and applied to the outer edge until 100% of the working face of the pad is primed with product. This helps if you're buffing panels that the edge of your buffing pad may come into contact with.

❚❚ The Circle-Pattern And X-Pattern Method Of Applying Products

The circle pattern

As you work around the car, you'll find that your product will migrate to the center of the pad on its own, leading to saturation.

Cut down on product after your first section pass

At this point, you could clean your pad or add fresh product. When you add fresh product, you can adjust how much you apply.

Adding "working product"
Some people will recommend 3 to 4 pea-sized drops of product. This can be correct for concentrated products or working small sections, but if you follow this advice, make sure you are not under-lubricating the surface.

This can cause problems because wet foam will retain heat better than dry foam. Over time, this can accelerate delamination between the hook and loop material and the surface it is attached to. For these reasons, I prefer applying product to the outer edge of the pad, also known as the circle pattern.

In this example, I used half a circle of product since 100% of the face of the pad is now primed.

If you're placing pea or dime-sized amounts of product to the face of your pad, then it's also a good idea to avoid placing the product directly in the center of the pad.

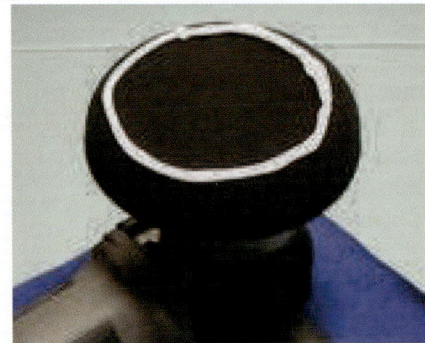

The X-pattern
Applying product using an X-pattern is a fast and simple way to get product out of the bottle and onto the pad in a measured way. This

method is easy to teach others and is easy to duplicate.

X-pattern on a clean dry pad and then worked for a section pass

Cut down on product after your first section pass

After making a thorough section pass, the pad is now equally primed with residual product. At this point, you could clean your pad or add fresh product. In this example, I used half an X-pattern, or a single strip of product since the pad is already primed.

How Much Product Do I Use With My DA Polisher?

Use an "ample" amount of product. This means not too much and too little product.

- **am·ple** - *adjective* - Fully sufficient to meet a need or purpose: had ample food for the party.

Using too much product

This will over-lubricate the pad and paint. Excess liquid will interfere with the abrasives' ability to abrade the paint and they will tend to glide over instead of biting into the surface.

Using too little product

Under-using product reduces lubricity and will make it more difficult for your pad to rotate efficiently. You need the pad to rotate so that it will engage or force the abrasives against and into the paint.

The question then becomes,

How much is an ample amount?

In this chapter, Priming and Prepping Pads Before Use, I showed three ways to prime and apply product to a clean, dry pad.

After you have broken-in a clean, dry pad by making your first section pass, it's time to clean the pad and then apply fresh product.

Pea, dime or nickel-sized portions of product.

In some applications, a pea-sized amount of product will be sufficient. This depends upon the condition of the paint, what you're trying to accomplish and how concentrated the products are that you're using. If this doesn't give you a long enough buffing cycle, increase the size of the portion from a pea-sized drop to a dime or even nickel-sized portion.

Half circle - quarter circle

If you use the circle pattern to apply product, then after your first section pass the pad should be broken in and have the same appearance as though you primed it initially by spreading product out over the face of the pad with your finger.

Now that it's broken in, you can cut down on the amount of product you're using. A good rule of thumb is a half or quarter circle of product.

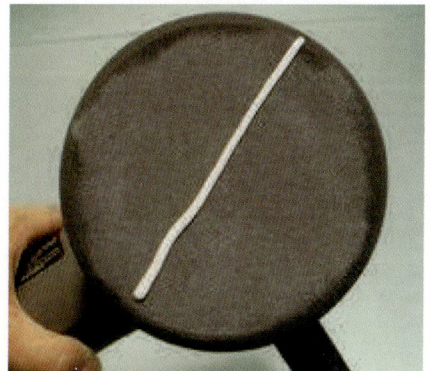

Half x-pattern - quarter x-pattern

If you're using the X-pattern to apply product to your pad, it is quick and easy to re-apply in a straight line across the face of the pad.

Pad Conditioners

Another option to prep a clean, dry pad before first use is to use a pad conditioner to lubricate and condition the surface. This will improve the buffing cycle and provide protection to the paint surface.

Pad conditioners are wetting agents that contain ingredients that will moisten and

soften the surface of the pad. They also provide some lubricating agents to ensure the face of the pad is lubricated.

How To Use

Mist a spray or two onto the face of the pad. Using your clean hand, massage the face of the pad to work the spray over and into the foam.

You're now ready to apply your choice of product to the pad.

Note: Pad conditioners are primarily for use with wool and foam cutting and polishing pads when using compounds and polishes.

Exception: applying waxes and sealants
It's not necessary or a good idea to condition pads before applying waxes and paint sealants, unless the manufacturer states to do so.

Why?
You don't want to introduce foreign liquids to a wax or paint sealant. This will adulterate the formula. It might not harm anything, but the idea is to use the wax, paint sealant or coating in its virgin form.

Cleaning Foam Buffing Pads

There are four general ways to clean foam buffing pads.

- Washing by hand
- Cleaning on the fly
- Pad washer
- Pad conditioning brush

Washing By Hand

You can generally use buffing pads multiple times before they need to be replaced. However, during and after use, you need to clean them and remove any built-up compound, polish or wax residue.

The way most people do this is either by washing and rinsing their pads in a sink or a bucket. This actually works pretty well as you can stand up as you clean the pads as most sinks are at waist level. Plus, you have running water to flush residue out of the pad.

Because there are all kinds of chemicals involved (compounds, polishes, waxes, paint sealants and the soap, cleaner, degreaser or detergent) and there's no way of knowing the safety of factor of all these different chemicals on their own or mixed together, I recommend wearing some type of chemical resistant gloves.

- Place a few pads into the sink and then add your choice of cleaning product. Agitate the foam pads, squeezing and kneading them to work both the cleaning solution into the foam and the built-up residue out of the foam.
- As you work the cleaning solution

into the foam, the cleaning agents will break down, dissolve, and emulsify whatever products are in and on the pad. Once the products are liquified and embodied together with the

cleaning agents, you should rinse the pad by placing it under running water and continuing to squeeze, knead and work the pliable foam into itself.

Once you see clear water coming out of the foam as you rinse and you're satisfied with the level of cleanliness, you can then set the pad aside to dry and move onto the next one.

Washing By Hand In A Bucket

This is pretty easy to do and it keeps all the different residue from your paint care products out of your sink.

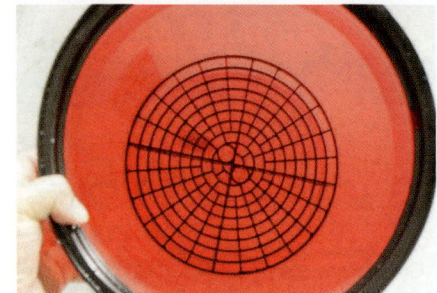

- Start by placing a Grit Guard insert into your wash bucket to help trap any dirt or abrasive particles on the bottom of the bucket.

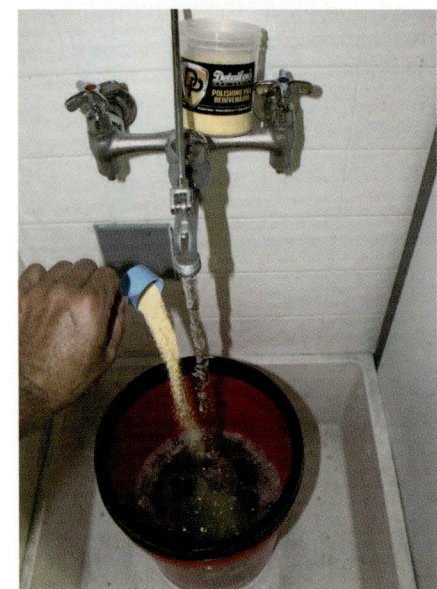

- Then, add water and some pad cleaning soap and mix thoroughly.

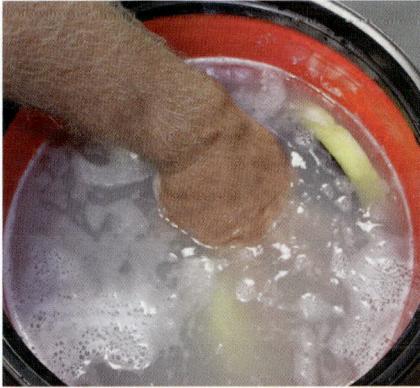

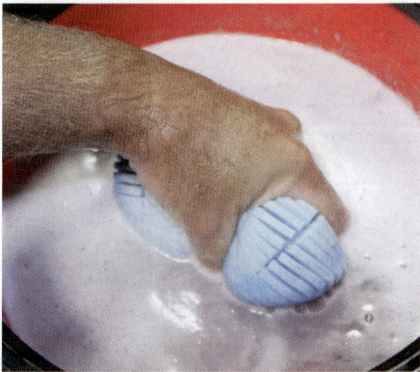

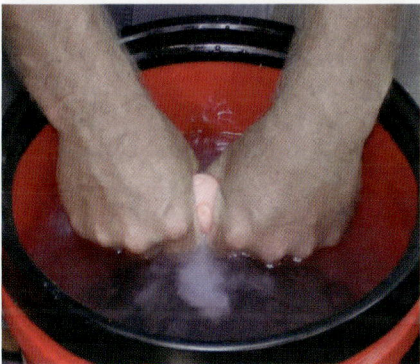

- Use the same approach listed above for washing pads in a sink.

Rinsing your pads
The benefit to washing in a sink is you have running water right at the sink. With the bucket method, you can tackle this issue a few different ways.

Secondary rinse bucket
Have a separate bucket with clean rinse water. Once you're satisfied with how clean you've gotten the pad, hold it above the bucket and squeeze out as much of the cleaning solution and product residue as possible. Then, place the pad into your rinse bucket.

Keep your bucket near a source of running water
If you use a hose, have either a sprayer or a brass quick-change valve to make controlling the water easier. Simply rinse your pads by squeezing them at the same time you're flushing them with water.

Time Saving Tip - Soak pads after use regardless of whether you're going to wash your pads in a sink or in a bucket. Before you begin buffing your car, mix up a bucket of pad cleaning solution. When you're finished using a buffing pad, place it into the bucket of pad cleaner.

Soaking your pads after use but before washing them enables the cleaning agents to dissolve and emulsify any compound, polish or wax residue. This will make washing your pads faster and easier.

Another benefit to this technique is the polish residue won't have a chance to dry and harden on and in the pad.

Don't cross-contaminate
If you're washing pads in a bucket or sink, wash your compound and polishing pads first. Then, wash any pads with waxes and paint sealants. This will keep your wash water cleaner and will make cleaning multiple compounding and polishing pads easier.

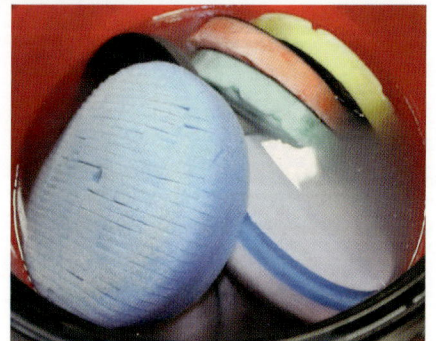

- **Compounds and polishes = water soluble**
Because most compounds and polishes are water-soluble, they are fairly easy to clean and rinse from buffing pads.

- **Waxes and paint sealants = water insoluble**
  Waxes and paint sealants, on the other hand, are not water soluble. They will not easily dissolve when agitated in a solution of water with a pad cleaning soap. You can clean pads used for applying waxes and paint sealants, but it will take a little more time and effort.

Cleaning On The Fly

» **Products needed:**
  Clean, medium-sized terry cloth towel

When using a dual action polisher to remove below-surface defects with any type of abrasive product, you're going to have two things building up on the face of the foam pad that you need to clean off.

- **Spent residue**
- **Paint**

You can't see clear
If you're working on a clearcoat finish, you won't see the paint residue building up on the pad because the paint is clear.

You can see color
If you're working on a single stage paint, then you'll see the color of the paint building up on the face of your foam pad. For example, if you're working on single stage blue paint, you'll see blue paint on the face of your foam pad.

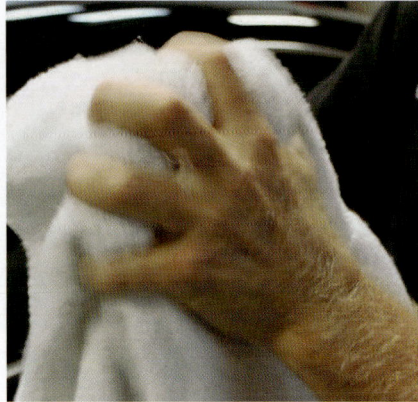

The important thing to understand is that as you work on any paint system, whether it's a basecoat/clearcoat, single stage or a tinted clearcoat, you're going to be removing a little paint. Both the paint you've removed and the spent residue from the compound or polish you're using are going to be building up on the face of the foam pad. It's important to clean this gunk off your pad often.

On the fly
The whole idea and success behind the "cleaning your pad on the fly" technique is that it allows you to quickly clean your pad and quickly get back to work.

In this technique, you hold a terry cloth towel against the face of the pad with one hand and holding the polisher in the other hand, turn the polisher on and press the towel into the face of the pad.

Sometimes it works well to fold your towel in half, depending upon how large the towel is. Smaller towels are easier to manage. You also need to make sure your towels are clean, as a dirty towel can contaminate your buffing pad.

The speed setting should be the same as when doing your correction work, which is usually the 5 to 6 speed setting. You don't want to continually adjust the speed setting in-between buffing sections of paint just to clean the pad. Plus, the higher speed setting actually helps to do a better job of

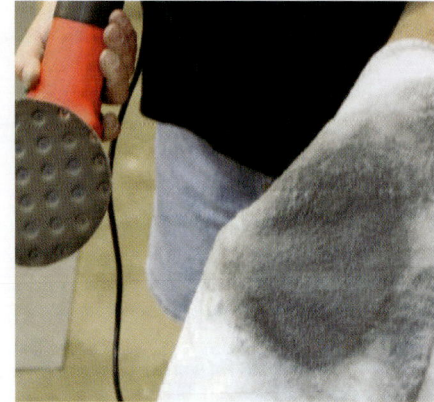

cleaning the pad.

💬 Tip: I will tend to use my extended fingers to grip around the pad and grab the backing plate and actually pull the face of my hand (against the towel) against the pad as this will help to blot out or astringe any excess liquid from the pad.

Question: *Why use terry cloth instead of microfiber?*

Answer: *Great question!*

Terry cloth is very good at absorbing liquid, so when you push the terry cloth into the foam, the liquid in the foam will transfer into the terry cloth fibers through capillary action.

The nap of terry cloth will help to slice into the caked-up and gummy residue, which will loosen its hold so the residue will transfer from the pad to the towel.

Compared to most microfiber polishing cloths, the terry cloth is more stout, allowing it to work better to break up the residue on the pad.

The tiny cotton loops, also called the nap of 100% Cotton Terry Cloth Toweling

Using A Pad Washer

A pad washer is a device used to clean or remove built-up residue from the face of a buffing pad quickly, efficiently and painlessly.

How it works

There's a Grit Guard insert resting on top of four spring loaded plastic cups (water pumps) that ride on what is called the Vortex Base. This sits inside a 5-gallon bucket that you fill to a specific volume with water or pad cleaning solution.

» **Step 1:** With the buffing pad attached to your DA polisher, insert the pad into the Grit Guard Pad Washer with the face of the pad against the Grit Guard insert.

» **Step 2:** Close the Splash Guard Lid; this prevents splatter from escaping the bucket as you clean pads.

» **Step 3:** Turn the polisher on. Use a medium speed setting (around the 4 setting) and as the pad is rotating, push it against the Grit Guard insert and pump the polisher up and down.

» **Step 4:** After you've cleaned the pad for about a minute or so, slowly lift the pad away from the Grit Guard insert and allow the it to spin freely while still inside the bucket and under the Splash Guard Lid.

Adjust the speed setting to ensure the pad is rotating. Don't simply use the highest speed setting as this is too fast for proper cleaning and will also splatter and sling cleaning solution out of the bucket.

What's happening inside the pad washer?

When you pump the polisher up and down against the Grit Guard insert, the spring loaded water pumps squirt or inject the pad with water and/or cleaning solution.

The pad cleaning solution mixes with the residue on the face of the pad and even penetrates into it and dissolves and loosens the built-up compound or polish residue.

At the same time you're pumping the pad up and down against the Grit Guard insert and extension, the pad is also rotating against the grill design of the insert. This acts like a squeegee, which extracts the dissolved gunk and product residue from the face and inside of the pad.

As the pad spins, inertia will cause any excess liquid inside the pad to sling out and deposit against the inside wall of the bucket. Any solids will settle to the bottom of the bucket. Open the Splash Guard Lid and remove the polisher.

At this point, you can extract even more water out of the pad one of two ways.

- **Grit Guard Extension**
  Remove the Grit Guard Extension from the Grit Guard insert and place it into the slotted holes on the lid. Next, press the foam pad against it with medium to firm pressure and turn the polisher on at a medium speed. The Grit Guard Extension will act like a

How the Grit Guard Universal Pad Washer Works - Here's a cutaway view of the internal components of the Grit Guard Universal Pad Washer.

3. Splash Guard Lid

4. Grit Guard insert with blank insert on center top

5. Spring Loaded Water Pump Cups

6. Stainless Steel Springs

7. Vortex Base

8. Rubber Grip Boots on Feet of Vortex Base

9. Housed inside a 5-Gallon Bucket

squeegee and squeeze excess water out of the pad as it rotates against it.

- **Drying towel**
  Take any clean, dry absorbent towel and press it into the buffing pad and hold it for a few moments. This will extract most of the excess cleaning solution.

At this point, you can return to work using your clean pad or place the pad aside in a dust and dirt-free environment.

Clean pad washer - replace water
The more you use the pad washer, the more often you should replace the water and cleaning solution.

If you're doing heavy compounding work, then your pad washer is going to load up with compound residue and paint solids faster than if you're lightly polishing a car in good condition. For this reason, you'll want to clean out the pad washer more often. The same goes for buffing either an oxidized gel-coat boat or single stage paint finish. Projects like these remove a lot of dead, oxidized material and you also generate a lot of compounding residue. Monitor your pad washer and clean and refresh the water as needed.

Cleaning Dry Pads Using A Pad Conditioning Brush

The fastest way to clean residue from a dry pad is to simply take a nylon pad conditioning brush and carefully scrub the dried product from the face of the pad.

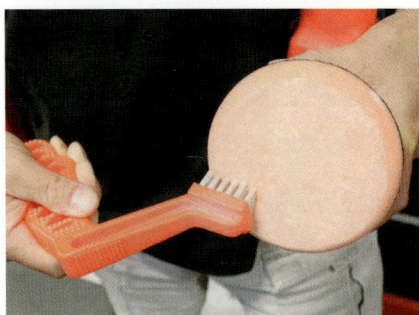

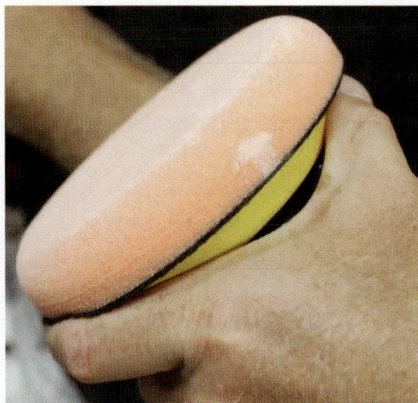

To use a pad conditioning brush, you must do so with the polisher in the off position. Hold the polisher in a way that you also grip the back of the backing plate to keep it from spinning and then draw the bristles of the brush over the face of the pad.

Pad Cleaners And Soaps

Pad cleaning soaps are important because water by itself is not very good at dissolving and removing all compounds and polishes quickly and easily from buffing pads. A good quality pad cleaning solution or soap will dramatically help get your buffing pads clean and ready to go back to work.

There are two options when it comes to pad cleaning solutions.

1. Spray-on pad cleaners

- Pinnacle XMT Polishing Pad Cleaner
- Grit Guard Pad Renewing Solution

This type of pad cleaner comes in a spray bottle and is sprayed directly onto the face of the pad.

- **Benefits**
  Concentrated cleaning solution instantly dissolves and loosens built-up product residue from the buffing pad.

  For extremely dirty pads, you can

Spraying XMT Polishing Pad Cleaner onto built-up residue on foam pad

agitate and work the cleaner with your hand before placing the pad into a pad washer.

Because there is no cleaning solution in the water, you get a cleaner rinse initially. The cleaner your pads are, the more cleaning solution and product residue mixes into the water. At some point, what was once clean rinse water will now be similar to a cleaning solution created by mixing a pad cleaning soap into water like option 2.

2. Powdered pad cleaning soaps

These citrus-based cleaning soaps work really well for dissolving and emulsifying compound and polish residue.

- 🖥 *Detailer's Pro Series Pad Rejuvenator*
- 🖥 *Snappy Clean Pad Cleaning Powder*

This type of pad cleaner normally comes in a concentrated powder form. Mix a measured amount of the powdered cleaning solution into your bucket of water before installing the Vortex Base. Then, mix the pad cleaning soap and water until you have a uniform cleaning solution. Then, re-insert the Vortex Base and the Grit Guard insert. Add or remove water until the level of cleaning solution in the bucket measures about 1/4" above the Grit Guard insert with it depressed against the spring loaded water pumps until they bottom out.

- **Benefits**
  Cleaning solution floods the pad with cleaning agents as it's being pumped and rotated against the Grit Guard insert.

- **Drawbacks**
  Some people have concerns that not enough of the cleaning solution will be removed from the pad. If put back into service, the cleaning solution could interfere with or affect the compound or polish being used.

The benefit to being able to clean your pads quickly and easily far outweighs and drawback to residual cleaning solution that remains in the pad. I've never seen any of my own work suffer from this concern, and given the choice, I will choose a pad washer over all the other options every time.

↪ Recommendation

If you routinely use a machine polisher, invest in a pad washer.

🗨 ***Note:*** The Grit Guard Universal Pad Washer works with all modern and popular polishers, including:

- DA polishers
  Porter Cable 7424XP, Griot's Garage DA polisher, Meguiar's G110v2 and the Shurhold Polisher
- All Rotary Buffers
- Cyclo Polisher
- Flex 3401
- Even a drill with a pad attached in some fashion.

🔴 How Often Do I Need To Clean My Pads?

» **Option 1: After each section pass**
In a perfect world, you would clean your pad after each section pass. Each time you buff a new section of paint, you'll be removing some level of paint from the surface if you're using any type of abrasive product (even a cleaner/wax), along with other substances like stains, road grime, impurities and anything detailing clay didn't remove. Plus, you'll have the spent product residue on the face of the pad. If you are a perfectionist, you'll want to clean your pad on the fly after each section pass.

» **Option 2: After every other section pass**
While perfection is a nice achievement, not everyone is trying to perform this type of work. For most people that are trying to balance doing great quality work

in a timely manner, then cleaning your pad on the fly after every other section pass is a faster and still very effective approach.

» **Option 3: After each panel**
Cleaning your pads after buffing an entire panel will get you by. If your pad is not rotating very well, this is an indicator of built-up residue and removed paint on the face of the pad and a sign you need to clean it.

↪ Problems Caused By Not Cleaning Your Pad Often

Compounds and polishes become less effective during application. If you don't remove the spent product, then it will act to dilute the strength or power of any fresh product you apply.

↪ Product Becomes More Difficult To Wipe Off

After buffing a section, the residue will become more and more gummy as it's continually becoming a mixture of product residue, removed paint and any contaminants that were on or in the paint. Add to this a little heat and evaporation of any carrying agents and you're left with a gummy residue that's going to be hard to wipe off.

↪ Harder For The Tool To Rotate The Pad

A build-up of gunk on the face of the foam pad makes it more difficult for the tool to rotate it.

↪ Increased Risk For Instilling Swirls Back Into Paint

As product residue and removed paint builds on the face of the pad, the potential for abrasive particles to accumulate and embed into this mixture of gunk increases and the potential to instill swirls as you're buffing increases.

Foam And Fiber Buffing Pads

◉ Cleaning Pads In A Washer And Dryer

There are some pads on the market that are designed so that they can be machine washed and dried in conventional washers and dryers. This makes cleaning and drying your buffing pads as simple and easy as possible.

Tips For Washing Pads In A Washing Machine

Separate pads for dedicated wash loads
One recommendation would be to wash pads used with compounds and polishes separate from pads used with waxes and paint sealants due to the fact that most compounds and polishes are a lot more water soluble than waxes and paint sealants. By doing this, you'll reduce the chance of cross-contaminating waxes and paint sealants onto your compounding and polishing pads.

Soak cycle
If your washing machine has a soak cycle, use this feature especially if your pads are extremely dirty with caked-on polish and wax residue.

Extra rinse
If your washing machine has an extra or secondary rinse cycle, consider using this feature as another chance to flush residue from your pads.

Hot or warm wash and rinse
Hot and warm water cycles are going to help soften polish and wax residue and also help the pad cleaning solutions emulsify and remove this residue from your pads.

Tips For Top Loading Machines

Don't overload the washing basin.
Your pads need room to move around during the washing and agitating cycle. If you overload the machine, you'll reduce the machine's ability to properly clean your buffing pads.

Add soap and fill wash basin first
This tip is actually on the label of some laundry detergents and it just makes sense. The idea is to create a uniform mixture of soapy water before placing buffing pads into the washing machine. To do this, set the water level to low or medium and then add your cleaning solution and allow the washing machine to fill to set level and begin its agitation cycle. This will thoroughly mix the water with the cleaning solution, creating a uniform mixture.

Once the water and cleaning solution are thoroughly mixed, place your foam pads into the washing machine and then set the correct water level. This technique will maximize the time the pads are being agitated from the very start of the cycle.

Follow manufacturer's recommendations
Use a recommended pad cleaning solution or a quality laundry detergent approved for your type of washing machine. Many new front loading washing machines recommend using specific types of laundry soap to prevent problems, so follow the recommendations from the manufacturer of your washing machine.

Tips For Drying Pads In A Clothes Dryer

If you separated and washed your pads using dedicated wash loads, then continue this practice when drying them. Removing absolutely 100% of any "quality" wax or paint sealant from a buffing pad is difficult to do. Since a dryer forces hot air into an enclosed chamber, it's possible that any wax or paint sealant not removed during the rinse cycle could transfer to any pad during the drying cycle.

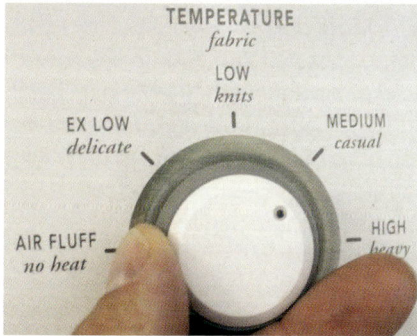

Use the warm setting for foam pads, not the high or hot setting. This is an extra safety precaution as warm flowing air will be more than enough to dry a load of foam pads. Select a time setting based upon how large of a load you're drying.

Important: *When washing buffing pads and microfiber towels, don't use a fabric softener sheet in the dryer.*

Pad cleaning products
There are all kinds of products that can be used to clean residues from buffing pads, but for the context of this how-to book, the only ones I'm going to list are products that specifically state on the label they are formulated for this type of job.

- Detailer's Pro Series Polishing Pad Rejuvenator
- Wolfgang Polishing Pad Rejuvenator
- Pinnacle XMT Polishing Pad Cleaner
- Snappy Clean Pad Cleaning Powder
- Grit Guard Pad Renewing Solution

Pad cleaning tools
Here are some pad cleaning tools specifically made to help you clean foam buffing pads.

- Foam Pad Conditioning Brush
- Duo Spur Wool & Foam Pad Cleaning Tool

How To Dry Foam Pads After Washing

After you've washed your pads, you need to dry them in a clean, dust-free area. Then, store them in a way they will remain clean until you need them for your next detailing project.

Here are some tips…

Upside down or right side up?
Dry your pads with the hook and loop material facing upwards so any water can drain out through the foam unhindered. This way, you won't have water or any remaining residue pooling between the foam and the hook and loop material, potentially affecting the adhesive.

Drying with Grit Guard inserts
If you own a Grit Guard insert, here's a tip from *Tad aka DarkHorse* on the AutogeekOnline.net Detailing Discussion Forum.

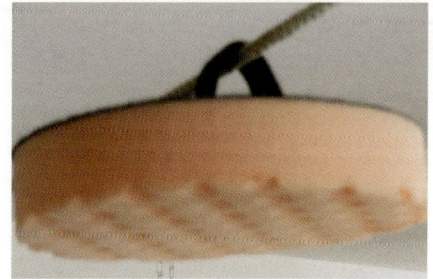

Hang drying pads
Here's a creative way to hang your pads up in the air to dry that uses the hook and loop interface. This method was submitted by *John aka Swimmer* on the AutogeekOnline.net Detailing Discussion Forum.

Cut a strip of hook material about 6"' in length so you can attach it in a loop fashion to the loop material on the back of your buffing pad. Then, run a clothesline on which you can hang your pads to dry. This positions them out of the way, where air can flow around them but airborne dust cannot land and settle on the face of the pads.

Box fan pad dryer
From Truitt aka Bill - Position and suspend a box fan from a clean, flat surface and then place your foam pads onto it face-down. Because your

Foam And Fiber Buffing Pads

pads are face-down, dirt particles won't land and lodge into the pores and the air being drawn past them will dramatically increase drying time.

Towel drying
Using a clean, dry terry or microfiber towel, roll your washed and rinsed pad inside the towel.

Press the towel into the foam as you're folding and rolling the pad into it. Then, squeeze and wring the pad inside the towel, forcing any excess water out of the foam and into the absorbent towel.

Afterwards, place your foam buffing pads where they will stay clean and air can circulate around them so that moisture can evaporate.

⬤⬤ How To Store Clean, Dry Buffing Pads

Clean cupboard - enclosed shelves
If you have an empty cupboard in your laundry room, utility room, or garage, this will make an ideal place to store your clean, dry pads.

Plastic Storage Containers
These containers work great not only for storing your foam buffing pads, but also microfiber towels and other detailing tools you want to keep clean like wash mitts, sponges, brushes, etc.

Tip: Mold and Mildew - If you're going to store foam pads in any kind of air-tight container or bag, be sure the pad is 100% dry to prevent the potential for mold and mildew forming. If it does form, you can simply wash the pad to remove any mold or mildew.

Original packaging bags
Some pads come with a re-closable plastic bag. Keep the bag and use it for storage.

Large sealable plastic bags
These work great for storing clean buffing pads. Just make sure your pads are 100% dry if you choose to seal the bag shut.

⬤⬤ Foam Pad Color Coding

Each pad manufacturer uses a different color coding system for the pads they manufacture. Even inside a single company's pad lines, there can be confusion. Below is a snapshot of colors used for popular pads in the detailing world.

💻 *Lake Country Foam Pads*
CCS Pads - Color Coding is identical for all CCS Pads

- **Yellow** = Cutting
- **Orange** = Light Cutting
- **Green** = Cutting/Polishing
- **White** = Polishing
- **Green** = Polishing
- **Gray** = Finishing
- **Blue** = Finishing
- **Red** = Finishing
- **Gold** = Jewelling

💻 *Flat Pads - Both 5 1/2 and 6 1/2 inch*

- **Yellow** = Cutting
- **Orange** = Light Cutting
- **White** = Polishing
- **Gray** = Finishing
- **Blue** = Finishing

Mike Phillips' - The Art of Detailing

⊙ Surbuf MicroFingers

Surbuf MicroFingers Buffing Pads are an interesting pad that has its roots in the woodworking industry as a pad used to stain wood by machine.

In the woodworking industry, wood stain is applied to the center of the pad and on a low speed setting and with very light pressure, the polisher is moved over a wood surface and the stain is worked into the grain of the wood by the MicroFingers.

While Surbuf pads are used to apply stain in the woodworking industry, in the detailing world, they are used on DA polishers for correction work.

» **The benefit**
Generally speaking, the fibers of this type of pad work as a type of abrasive to compliment the abrasives in the compound or polish. When used with a DA polisher, you will in effect have two types of abrasives (the mechanical abrasives in the compound and the MicroFingers) working for you to level the surface.

» **The drawback**
The MicroFinger fibers tend to leave micromarring in the paint, also called DA haze. This isn't a big deal because an aggressive foam cutting pad on a DA polisher will also leave micromarring or haze. Anytime you use a Surbuf pad, just keep in mind that after using this pad for your correction step, you need to follow it by re-polishing the paint using a softer pad and a less aggressive polish to remove the micromarring and create a clear, defect free finish.

Sizes Available
- 4 inch
- 5 1/2 inch
- 6 1/2 inch
- 7 inch

⚑ Tips For Using Surbuf Pads

Match the pad to the correct sized backing plate and center the pad onto the hook and loop interface. Always hold the pad flat to the surface and use light to moderate pressure, letting the combination of MicroFingers, abrasives and oscillating/rotating action do the abrading work.

- 4 inch = 3.5" Backing Plate
- 5 1/2 inch = 5" Backing Plate
- 6 1/2 inch = 6" Backing Plate
- 7 inch = 6" Backing Plate

Use firm pressure and slow arm speed
When removing swirls and scratches, you want to use firm pressure and slow arm speed. Some people recommend using light pressure so you don't flatten down the MicroFingers. While that sounds good, the truth is, after you make a few passes with any pressure, the MicroFingers naturally lay down and

Foam And Fiber Buffing Pads

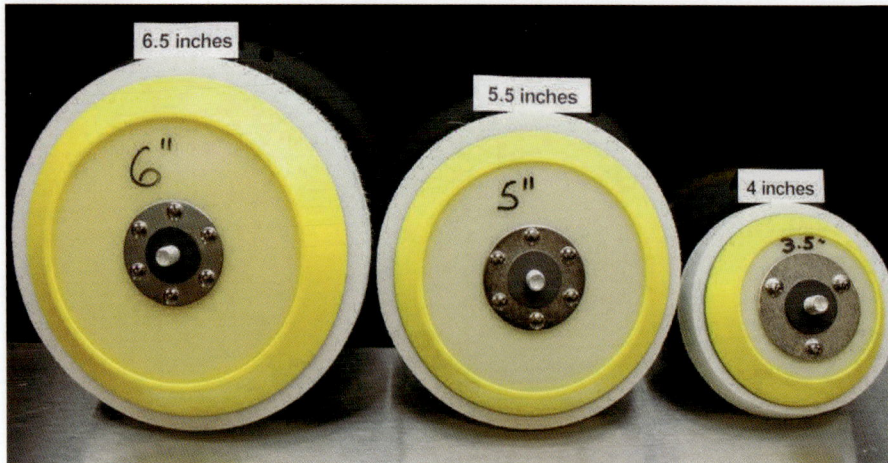

6.5 inches / 5.5 inches / 4 inches

flatten out. You can't stop this from happening and the pads still cut well. If you try to only use light pressure in an attempt to keep the MicroFingers from laying down, you won't engage the abrasives with the paint.

When to clean
Clean your Surbuf pads after each section pass. As the MicroFingers lay down, your product and any paint you're removing will build up on the surface of the pad. You want to remove this residue before adding fresh product. You should always be wiping any product residue from the paint after doing a section pass. Compound and polishes shouldn't be allowed to dry. There's no benefit to this and normally it makes wiping this type of residue from the paint more difficult.

How To Clean Surbuf Microfiber Pads

Compressed air
The best way is using an air squirter with an air compressor. Always use safety glasses when using compressed air.

Pad conditioning brush
If you don't have an air compressor, you can use the nylon bristles of a pad conditioning brush to agitate the working face of the Surbuf pads. Hold the polisher in such a way that you can keep the backing plate from spinning freely, and then draw the brush against the MicroFingers. This will remove caked-up product and re-fluff the fibers.

What I do is brace the pad from behind by holding my thumb and index finger against the backing plate. This keeps the assembly from spinning while I run the brush over the face of the pad to remove built-up residue.

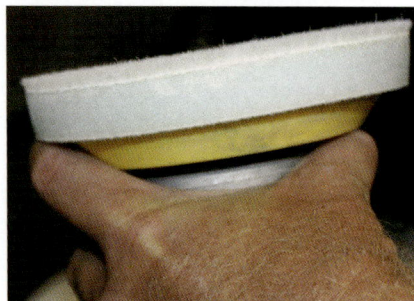

Pad Washer
The Grit Guard Universal Pad Washer works excellent for cleaning Surbuf pads. Use the same technique shared in this chapter.

For more information:
📖 *Cleaning Pads using a Pad Washer*

Wash by hand
You can also wash your Surbuf pads by hand in either a sink or a bucket in the same way you would wash a foam buffing pad by hand.

💬 **Note:** It's not recommended to wash Surbuf pads in a washing machine or dry them in a clothes dryer.

Meguiar's DA Microfiber Pads

Microfiber pads were first introduced and used at the OEM level for spot repair on the assembly line. The technology has since been improved and introduced to the detailing industry as part of a complete high production, swirl-free system for reconditioning the paint on used cars.

What is a Microfiber DA pad?
Microfiber polishing pads use a specific type of open-ended microfiber material that is extremely soft to the touch when new, clean and dry. The

microfiber material is attached to a foam backing interface that comes in two styles, cutting and finishing. The noticeable difference between the two types of discs is the foam backing material. If you look closely and compare the microfiber material between the cutting and finishing discs, you can also see there is a subtle difference in the microfiber pile.

Three sizes available in both cutting and finishing discs

Meguiar's microfiber pads are available in 3 different sizes - 3", 5" and 6". The actual exact size for pads and backing plates varies as is the norm for all buffing pads and backing plates. Normally, you want the backing plate to be a little undersized so there's a safety margin around the pad preventing you from gouging the paint with the edge of the backing plate. At the same time, it's important to have equal and uniform pressure applied over the entire working face of the pad to maximize efficiency.

Cutting Discs

- **Foam backing**
  Maroon foam backing that is approximately 1/4" thick with a medium density cushion to it.

- **Microfiber pile**
  Open-ended microfiber material that is very soft, yet different when compared to the microfiber used for the finishing disc. The fibers appear to be longer in length and slightly larger in diameter. The microfiber pile is also more dense than the finishing pad with more fibers per square inch.

Finishing Discs

- **Foam backing**
  Black foam backing is approximately 3/8" with a soft cushioned feel to it that's slightly softer than the maroon foam backing of the cutting disc.

- **Microfiber pile**
  Soft, open-ended microfiber material that is even softer than the microfiber pile used for the cutting pad. The fibers themselves are both shorter in length and smaller in diameter than the

microfiber pile used to make the cutting disc. The microfiber pile also appears to be less dense with less fibers per square inch as compared to the microfiber cutting discs.

Meguiar's DA Microfiber discs are part of a multi-component system designed and optimized specifically for use with DA polishers and their matching D300 Compound and D301 Finishing Wax for a 2-step approach for removing swirls and scratches and restoring a swirl-free, high gloss finish.

Factory paint

The first thing to understand about this system is that it is specifically designed for and formulated for use on factory paint. When used as intended, this two-step approach produces phenomenal results with no chance of instilling swirls. One advantage this system offers is time savings because it's a two-step system that delivers results normally associated with three or more steps.

First Step - Remove Swirls And Scratches

The microfiber cutting discs, when used with the matching compound, will remove most swirls and scratches in one step with a residue that wipes off easily. Deeper swirls and scratches would require more applications or more aggressive products, pads and tools. This system is targeted at high volume detailing, not show car detailing. In high volume detailing, the goal is not to remove 100% of all defects - it's to remove the majority of medium to shallow swirls and scratches and do it without instilling swirls at the same time.

First, prime a clean, dry pad.

Once it is primed, apply your working product using 3-4 pea-sized to dime-sized drops of product to the face of the pad.

Second Step - Refine Results, Create Gloss And Seal Paint

The microfiber finishing disc, when used with the matching polish/wax, has the ability to lightly abrade the paint to remove any haze left by the aggressive first step and refine the results to create a high gloss finish.

Official product recommendations
Use the Microfiber Cutting Disc with D300 Correction Compound and use the Microfiber Finishing Discs with D301 Finishing Wax. There are no official recommendations for using these types of pads outside of the matching compound and polish/wax that makes up the DA Microfiber System. When used as intended, they work very well and reduce the overall time it takes to restore the finish on cars with factory paint.

Using with non-system products
I've included these two discs in this how-to book because they are an available option for DA polishers besides conventional foam buffing pads and other fiber-type pads like the Surbuf pads. They should be used as intended and that's with their matching compound and polish/wax. If you choose to use them with any product outside the system, I would strongly recommend doing a test spot to a small section of paint and checking your results. Make sure you're getting the results you want and hope for before attempting to buff out the rest of the car.

How To Clean Meguiar's Da Microfiber Pads

Compressed air
The best way is using an air squirter with an air compressor. Always use safety glasses when using compressed air.

Bug scrubbing sponge
Interestingly enough, this simple bug scrubbing sponge works really well to remove caked-on product residue while also re-fluffing the microfibers.

Pad conditioning brush
If you don't have an air compressor, you can use the nylon bristles of a pad conditioning brush to agitate the working face of the Meguiar's microfiber pads. Hold the polisher in one hand in such a way that you can keep the backing plate from spinning freely, and then draw the brush against the microfibers. This will remove caked-on product and re-fluff the fibers.

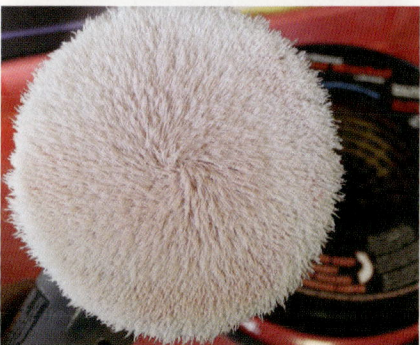

Pad Washer

The Grit Guard Universal Pad Washer works excellent for cleaning Meguiar's microfiber pads. Use the same technique shared in this chapter.

For more information:

📖 *Cleaning Pads using a Pad Washer*

Machine washing and drying

The Meguiar's Microfiber DA Discs are made to be washed and dried in conventional washing machines and clothes dryers. Use the same techniques shared in this chapter.

For more information:

Cleaning pads in a washer and dryer

Wash by hand

You can also wash your Meguiar's microfiber pads by hand in either a sink or a bucket in the same way you would wash a foam buffing pad by hand.

Drying and storage

Same as foam pads.

👀 How To Choose The Right Pad For The Job

Any time you're buffing out a car for the first time, it's a good idea to do what's called a test spot to one of the horizontal panels. Dial in a system approach that removes the defects to your satisfaction and creates the quality of finish appearance that you're looking and hoping for before buffing out the entire car.

- If you can make one small section of paint look great, if you duplicate the same process to the rest of the car, you should get the same results throughout.

- If you run into any kind of problems or issues working on your test spot, then you'll be glad you didn't just start buffing out the entire car only to find out towards the end of the project you're not getting the results you wanted.

- If you have already worked on the paint for your current detailing project, then you probably already have an idea as to which pad to start out with. If not, then hopefully the information below will help to guide you to pick the right pad.

Why test?

Hardness of the paint you're buffing is a huge variable. Paint manufacturers are continually introducing new paint lines and modifying existing ones. This means the paint on a 2011 Ford manufactured in January can buff differently than the paint on a 2011 Ford manufactured in March. It all depends upon the paint system being used at the time.

So don't rely on past experiences to base future product choices upon for your next detailing project. If you're working on a car you've never worked on before, new or old, before buffing out the entire car, do a little testing and dial-in a system that works great in one location. Theoretically and

Foam And Fiber Buffing Pads

hopefully, this same process will work perfectly over the rest of the car. Always do a test spot.

💬 *"Use the least aggressive product to get the job done"*

Some people read the above quote and think it applies to the liquid paint care products used to buff out a car. While this is true, it's not limited to just the liquid products. It actually includes everything that is going to touch the paint, including your choice of pads.

There are 3 basic categories of buffing pads:
- **Cutting**
- **Polishing**
- **Finishing**

Inside these 3 groups are sub-groups
- » **Cutting**
  - Aggressive
  - Medium
  - Light

- » **Polishing**
  - Medium Polishing
  - Light Polishing

- » **Finishing**
  - Finishing pads
  - Jewelling pads

In most cases, the differences are subtle. But, because modern clearcoat paints are thin and scratch-sensitive, little differences can have huge effects, thus the variety of different types of pads and levels of aggressiveness.

🔴 Paint Conditions And Pad Recommendations

Here are the basics of choosing the right pad for the job. The first step is to evaluate your car's finish as explained in this chapter, *Visual and Physical Inspection.* After reading that chapter, you should be able to inspect your car's paint and determine where it falls into one of these 11 categories.

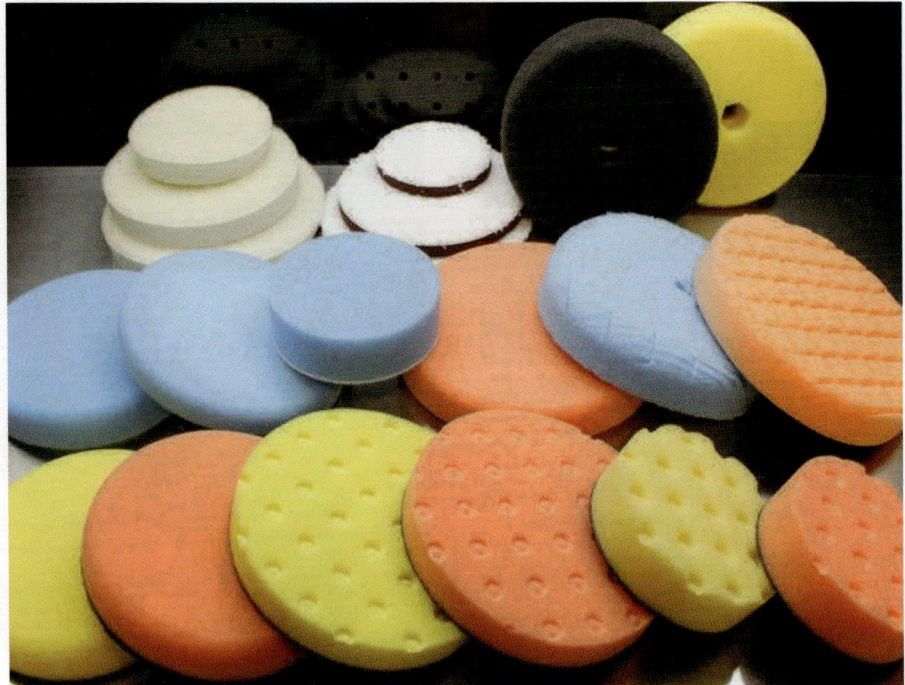

- **Show Car Quality**
  Foam Polishing Pad, Finishing Pad or Jewelling Pad

- **Excellent Condition**
  Foam Polishing Pad, Finishing Pad or Jewelling Pad

- **Good Condition**
  Foam Polishing pad

- **Mildly Neglected**
  Foam Polishing or Cutting Pad

- **Severely Neglected**
  Aggressive Foam or Fiber Cutting Pad

- **Horrendous Swirls**
  Aggressive Foam or Fiber Cutting Pad

- **Extreme Oxidation**
  Aggressive Foam or Fiber Cutting Pad

- **Extreme Orange Peel**
  Remove by sanding and compounding

- **Unstable**
  Correction not possible - repaint

- **Clearcoat Failure**
  Correction not possible - repaint

- **Past the point of no return**
  Correction not possible - repaint

Which type of foam pad to use
All of the foam pads listed in this book work great - CCS pads, Flat Pads, Kompressor Pads, Cobra Pads, Hydro-Tech Pads, Edge, etc.

Which pads are best
Personal preference is a huge factor when it comes to what's best. Flat pads have been around the longest and have a long track record of success. CCS pads have been around for close to 20 years and have a large and loyal following.

💬 Start with either the 5 1/2" CCS or Flat open cell pads and gain experience with them. If you can afford to, then get a selection of pads from both styles. The CCS and Flat pad styles are really easy to use and make learning to machine polish a cinch.

As you tackle more detailing projects, test out the Hydro-Tech, Kompressor, or any of the other pads available for use with DA polishers including the Surbuf and microfiber pads.

Mike Phillips' - The Art of Detailing

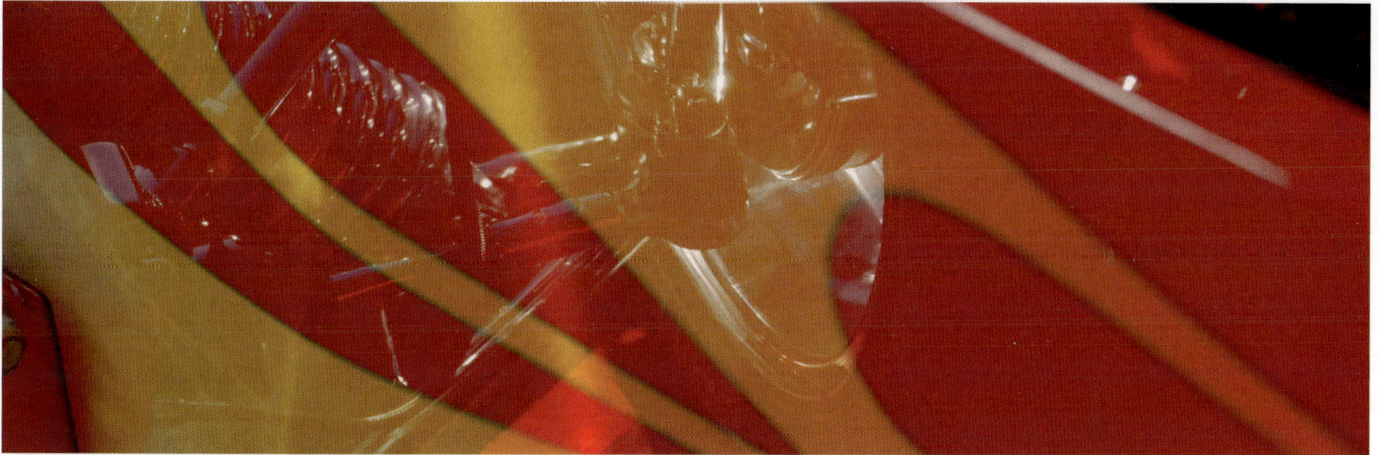

Compounds, Polishes And Waxes Overview

There's always a lot of confusion when it comes to words and terms used in the car detailing industry and hobby.

Part of the reason for this is because there's no organization in the auto appearance industry that regulates or has oversight over the language used to describe and market car appearance products. Manufacturers, marketers and distributors of car care appearance products can and do name their products using whatever terms they like, regardless of the confusion it may cause or any historical precedents.

Judge a product by the function it performs, not the name on the label
Because there's no universal standard definitions for words and terms used in the car care appearance world, my practice and recommendation to others is to judge a product not by the name on the label, but by what function the product serves.

For example, if a product is referred to as a polish but acts as a paint sealant, then the product is in fact a paint sealant and not an abrasive polish in the historical use of the word.

If a product is referred to as a glaze but acts to seal the paint, then the product is a wax or paint sealant and not a glaze in the historical use of the word.

Here's a list of commonly used words in our industry and my attempt at creating some type of standardized definition for each word.

- Aggressive Cut Compound
- Medium Cut Polish
- Fine Cut Polish
- Ultra Fine Cut Polish
- Non-Abrasive Glaze or Pure Polish
- Pre-Wax Cleaner
- Paint Cleaner
- Carnauba Wax
- Synthetic Paint Sealant
- Hybrid Sealant/Wax
- Paint Coating
- Cleaner wax or AIO

Aggressive Cut Compound

A very aggressive liquid or paste that uses some type of abrasive technology to cut or abrade paint quickly. In the body shop world, compounds are used to remove sanding marks. In the detailing world, compounds are used to remove deep below-surface defects like swirls, scratches and water spot etchings. Depending upon the abrasive technology and the application method and material, some automotive compounds can remove down to #1000 grit sanding marks. Of course, topcoat hardness is an important factor that affects effectiveness.

Historically, the more aggressive the compound, the more follow-up polishing will be required to restore a defect-free finish. Due to major advancements in abrasive technology, the trend is for very aggressive compounds that finish out like medium and even fine polishes.

In most cases, an aggressive compound should be followed with either a medium or fine polish to refine the surface to a higher degree than the results produced by only the compound. Most compounds are dedicated products in that their function is primarily to abrade the paint. For this reason, after the compounding step, further polishing and sealing steps are required. Most compounds are water-soluble, so that they can be washed off body panels and out of cracks and crevices.

Compounds, Polishes And Waxes

Medium Cut Polish

A liquid or paste that uses some type of abrasive technology to cut or abrade the paint, but is less aggressive than a true cutting compound. Depending upon the abrasive technology and the application method and material, some medium polishes can remove down to #2000 grit sanding marks and finish Last Step Product (LSP) ready. Topcoat hardness is an important factor that affects a medium polish's effectiveness at removing below-surface defects.

Most medium polishes are dedicated products in that their function is primarily to abrade the paint. For this reason, after the polishing step, further steps are required. This may include another final polishing step depending upon the results after using the medium polish. At a minimum, the paint should be sealed with a wax, paint sealant or coating.

Fine Cut Polish

A liquid or paste that uses some type of abrasive technology to cut or abrade the paint, but is less aggressive than a true medium polish. Depending upon the abrasive technology and the application method and material, some fine polishes can remove down to #2500 grit sanding marks while still finishing out LSP ready. Topcoat hardness is an important factor that affects a fine polish's effectiveness at removing below-surface defects.

Most fine polishes are dedicated products in that their function is primarily to abrade the paint. For this reason, after the fine polishing step, further steps may be required. This could include another final polishing step depending upon the results after using the fine polish. At a minimum, the paint should be sealed with a wax, paint sealant or coating.

Ultra Fine Cut Polish

A liquid or paste that uses some type of abrasive technology to cut or abrade the paint, but is less aggressive than a true fine polish. Depending upon the abrasive technology and the application method and material, some ultra fine polishes can remove down to #2500 grit sanding marks while still finishing out LSP ready. Topcoat hardness is an important factor that affects an ultra fine polish's effectiveness at removing below-surface defects.

Most ultra fine polishes are dedicated products in that their function is primarily to abrade the paint. For this reason, after the ultra fine polishing step, at a minimum, the paint should be sealed with a wax, paint sealant or coating.

Non-Abrasive Glaze or Pure Polish

Historically, the term glaze is used to describe a bodyshop safe, hand-applied liquid used to fill-in and mask fine swirls while creating a deep, wet shine on fresh paint. It's a category of products used on fresh paint in body shop environments, which will not seal the paint surface.

A bodyshop safe glaze is used in place of a wax, sealant or coating because it won't interfere with the normal out-gassing process of fresh paint for the first 30 days of curing. The function of a bodyshop glaze is to hide rotary buffer swirls while giving the paint a uniform, just waxed appearance to ensure customer satisfaction. After 30 days cure time, it's normal to the seal the paint using a wax, paint sealant or coating.

- **Hiding swirls**
  There's a number of reasons why body shops use a glaze on fresh paint to hide swirls. Most body shops are production oriented

and perform a limited number of machine buffing steps due to time restrictions and profitability. This would include machine compounding with a wool pad and polishing with either a wool finishing pad or a foam polishing or finishing pad, both steps using rotary buffers.

The end result is normally an excellent shine, but with rotary buffer swirls in the paint that can be seen in bright light. The glaze is normally hand-applied to fill in and hide the swirls as hand application is fast and relatively effective as long as the swirls are shallow. This glazing procedure produces a finish that customers will accept at the time of vehicle pick-up. The results are somewhat misleading, however, because bodyshop glazes are water soluble. As such, they will wash off after a few car washes or repeated exposure to rainy weather, making the swirls visible again. This is the standard and accepted practice in the body shop industry.

💬 **Note:** Because there are no rules or regulations governing the definition or the use of the word "glaze", manufacturers and sellers of paint care products use it as a name for all types of products that are not true glazes in the historical sense of the word. Most common is the use of the word glaze in the name of a car wax or paint sealant.

- **Paint cleaner**
  A liquid, paste or cream that relies primarily on chemical cleaning agents to remove any light topical contamination or surface impurities to restore a clean, smooth surface as part of a process to prepare a painted finish for application of a wax, paint sealant or coating. Paint cleaners are for very light cleaning and not normally intended to be used

like an abrasive polish to remove below-surface defects.

Pre-Wax Cleaner

Similar or the same as a paint cleaner. Most pre-wax cleaners are complimentary products in that they are part of a specific brand's system in which the pre-wax cleaner is matched to a wax or paint sealant. There's a chemical synergistic compatibility to ensure maximum performance between products that might not be achieved using products from outside the brand.

Carnauba Car Wax

Generally defined as a product that contains some type of naturally occurring waxy substance intended to protect the paint while creating a clear, glossy finish. Carnauba wax is the most commonly used naturally occurring wax found in car wax formulations. This category of traditional waxes will wear off under normal wear and tear, repeated washings and exposure to the environment and should be reapplied

on a regular basis to maintain a protective coating on the surface of the paint.

Synthetic Paint Sealant

Generally defined as a product that contains some type of man-made or synthetic protection ingredients to protect the paint while creating a clear, glossy finish. Perception on the part of the public is that a paint sealant is made from synthetic polymers with no naturally occurring wax type substance or other naturally occurring protection ingredients.

The general consensus among car enthusiasts is that because the protection ingredients are synthetic, a paint sealant will protect better and last longer than a traditional car wax made using naturally occurring waxes. Paint sealants will wear off under normal wear and tear, repeated washings and exposure to the environment and should be reapplied on a regular basis to maintain a protective coating on the surface of the paint.

Compounds, Polishes And Waxes

◈ Hybrid Sealant/Wax

The term "car wax" refers to a category of products that uses naturally occurring wax ingredients for protection and beauty, while the term "paint sealant" refers to a category of products that uses synthetic polymers. The fact is, most products are a blend of both natural and synthetic ingredients and are thus hybrid sealant waxes.

◈ Paint Coatings

Generally defined as any paint protection product that contains man-made or synthetic protection ingredients that are intended to permanently bond to the paint to both provide a barrier-coating of protection as well as create a clear, high gloss finish. The products available in this category are considered permanent coatings because like your car's paint, they cannot be removed unless you purposefully remove or neglect them.

◈ Cleaner Wax or AIO

A cleaner wax, or what is also referred to as an All-In-One (AIO), is a one-step product. These formulations use a blend of chemical cleaners and often some type of abrasives, plus some

type of protection ingredients that will remain on the surface after the cleaning action is finished and the residue is wiped from the paint.

The combination of chemical cleaners and abrasives will remove topical defects like oxidation and road grime from the surface, which will restore clarity to the clearcoat.

At the same time, the product will leave behind a layer of protection using some type of protection ingredients to help lock in the shine and protect from the elements.

- **Abrasive cleaner waxes**
  Some cleaner waxes have the ability to remove below-surface defects like swirls and scratches. To what degree depends upon how aggressive the abrasives are in the formula. There are some fairly aggressive cleaner waxes available and these are normally marketed at the production detailing industry.

- **Retail car waxes = cleaner waxes**
  When you go to your local auto parts stores, most of the retail waxes on the shelves do in fact fall into the cleaner wax category. They are targeted at the average person, driving what we refer to as a daily driver. Over time, the

finish quality deteriorates and in order to restore it with just a single product, it must offer some level of cleaning ability or abrasive action.

- » **Production detailing**
  Cleaner waxes are the norm for production detailing. The goal in this industry is to restore shine to the paint on a car as fast as possible to maximize the profits for the detailer or detail shop. For this reason, multiple step procedures are not ideal - you want to clean, polish and protect in one step.

- » **Maintenance wax**
  Some cleaner waxes are formulated to be very light in their cleaning ability. As such, they make great one-step maintenance products for cars that are in good to excellent condition. Because they will clean, polish and protect in one step, a lot of people prefer to use a light cleaner wax to maintain their car's finish.

⚏ Factors That Affect How Aggressive Or Non-aggressive A Product Is

When working on automotive paints, it's important to remember that it's not just the compounds and polishes that determine total correction ability, it's anything that touches the paint and even the way the paint is touched. *Here are some factors:*

Application Materials

Wool cutting pads are more aggressive than soft foam finishing pads. Applying any product with a more aggressive pad will make the process more aggressive overall, while applying any product with soft foam will tend to make the process less aggressive.

Buffing Pads

Most Aggressive to Least Aggressive

- Fiber cutting pads
- Foam cutting pads
- Foam polishing pads
- Foam finishing pads

Application Process

The application process is how you apply your compounds, polishes and waxes, whether it's by hand or machine.

Listed in order of most to least powerful

- **Rotary buffer**
  Out of all the common tools used to polish paint, the rotary buffer is the most powerful and has the ability and potential to make any product and/or any application material more aggressive than other tools simply by its power.

- **Forced rotation dual action polishers**
  The Flex XC-3401VRG is a forced rotation dual action polisher. While it doesn't have the same ability for powerful correction work as a rotary buffer, it does offer a lot of correction power.

- **DA polishers**
  DA polishers use a free floating

spindle bearing assembly, which means if you push too hard on the head of the unit or hold the tool so that pad is on edge, you can stop the pad from rotating. This is the feature that makes it very user friendly for people new to machine polishing. However, this also means it doesn't have the same power for correction work as either the forced rotation dual action or rotary buffers.

- **Cyclo polishers**
  The dual counter rotating heads of a Cyclo polisher use a combination of a direct drive and a free floating spindle bearing assembly. This dual drive feature provides a lot of power while being safe at the same time. The Cyclo is about equal to a DA polisher in terms of correction power, but there are more new pads and chemicals being introduced for the single head DA polishers to increase and improve their abilities.

- **The human hand**
  The human hand is actually very powerful in terms of correction power. Using your 4 fingers, you can exert a lot of pressure to a small area and using a quality compound and applicator, you

can remove a lot of paint fast. However, your finger, hand, arm and shoulder muscles get tired whereas the all the above tools offer consistent power output.

- **Big picture**
  No matter which tool you're working with or if you're working by hand, you can increase or reduce how aggressive or non-aggressive any procedure is by changing the type of application material you're using.

- **Size of work area**
  To increase aggressiveness of a process, you can shrink the size of your work area. This will concentrate more product to the process. To decrease the aggressiveness of a process, you can increase the size of the work area. This will act to dilute the strength of the product being used.

- **Product amount**
  Normally, you want to use an ample amount of product for the procedure you're doing. Using too much product can hyper-lubricate the surface, making it more difficult for abrasives to work. Using too little product means not

having enough product on the surface to actually do a good job. When it comes to using cleaner waxes on neglected surfaces, you should lean towards using the product heavy or wet so that you err on the side of caution and have plenty of chemical cleaning agents and abrasives working for you. Using too little will result in less overall cleaning ability.

- **Number of applications**
  Applying a product multiple times can affect how aggressive it is after the first application. The first application will tend to do the initial grunt work, removing all the topical impurities, enabling second and third applications to go right to work on freshly cleaned paint.

- **Technique**
  Using proper technique is vitally important. For example, moving a DA polisher too quickly over the surface will decrease a product's aggressiveness because you don't give the combination of oscillating action, rotating action, the pad material and the product time to affect the paint in one area before moving the polisher further along the paint.

- **Summary**
  When working with a DA polisher, for more powerful and aggressive cutting or correction power, use foam cutting pads, Surbuf pads or microfiber cutting pads. To reduce the aggressiveness of a DA polisher, switch to foam polishing and finishing pads or microfiber finishing pads.

Use The Least Aggressive Product To Get The Job Done

I'm a strong advocate of giving credit where it is due, for both professional and personal reasons. To this point, I want to give credit to Meguiar's for this quote and philosophy towards working on automotive paints. I learned this when I worked for them in 1988 as an outside sales rep and trainer for Oregon, Washington and Idaho.

"Use the least aggressive product to get the job done"

The reasoning and logic behind this statement and approach towards working on car paint is for two reasons.

- **Reason 1 - Automotive paints are thin**
  Factory applied paint, whether it came on a Model T or a brand new Ford Mustang, is thinner than most of us prefer. It's thin because it costs more to apply more paint in the way of materials and time.

- **Reason 2 - Removing below-surface defects means removing a little paint**
  Below-surface paint defects are things like swirls, scratches, and etchings like Type II Water Spots. Because these types of defects are below the surface level, the only way to remove them is to level the paint.

Now, let's tie the two concepts together. Paint is thin, and removing defects means removing paint, but there's not a lot of paint available to remove. This is why the "use the least aggressive product to get the job done" philosophy is so important.

Here's the "why" part
The reason why you want to use the least aggressive product to get the job done is so that you'll leave the most amount of paint on the car to last over its service life.

- **Digging deeper**
  In order to use the least aggressive product to get the job done, you need to do some testing. This means you have to have more than one product in your arsenal of detailing supplies.

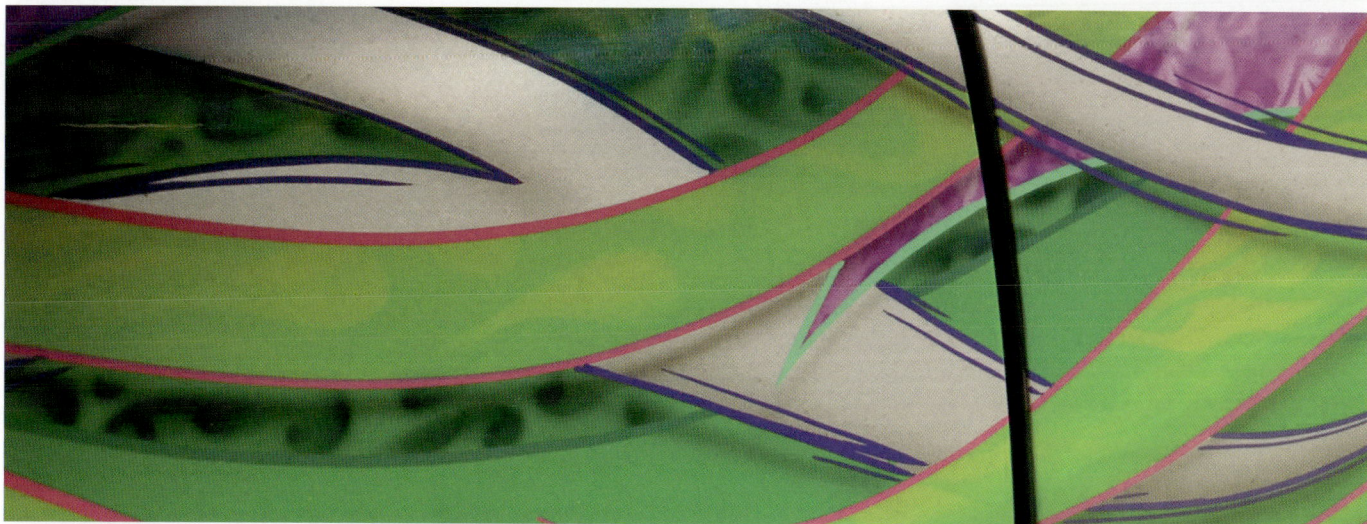

Tool time

Products are like tools. They enable you to perform a specific procedure or task that you couldn't do otherwise. Just like a screwdriver enables you to either remove or install a screw, a quality compound or polish enables you to remove defects and restore a show car finish.

In the context of detailing, this means you don't know if you can remove the swirls with a fine polish and a soft polishing pad until you try.

Sure, you can remove them with an aggressive compound and cutting pad, but if your goal is to preserve your car's precious, thin coat of beauty, then start each project by doing some testing. Try to find the least aggressive product in your detailing arsenal that will enable you to get the job done.

You need some tools in your tool box!

If you haven't already, consider adding a few tools to your tool box. Any time you're working on a car's finish, you'll already have the tools you need to do some testing and then tackle the job.

A well rounded inventory would include:

- Aggressive compound for serious paint defects
- Medium cut polish
- Fine cut polish
- Ultra fine cut polish
- Hand applied paint cleaner
- Non-abrasive glaze or pure polish
- Cleaner wax
- Finishing wax or sealant

The Graphic Equalizer Analogy To Polishing Paint

Mike Pennington, the Director of Training for Meguiar's, gave me this analogy a long time ago so I want to give him credit for it.

You can adjust your pad, product, tool and technique just like you can adjust music using a graphic equalizer. When everything is dialed in perfect for the paint you're working on, you'll get the results you're looking for.

It does mean sometimes playing around a little to find the perfect combination of products and procedures, kind of like adjusting a graphic equalizer for a single song so it sounds perfect to your ears.

When everything is right, you'll make beautiful music, or in this case, you'll create a show car finish.

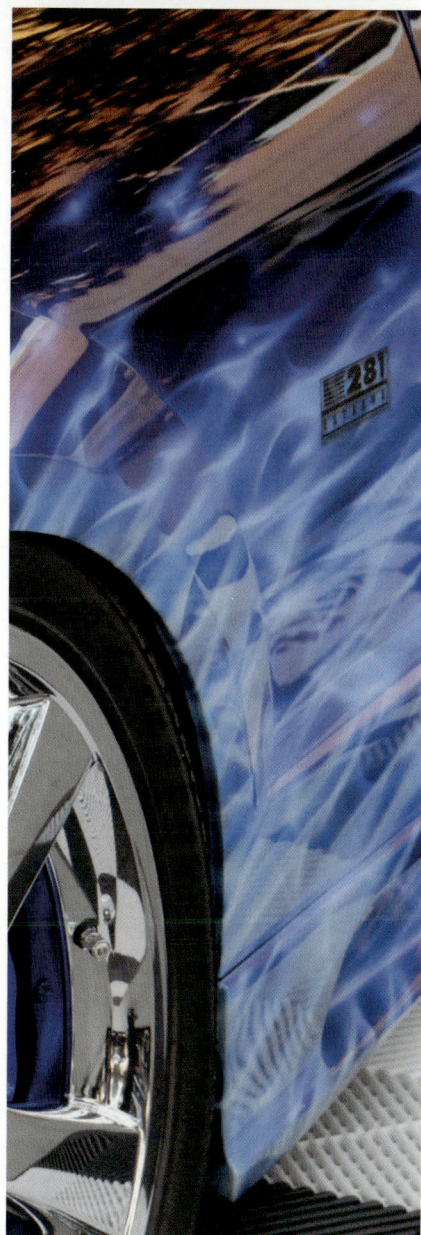

Work Clean, Get Organized And Dress Casual

Anytime you're using a power tool it's a good idea to wear safety glasses.

👓 Work Clean, Get Organized And Dress Casual

Before you begin buffing out any car, you should also have a clean and well-lit work environment.

Work clean

Do the simple things like sweep the garage or shop floor. You don't want any dirt or dust to get on the paint as you're working through your paint polishing procedures via foot traffic and air circulation in your work environment.

Get organized

If you have a workbench or any kind of table, clean it off and make a place for all your detailing tools.

Microfiber towel supply

Not only do your microfiber towels need to be clean, but you need a clean area to place them where they're readily accessible.

After using microfiber towels, it is a good idea to store them in a clean container so they don't end up on the garage floor. When you're done using a microfiber towel, you still need to prevent it from becoming contaminated before you wash and dry.

Paint care products

Have all your compounds, polishes and waxes in one place for easy access.

Buffing pads

You're going to need a clean area to place your buffing pads so they're readily available, but won't get dirty as you're working around the car. You'll also need a place for dirty pads as you go through them until you can clean them and put them away.

Miscellaneous tools and supplies

Painter's tape, wheel maskers, plastic drop cloths, beach towels, etc.

More light is better

Good lighting is important because you need to see the paint as you're working on it. Turn all garage or shop lights on, and if needed, replace worn out bulbs. Some people go to great extents to increase the light in their garage by mounting fluorescent lights on the sides of the walls to light up the vertical panels.

Power-up

Have heavy duty extension cords ready and accessible for all sides of the vehicle. A heavy duty 14 to 12 gauge extension cord is recommended with a 12 gauge recommended for any extension cord over 25 feet in length.

Get comfortable

Wear comfortable clothing. Avoid wearing things like belts, watches, ties and jewelry. Also avoid wearing hot or uncomfortable clothes as well as shoes or sandals that don't provide good ankle support.

Miscellaneous Items

- Cold drinks
- Snacks
- Music for when you're not running the polisher
- Ear protection
- Eye protection
- Camera
- Assortment of nylon detailing brushes for removing residue from cracks and crevices
- Fan to blow air on hot days

Having a clean, well organized work environment will speed things up and make the project a lot more enjoyable.

After each step, take a moment to do a little clean up and organization.

Mike Phillips' - The Art of Detailing

IMPORTANT *This section and the next are purposefully placed in this how to book at this point in time because you need to know how to carefully wipe compounds, polishes and waxes off paint so you don't put scratches back in during the wipe-off process.*

You're going to need to wipe off compound or polish residue when you do your first test spot and you don't want to skew your results by inflicting toweling marks. Learn how to properly use a microfiber towel to carefully wipe compound and polish residues off.

People watching

I often try to observe people and the techniques they use for any and all aspects of detailing cars. The goal is to help them tweak their technique if anything they're doing could use some improvement. Most pros would agree, when it comes to taking a car's finish to its maximum potential, that even more important than pad, product and tool selection is technique. All techniques, not just how you move the polisher.

Technique is everything

A basic technique that's vitally important

One common procedure that is as basic as you can get is also one of the most important procedures involved in creating a true show car shine, and

that's correctly folding and using a microfiber towel to remove a coating of polish, wax, paint sealant, spray-on-wax or spray detailer.

Good technique - Used correctly, your hand and a microfiber towel will create an eye-dazzling finish that that will hold up under intense scrutiny under bright light conditions, like full overhead sunlight or while on display at an indoor car show.

Wrong technique - Used incorrectly, you can easily instill swirls and scratches into the paint, requiring machine polishing to remove them. You're then back to wiping the polish off without instilling swirls all over again. Are you starting to get the idea of how important it is to carefully wipe anything off paint?

👀 How To Correctly Fold And Use A Microfiber Towel

Here are the basics of how to correctly use a microfiber towel.

🚶 *Correct Technique*

1. Start with a clean, microfiber towel. If the towel has been washed and dried, I will usually inspect each side to make sure there are no contaminants stuck onto the fibers of the towel. Microfiber acts like a magnet and can easily attract and hold all kinds of things to itself

that you don't want to rub against your car's paint, so take a moment to visually inspect your microfiber polishing towels.

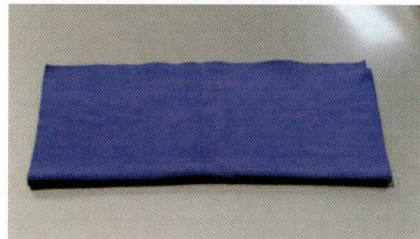

2. Fold the microfiber towel in half and then in half again...

Control over the towel

By folding your microfiber towels into quarters, you will now have 8 dedicated sides to wipe with and you have control over all 8 sides. When you simply lay a microfiber towel flat or scrunch it up into a wad, you don't have any control over it because it's too hard to gauge and remember how much of the towel has already been used. This is what I mean by having control over the towel - it's being able to monitor how much of the towel has already been used. You can only do this if you have a repeatable system in place like folding your towels.

Cushion to spread out the pressure from your hand

Folding your microfiber towel also provides cushion to spread out the pressure from your hand. This provides two benefits:

1. Helps reduce the potential for fingermarks, caused by excess pressure from your fingertips.

2. Helps to maintain even contact between the working face of the folded microfiber towel and the surface of the paint. This is important at all times, but especially whenever you're working on any panel that is not flat.

⚘ Incorrect Technique

Unfolded Microfiber Towel
Simply laying the towel flat against the paint increases the potential for swirls and scratches due to pressure points against the towel. Using a towel flat and unfolded offers little to no cushion and reduces even pressure between the cloth and the paint. I cringe when I see someone wiping a nice finish by simply placing the towel down flat on the paint and then placing their hand flat on the towel.

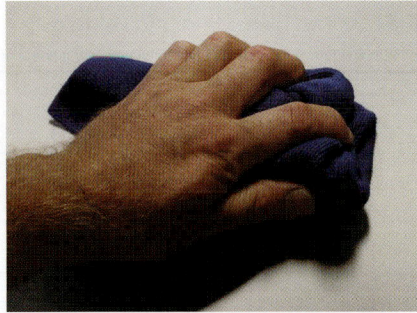

🔳 How To Carefully Wipe Off Compounds, Polishes And Waxes By Hand

Now that you know how to correctly fold and use a microfiber towel, let's take a look at how to correctly wipe compound, polish and wax residues without harming the paint.

- **Waxes and paint sealants**
  Applying a thin, uniform coating of any wax or paint sealant will ensure easy removal.

- **Compounds and polishes**
  Compounds and polishes should be wiped off immediately after polishing when the residue is still a wet film. If you do this, the wetness acts to lubricate the surface during wipe-off.

When using the the wet buffing technique, immediately after you buff a section, turn your polisher off, allow the pad to stop spinning and then set the polisher aside. You should have a clean, dry microfiber towel nearby so you can quickly start wiping the leftover compound or polish residue off the paint.

Big picture
When it's time to wipe any product off the paint, your job is to remove it without struggling and without inflicting toweling marks back into the paint.

The words "toweling marks" are a nice way of saying light or shallow swirls and scratches from pushing too hard with your wiping towel. In other words, you're struggling as you're trying to remove something that's not coming off easily.

Let me share with you the technique I call, "breaking open a coat of wax and then creeping out".

This technique also works with any film on a painted surface. First, let me share the problem.

Trying to wipe off too much product at a time
Most people try to wipe off huge sections of product with each wipe. For some products, this works well because the product is incredibly easy to wipe off in the first place. But for a lot of other products, wipe-off requires a little more work and effort.

If a product is difficult to wipe off, trying to take huge chunks of it off in a single stroke doesn't work very well. When you try to remove huge amounts of product in a single wiping pass, the surface tension between the layer of product and the paint is greater by the shear volume of surface area compared to what your hand and a wiping cloth can pull away from the paint and onto the cloth.

Solution: Take little bites
Instead of trying to wipe off huge sections at a time, just wipe little bites of product off using an overlapping, circular motion with your hand and microfiber polishing towel. When you only try to take off little bites of product at a time using overlapping circular wiping passes, taking off any product is easy.

You need a starting point
Before you can remove any type of residue, you need a clean starting point. After you remove the product from one small area, you will uncover the paint you have just compounded, polished or waxed and thus you'll have a shiny spot.

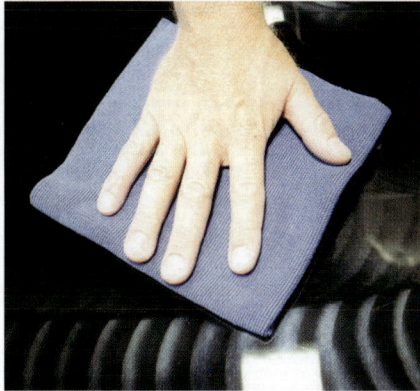

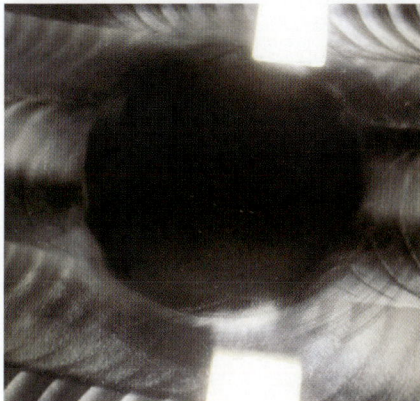

You can do this anyway you'd like, but here's how I usually do it. Place a clean microfiber towel folded 4-ways flat on a panel, and then gently but with firm pressure, twist the microfiber in a circle. This will usually remove most of the wax in that area and create a shiny spot. This is called "breaking open a coating of wax".

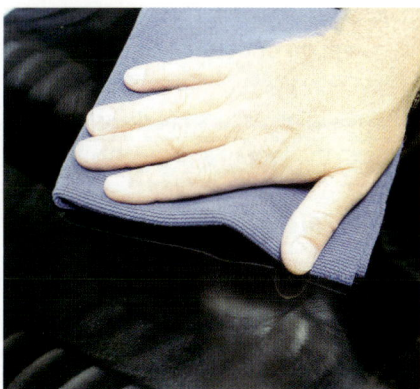

Now, you can start taking small bites of wax off the paint by making small overlapping circular swipes with your microfiber towel and then creeping outward from the shiny spot.

Washing Microfiber Towels

Most importantly, don't overload the washing basin. Your microfiber towels need room to swish around during the washing and agitating cycle. If you overload the machine, you'll reduce the machine's ability to properly clean your microfiber towels.

Most important: Add soap and fill wash basin first
The idea is to create a uniform mixture of soapy water before placing microfiber towels into the washing machine.

1. To do this, set the water level to low or medium. Then, add your cleaning solution and allow the washing machine to fill to set level and begin its agitation cycle. This will thoroughly mix the water with the cleaning solution for a uniform mixture.

2. Place your microfiber towels into the washing machine and then set the water.

3. Reset the switch/timer for it to run through the entire washing cycle.

This technique will maximize the time the microfiber towels are being agitated because from the very start of the cycle, your microfiber towels are saturated with a uniform mixture of water and cleaning solution.

If you wash your microfiber towels or anything by adding them to the washing machine first and then

adding soap, part of the washing or agitating cycle will be wasted while the cleaning soap uses valuable time to mix throughout the water.

Second rinse cycle
If your washing machine has the option for a second rinse cycle, use this to ensure all laundry detergent as well as any other residues are completely rinsed from your microfiber towels.

Microfiber cleaning detergents
When it comes to cleaning your microfiber towels, you want to use a good quality detergent soap to emulsify and remove any compound, polish or wax residues.

- *Pinnacle Micro Rejuvenator Microfiber Detergent Concentrate*
- *Detailer's Pro Series Microfiber Cleaner*
- *Sonus Der Wunder Microfiber and Pad Wasche*

Pre-wash maintenance
One of the best things you can do to maintain the quality of your microfiber towels is to sort them as you use them into dedicated laundry bins.

- **Bin 1** - Water-soluble residues - compounds, polishes, glazes, paint cleaners
- **Bin 2** - Waxes, paint sealants
- **Bin 3** - Everything else - Don't use these to wipe polished paint.

By separating your microfiber towels by the type of product they are used with, you can avoid any chemical cross-contamination. You can pick up laundry bins like the one you see here to help keep your laundry organized and clean.

👀 The 4 Minimum Categories Of Wiping Towels

Just as important as any product or tool in your detailing arsenal are your wiping towels. You can use the best compound, polish, LSP and buffing pads and top of the line polishers, but if you're using any type of wiping towels that are in some way, shape or form contaminated, then you risk putting swirls and scratches into your car's finish.

4 categories minimum
Everyone should have at least 4 types of wiping towels. These are the minimum, so feel free to separate your wiping towels as much as you'd like.

- **Good microfiber towels**
  You can "touch" paint with microfiber polishing towels from this collection. These are the microfiber towels in your collection that are new or you have washed and dried and you trust them to be safe on a high gloss, polished finish.

- **Secondary microfiber towels**
  These are washed, dried and clean, but their quality has fallen to a level that you have deemed them not worthy of touching a high gloss, polished finish. You don't throw them away because they still have value for wiping spray detailers or cleaner/waxes out places like door jambs, chrome wheels or bumpers, or some components in the engine compartment. The point is they are still great at removing residue, just not off a swirl-free, scratch-free, high gloss surface.

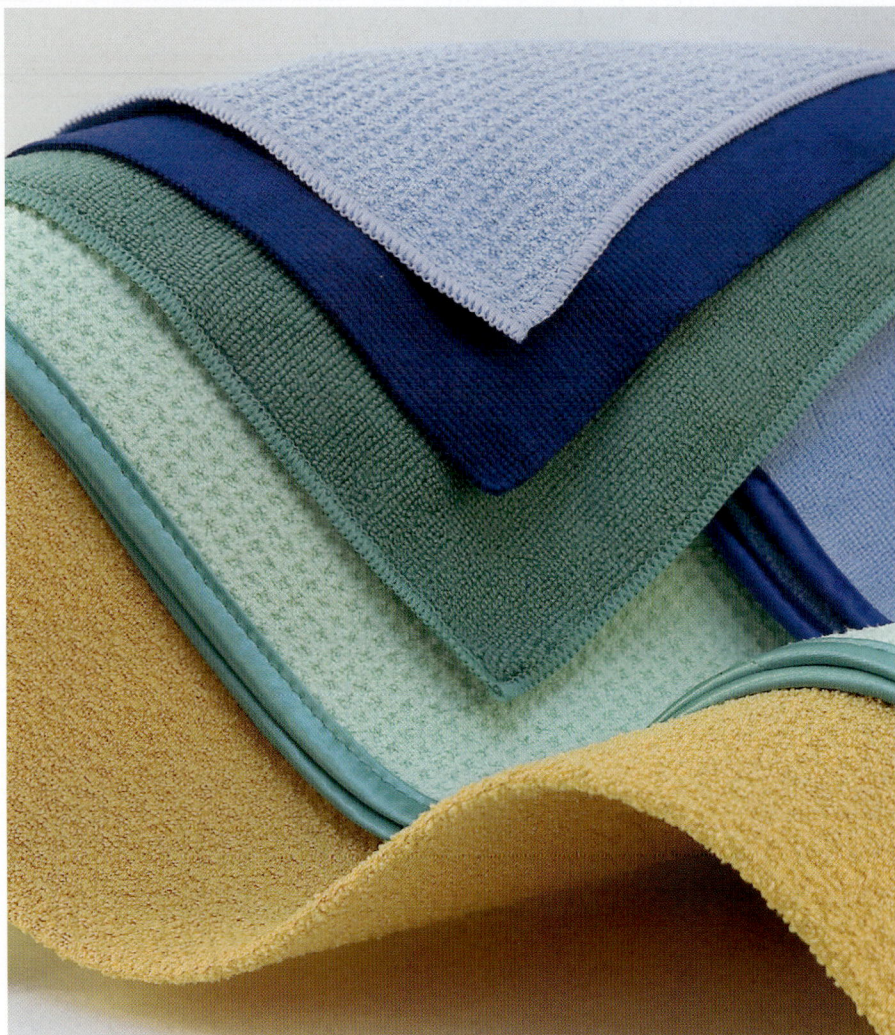

Good cotton towels
While microfiber towels are superior for removing products from smooth, high gloss finishes, there's still a place for good quality cotton towels. For example, cleaning your pad on the fly. Cotton towels with a large nap work better than microfiber towels. Some people prefer a cotton towel with a large nap to remove compounds because they offer a more aggressive bite, but then switch over to microfiber for removing polishes and LSPs. Your good cotton towels should be clean and soft and worthy of working on paint in good condition or better.

- **Secondary cotton towels**
  Secondary Cotton Towels are

washed and dried, but for whatever reason, their quality is fallen off too far from what's acceptable to touch paint in good condition or better. They still have value, however, for mundane tasks like wiping excess tire dressing from the face of a tire, applying or wiping cleaners and dressings in the fender well area, applying or removing cleaners, dressings or cleaner/waxes in the trunk area or door jambs and engine compartments. They have value because they are absorbent, clean and ready to use and paid for. After some projects you might be better off discarding them versus trying to clean them well enough that they can be used again.

What Is A Section Pass?

When talking about machine polishing on discussion forums and in detailing classes, we talk about "making passes" with the polisher. During these discussions, people that are new to machine polishing always have one or all of the below questions:

- What's a pass?
- How many passes do I make?
- What's a section pass?

The Definition Of A Section - The Size Of An Area To Work At One Time

To understand what a section is, you first need to know what a panel is.

- **Vehicle** - Body shell with panels
- **Panels** - A door, hood, roof, etc. - the major portions of the vehicle
- **Section** - A portion of a panel

In order to buff out a vehicle, you need to divide or slice the various panels into smaller sections. In most cases, the size of a section should be in the 16" x 16" to 20" x 20" size.

Here's a trunk lid that is divided into sections for the correction step.

The tape is only to give you a reference point as to how to divide up a panel into sections. You would not use tape to create sections and then try to remove swirls and scratches. The section you see would be larger without the tape because in the real world, when you're buffing out the different sections, you'll be overlapping each new section into the previous section. This tends to naturally increase the size of the section you picture in your imagination when sizing up a panel and dividing it into a manageable section.

Because modern vehicles come in all different shapes, you can't always create perfectly squared-up sections of paint to buff out. What I teach people is to let the panel be your guide.

Avoid Buffing On Raised Body Lines

It's a good practice to avoid buffing on raised body lines. Knowing and practicing this will help you to divide a car's panels.

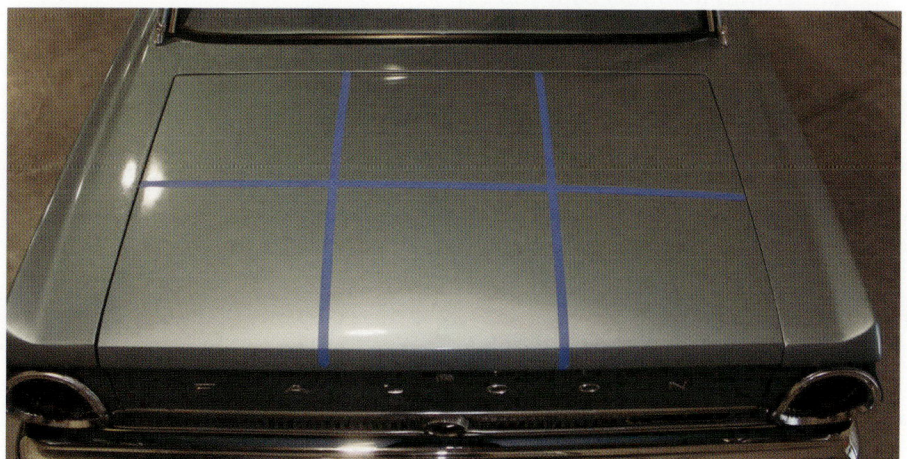

Time To Start Buffing!

You won't always be working on a perfectly square, flat hood. There are many places where you'll be buffing thin panels of paint, like around the top portion of a fender, the A-pillars and B-pillars, and other complex panels. In these cases, you need to let the panel be your guide and this may mean buffing very small areas or areas that are longer than they are wide.

Maximize buffing cycle

If you try to tackle too large of a panel at one time, you'll shorten the buffing cycle of your product. While you're polishing one section, the product not being worked will be drying. By working a smaller section, you'll be actively engaging the wet, working film of product, keeping it in liquid form. The longer any film of product sets undisturbed, the more quickly it will tend to dry and you'll decrease the buffing cycle.

Maintain equal downward pressure

The farther away from your body you move your hand, the more likely you are to exert less pressure. The longer your arm stroke, the more likely it is that you'll remove less paint. This makes for uneven material removal. It can also lead to removing too much material in the area closer to your body. By keeping your buffing area to a manageable size, you'll improve the likelihood that you'll only remove the necessary amount of material to get the job done. You'll also remove material equally over the section you're buffing.

👀 The Definition Of A Single Pass And A Section Pass

There are two definitions of the word "pass" as it relates to machine polishing.

- **Single pass**
  A single pass is when you move the polisher from one side of the section you're buffing to the other.

- **Section pass**
  A section pass is when you move the polisher back and forth with enough single overlapping passes to cover the entire section one time.

Question: *Which directions do I move the polisher when doing section passes?*

Answer: *Use a repeatable pattern.*

Successfully removing all the swirls out of the entire car means removing all the swirls out of each section you work. In order to do this, you need a method that you can control and duplicate as you buff out each section.

For most people, following a back and forth, side-to-side pattern works because it's easy to remember, easy to do and easy to duplicate. If you run a detailing business, it's an easy pattern to teach your employees to ensure they are successful.

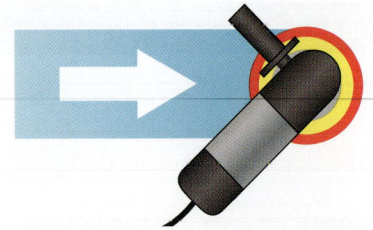

Here is a single pass with a polisher.

The first set of overlapping passes in a side to side direction is one section pass.

Next, make your overlapping passes in the opposite direction, which would be your second section pass.

Each time you go over the entire section that would be a section pass. For correction work you will make 6 to 8 section passes to each section to remove defects.

Mike Phillips' - The Art of Detailing

Question: *How many section passes do I do?*

Answer: *6 to 8 section passes minimum.*

In most cases, if you're removing any substantial below-surface defects, you're going to make at least 6-8 section passes before you either feel comfortable you've removed the defects or you're at the end of the buffing cycle for the product you're using.

When doing your test spot, remember how many section passes you make and the results you obtain. This will give you an idea as to how many section passes you'll need to be doing for each section as you move around the car. The deeper the defects, the harder the paint, the more section passes you'll need to do.

Arm Speed

Arm speed is the term for how fast you move the polisher over the paint.

- **Major correction work = Slow arm speed**
  For any major correction work, you want to use a slow arm speed.

- **Polishing work = slow/medium arm speed**
  For polishing work, you still want the combination the abrasives in the product, the aggressiveness of the pad, and the oscillating/rotating action to further abrade the paint to maximize gloss and clarity. For this reason, you don't want to move the polisher too quickly, but slightly faster than you would if you were removing swirls and scratches.

- **Waxing or sealing the paint = medium/fast speed**
  When it comes to applying a wax, you're no longer limited to a small area. You can work as large of an area as you can reach as long as

you have enough wax to spread out. You can move the polisher fairly quickly, because you're no longer trying to abrade the paint. My recommendation is to always make 2-3 passes over each square inch of paint.

Downward Pressure

- **Removing swirls and scratches = firm pressure**
  I recommend about 15 to 20 pounds of downward pressure, but you must be able to see the pad rotating. Swirls and scratches are best removed when the pad is rotating, not just jiggling or vibrating against the paint.

- **Polishing to a high gloss = medium pressure**
  I usually make my first two section passes with firm pressure. This ensures any haze left by the correction step is cut out by the abrasives while they are at maximum abrading ability. For the remaining passes, I reduce pressure and increase arm speed slightly. At this point, polishing paint becomes an art form due to the level of care used during the final 3-5 section passes.

- **Machine waxing = light pressure**
  When applying a finishing wax or paint sealant, you only need to apply light pressure - just enough to keep the pad flat against the surface.

💬 **Note:** If you were using a one-step cleaner wax, then you would be using firm pressure because you would be trying to restore neglected paint.

Tool Speed Setting

Here is a general range of speed setting used for most procedures. Specific speed settings can be subjective and vary based on numerous circumstances.

Always follow the manufacturer's recommendations for specific products being used.

Typical speeds for most procedures using most DA polishers
- 5 to 6 Speed setting for removing swirls
- 4 to 5 Speed setting for polishing after swirls are removed
- 3 to 4 Speed setting for applying wax.

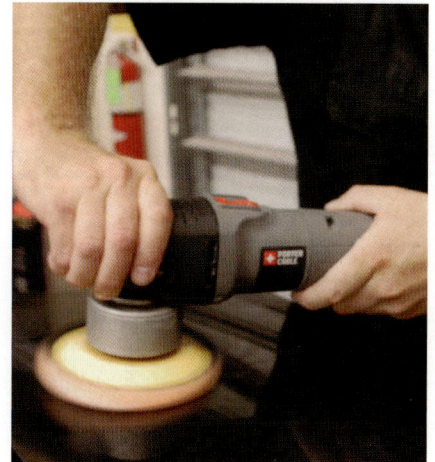

How To Hold The Polisher

When doing your section passes, you want to hold the body of the polisher in a way that the face of the pad is flat against the paint. Buffing pads rotate best when equal pressure is applied over the entire face of the pad. If you hold the body of the polisher so that more pressure is applied to just the edge of a pad, this increased pressure will cause the pad to slow down and even stop rotating in some situations.

How Much Product To Use

See the following chapters:
- 📖 *Priming your pad*
- 📖 *How much product to use*

Clean Your Pad Often

See the following chapter:
- 📖 *Cleaning Buffing Pad*

Time To Start Buffing!

✈ Remove Spent Residue

See the following chapter:
📖 *How to carefully wipe off compounds, polishes and waxes by hand*

👀 Buffing Cycle

The buffing cycle is the amount of time you are able to work the product before the abrasives have broken down and/or the product begins to dry. With most diminishing abrasive products, the diminishing abrasives will have broken down after around 6 passes using good technique, with firm downward pressure and slow arm movement.

Different products have different buffing cycles, depending upon the type of abrasives used in the formula and the different lubricating ingredients as well as carrying agents used to suspend the abrasives and provide lubrication.

🗩 **Note:** With SMAT (Super Micro Abrasive Technology) products, you can stop anytime during the buffing cycle if the defects are removed. The only limitation when using SMAT products is to make sure you always have a wet film of product on the surface.

Factors that affect the buffing cycle:
- Ambient temperature
- Surface temperature
- Size of work area
- Type of machine
- Type of pad material
- Humidity
- Wind or air flow surrounding the car
- Amount of product used
- Technique

👀 The wet buffing technique

Most compounds and polishes should be used so that there is enough product on the surface to maintain a wet film while the product is being worked. The wetness of the product provides lubrication so the abrasives don't simply scour the finish leaving behind swirls and scratches.

👀 Wet Film Behind Your Path-Of-Travel

As you're making a single pass with the polisher, the path of travel should have a visible wet film behind it. If the paint behind the pad is dry and shiny, you've run out of lubrication and you're dry buffing. Turn the polisher off. Wipe the residue off and inspect the paint. It's pretty rare to actually cause any harm, but pay attention when you're running the polisher and try to avoid dry buffing.

👀 Dry Buffing

There are some products on the market in which the manufacturer recommends buffing the product until it dries. As the product dries, you'll tend to see some dusting as the product residue becomes a powder and the paint will have a hard, dry shine to it.

Although some manufacturers recommend this, it's important to understand what's taking place at the surface level. As the product dries, lubricating features are lost. As this happens, friction and heat will increase and with this, so does the risk of micro-marring the paint.

👀 The Remedy To Dry Buffing

If you accidently dry buff, don't panic. You can quickly re-polish that section by cleaning your pad and adding fresh product and making a few new section passes.

IMPORTANT: *Read this before doing your test spot. You need to nail the test spot so your process is dialed-in and proven before you attempt buffing out the entire car.*

Here's a list of the most common problems

- Trying to work too large of an area at one time.
- Moving the polisher too fast over the surface.
- Using too low of a speed setting for removing swirls.
- Using too little or too much downward pressure on the head of the polisher.
- Not holding the polisher in a way to keep the pad flat while working your compound or polish.
- Using too much or too little product.
- Not cleaning the pad often enough.

Here are the solutions:

- **Trying to work too large of an area at one time.**
Shrink the size of your work area down. You can't tackle too large of an area at one time. The average size work area should be around 20" by 20". Most generic recommendations say to work an area 2' by 2', but for the correction step, that's too large. You have to do some experimenting to find out how easy or how hard the defects are coming out of your car's paint system and then adjust your work area to the results of your test spot. The harder the paint, the smaller the area you want to work.

- **Moving the polisher too fast over the surface**
For removing defects, you want to use slow arm speed. It's easy and actually natural for most people new to machine polishing to move the polisher quickly over the paint, but that's the wrong technique. One reason I think people move the polisher too quickly over the paint is because they hear the sound of the motor spinning fast and this has psychological effect, which causes them to match their arm movement to the perceived

fast speed of the polisher's motor.

Another reason people move the polisher too quickly over the paint is because they think like this,

"If I move the polisher quickly, I'll get done faster"

But it doesn't work that way. Anytime you're trying to remove swirls, scratches, water spots or oxidation using a DA polisher, you need to move the polisher s-l-o-w-l-y over the paint.

- **Using too low of a speed setting for removing swirls.**
When first starting out, many people are scared of burning or swirling their paint. They take the safe route of running the polisher at too low of a speed setting, but this won't work. You need the speed, oscillation, and rotation of the pad, along with the combination of slow arm speed, product abrasives, pad aggressiveness, and downward pressure to level the paint.

- **Using too little downward pressure on the head of the polisher.**
For the same reason as stated in #3, people are apprehensive to apply too much downward pressure to the polisher. The result of too little pressure is no paint is removed, thus no swirls are removed.

- **Using too much downward pressure on the head of the polisher**
If you push too hard, you will slow down the rotating movement of the pad and the abrasives won't be effectively worked against the paint. You need to apply firm pressure to engage the abrasives against the paint, but not so much that the pad is barely rotating. This is where it's a good idea to use a permanent black marker to make a mark on the back of your backing plate so your eyes can easily see if the pad is rotating or not. This will help you to adjust your downward

pressure accordingly.

- **Not holding the polisher in a way to keep the pad flat while working your compound or polish.**
Applying excess pressure to one side of the pad will cause it to stop rotating and thus decrease abrading ability.

- **Using too much or too little product.**
Too much product hyper-lubricates the surface. The abrasives won't effectively bite into the paint, but instead will tend to skim over the surface. Overusing product will also accelerate pad saturation as well increase the potential for slinging splatter onto adjacent panels.

Too little product means too little lubrication and this can interfere with pad rotation.

- **Not cleaning the pad often enough.**
Most people simply don't clean their pad often enough to maximize the effectiveness of their DA polisher. Any time you're abrading the paint, you have two things building up on the face of your buffing pad:

- Removed paint
- Spent product

As these two things build up on the face of the pad, they become gummy. This has a negative effect on pad rotation and makes wiping the leftover residue from the paint more difficult. To maintain good pad rotation, you want to clean your pad often and always wipe off any leftover product residue from the paint after working a section. Never add fresh product to your pad and work a section that still has leftover product residue on it.

For more information on cleaning your pad see this chapter:
📖 *Cleaning your pad on the fly technique*

Step-By-Step How To Do A Test Spot Car Preparation

A test spot is simply an area of paint in which four things are tested simultaneously.

- Products
- Pads
- Tool of choice
- Skills and abilities

The idea is to test out the products, pads and process you're thinking of using over the entire car to just one small section and make sure you can make it look great!

Good results
If you can make one small section look great, then you'll have proven your system approach and this will give you the confidence to duplicate the process over the rest of the car.

Bad results
If you run into any kinds of problems, you'll be glad you only worked on this one small section of your car. It's easier and faster to undo any issues and fix a small area of paint versus having to redo the entire car.

Where to do a test spot
The best place to do a test spot is on a horizontal panel that you can look down on, like a hood or trunk lid. You normally want to inspect the paint

using bright light like the sun or a Brinkmann Swirl Finder Light. The sun works best, but using it to inspect your results works best when it is directly overhead, thus a horizontal surface works best.

Before you start
- Wash and dry car - Paint must be clean before you do any testing.
- Inspect paint visually for swirls - this tells you whether or not you need to machine polish.
- Inspect paint physically with your sense of touch for above surface bonded contaminants. This tells you if you need to use detailing clay or not.

Option - clay only the test spot
If there's any question or doubt that the paint is so far gone that it cannot be saved, before claying the entire vehicle, you can just clay the area you're going to test on. Wait to clay the entire car after your test results confirm the paint can be saved.

Save your clay
Sometimes, a finish can be past the point of no return. This means no amount of work and nothing you pour out of a bottle or scoop out of a can will undo the damage and restore an

acceptable finish. For extreme detailing projects like this, you might as well save your clay until you confirm the paint can be successfully corrected and you're going to commit to buffing out the rest of the car.

Use a tape-line
I'm a big fan of using a tape-line on the paint when doing a test spot because it makes it really easy for your eyes to see and gauge before and after differences. This will make it easier for you to tell if you're making progress or if something's not working right.

The idea is to place some painter's tape onto the paint and only do your testing to one side of the tape. After applying, working and then wiping off each product, you can compare the side you're working on with the "before" condition of the paint. The goal, of course, is to remove the defects from the paint and restore it to like-new condition.

Use the least aggressive product to get the job done
If you've never worked on the vehicle you're planning on detailing, you should start your testing with the least aggressive products in your

Mike Phillips' - The Art of Detailing

Using a tape-line on the paint when doing a test spot because it makes it really easy for your eyes to see and gauge before and after differences.

collection and check to see if the safest approach will work. If the first product you test doesn't work fast or effectively enough, you can always substitute a more aggressive product.

Through some simple trial and error testing, you should be able to figure out which pad and product combinations work best. By testing first, you'll already know and have the confidence that you're going to get excellent results over the entire car.

For more information:
📖 *Use the least aggressive product to get the job done*

RIDS = Random, Isolated Deeper Scratches

When you do your testing, the goal is to find a product and pad combination that removes the majority of the defects, not each and every single scratch. Because you're using a DA polisher, chances are you cannot remove 100% of all the deeper swirls and scratches.

Chances are very good that you'll remove a majority of the shallow swirls and leave the deeper RIDS behind. Make sure as you're testing that your expectations are realistic. If you're aiming for a show car finish, then you should be working on an

actual show car or a garage queen, not a daily driver. If you're working on a daily driver that has swirls and scratches now, even if you're careful, you'll likely get a few more swirls and scratches in the future just from normal, day-in, day-out, wear and tear. For this reason, you don't want to try to remove 100% of all swirls and scratches out of a daily driver as it sacrifices too much paint.

For more information:
📖 *RIDS = Random Isolated Deeper Scratches*

New test spot = new section of paint

If you don't get the results you're looking for from your first test spot and want to be as accurate as possible, then each time you start a new/different test spot, try to use a fresh section of paint that has not been buffed yet. This is why a hood or a trunk lid works well for doing test spots. More often than not, they are large enough to allow you to easily do 2 to 5 test spots, but normally you'll dial in a process that works with the first one or two tests. If and when you move to a fresh section of paint to perform a new test spot, continue using painter's tape to make a tape-line so you can quickly and easily check your results and confirm you're

making progress.

Chemically stripping the test spot
The lubricating agents used in all high quality compounds and polishes will tend to remain on the surface and fill or mask any defects still remaining in the paint. If you want to make 100% sure your process is working, you can chemically strip the paint used for your test spot and then inspect the results. This is normally done after the polishing steps and before any wax, paint sealant or a coating is applied. Isopropyl alcohol is the most common solvent used to chemically strip paint. Mineral spirits is another option and there are a few products on the market formulated just for removing any polishing residues. Another option is to wash the test area using a detergent soap with a water rinse.

For more information on how to chemically strip the paint in order to accurately inspect and view the results, read the below article and pay attention to the warnings.

For more information:
📖 *How to Mix IPA for Inspecting Correction Results*

📽 Step By Step How To Do A Test Spot Using A DA Polisher

I'm going to show how to perform a test spot. This process will work with any collection of quality paint correction products.

Step-By-Step How To Do A Test Spot Car Preparation

Pad selection

For the following example, I'll use a specific pad system to walk you through the process. You can use any pad line or design you'd like. The key point is to use clean, high quality pads so you don't hinder the performance of the products being used.

✦ First Test Spot

Process:
1. *Finishing polish w/polishing pad*

To demonstrate "using the least aggressive product to get the job done", I'll start my first test spot using a fine or finishing polish and then progressively test with more aggressive pad and/or product combinations until an approach is dialed in.

- **Step 1** - Prime a clean, foam polishing pad with a finishing polish, then apply 3 dime sized drops of working product.

- **Step 2** - Turn polisher on using a slow speed setting (3 or 4), then spread the product out over an area of about 16" x 16".

- **Step 3** - Turn the speed setting of your DA polisher up to 5 or 6 and start making your overlapping section passes. Do anywhere from 5 to 8 section passes to your test spot.

- **Step 4** - After you finish making

your final section pass, turn the polisher off and carefully use a microfiber towel, folded 4-ways to wipe the leftover residue from the paint.

- **Step 5 - Inspect the paint**
Depending upon how bad the paint was before you started, you should be able to see a noticeable difference between the "before" and "after" sides divided by the tape-line. When inspecting, use a Brinkmann Swirl Finder Light or move the car into bright, overhead sunlight.

- **Step 6 - Optional - Chemically strip paint before inspecting.**
If you want to make sure you're seeing the true results and that no polishing oils or other fillers are masking defects, then chemically strip the paint and inspect the results.

For more information:
📖 *How to Chemically Strip Paint*

Questions after the first test spot

- **A:** *Does the paint look better?*
- **B:** *Are the defects removed to your satisfaction?*

Answers:
- **A:** Yes
- **B:** Yes

If the answer to both questions is "yes", then this combination of pad and product are aggressive enough to remove the defects. Theoretically, if you duplicate the same process over the rest of the car, you should get the same results.

If the defects are not removed to your satisfaction, then do a second test spot.

✦ Second Test Spot

Process:
1. *Medium polish w/polishing pad*
2. *Finishing polish w/finishing pad*

For this second test, you're going to be doing two steps since you were unable to remove the defects with one step.

Inspect after the polishing step
Keep in mind the first step, also known as the correction step, will be followed by the polishing step. The true results are gauged after both steps are completed.

As you become more aggressive in your choice of products and pads, it's possible that while the more aggressive pad and polish will remove the defects faster and more effectively, you could also leave behind what we call micro-marring, DA haze or tick marks. It just depends upon how polishable the paint is and how aggressive your pads and products are.

Questions after the second test spot

- **A:** Does the paint look better?
- **B:** Are the defects removed to your satisfaction?

After the second test spot, if you answered "no" to both questions, then perform a third test spot.

Mike Phillips' - The Art of Detailing

🏃 Third Test Spot

Process:
1. *Medium polish w/cutting pad*
2. *Finishing polish w/finishing pad*

If you're still not removing the defects fast enough using a medium polish with a polishing pad, try the same product but substitute a more aggressive foam cutting pad.

With the combination of a quality medium polish, a foam cutting pad and good technique, you should be able to remove the majority of swirls and scratches. Then, you'll refine the results during the polishing step. After performing both steps, inspect your results.

If you still cannot remove the defects to your expectations, it may have more to do with your technique than it has to do with the pad and product. At this point, you may want to re-read these two chapters.

📖 *What is a section pass and how to do one*
📖 *The DA Polisher Troubleshooting Guide*

Sealing the test spot - optional
After you remove the finishing polish, the paint should look awesome! It should be clear, with no defects blocking or clouding your view of the color coat under the clear layer of paint. What you have done is perfectly prepared the paint for application of a coat of wax, paint sealant or a coating.

At this time, if you really want to see how the entire car is going to look after you've completed the entire process, then apply a quality wax, sealant or coating. You should see a show car finish if you've done everything right.

What you see in your test spot is how the entire car is going to look and this should get you motivated.

🏃 What To Do Next?

The next step is to get busy!

Claying
If you only clayed the hood or the test spot area, then the first thing you want to do is finish claying the rest of the car.

Taping off and covering up
As an option, you can tape off or cover up any rubber, plastic or vinyl trim or components. These materials will tend to stain easily if you accidently get any polish or wax residue on them. This residue will tend to turn white and detract from the beauty of the car. It can also be difficult to remove this residue completely.

For more information:
📖 *How to Tape-off a Car*

Set-up a work station
Gather all your supplies and assemble them in one easily accessible area. This can be a workbench, a rolling cart or even a folding table. Having all your products, pads and plenty of clean microfiber towels all in one place will help you get the job done faster.

Start at the top and work your way down
After you've completed your test spot and dialed-in your approach, the next thing to do is start buffing out the car. People that are new to machine polishing usually inquire as to where to start and how to proceed to buff out a car.

For more information:
📖 *Start polishing at the top and work your way down*

Divide larger panels into smaller sections
Buffing out a car with any machine is simply a matter of slicing up each panel into smaller sections and then buffing only one section at a time. After finishing one section, move to a new section and overlap a little into the previous section.

📖 How To Tape-Off A Car

I love to polish paint, but I loathe getting the wax out of the cracks. That's why I tape off every car I detail, usually better than a painter getting ready to paint a car. That way, I don't have to dig wax out of the cracks or

off trim after the detail is finished. Before machine polishing any vehicle take a few moments to tape, cover and protect any rubber, vinyl or plastic trim, especially any pebble textured black plastic trim.

Cover any fresh air grills

Wheel maskers - Cover wheels and tires with wheel maskers, especially if you're going to be using a rotary buffer

Start Polishing At The Top And Work Your Way Down

People that are new to machine polishing usually have two common questions.

- **Question 1 - Where do I start?**
  Start by buffing out the highest point on the car, which is usually the roof.

- **Question 2 - Do I complete each step one at a time to the entire car, or all the steps to one panel then move onto the next panel?**
  Great question. I'll explain both approaches and let you choose which works best for you.

How To Buff-Out Your Car Step By Step

Most professional detailers will perform each step to the entire car at one time and then move on to the next.

- **Step 1 - Correction step**
  Whatever your more aggressive pad and product combination is that you dialed-in during your test spot, perform this step to the entire car starting with the highest point, the roof. Next, buff the horizontal panels below the roof, usually the hood and trunk lid. After you buff the horizontal panels, tackle the vertical panels. After buffing out the vertical side panels of the vehicle, tackle any paint on the vertical panels of the front and rear of the car. Depending upon the vehicle you're detailing, there may be very little or a lot of paint on the front and rear sections of the vehicle. For example, a lot of modern cars have a grill and a front bumper cover painted the same color as the car. A truck may have very little paint to polish at the front of the vehicle, but there's usually a large, rectangular tailgate to polish at the rear.

- **Step 2 - Polishing step**
  Perform your second step process to refine the results of the first step, following your original path of travel. For example, if you started on the roof for the first step, start there for the second step.

- **Step 3 - Sealing step**
  Whether you're going to apply your choice of wax, paint sealant or a coating for the protection or sealing step, again, start at the highest point and work your way down, following your previous path of travel.

- **Step 4 - Second coat of wax**
  A lot of people like to apply two coats of wax or two coats of a paint sealant for two reasons.

  1. Uniform coverage - This means to ensure that every square inch of paint was coated. Sometimes, you can accidently miss applying wax to some portions of the paint, especially on light colored cars on which it can be difficult to see there's an actual layer of product being applied.

  2. Uniform protection - Applying two thin coats of a wax or paint sealant ensures a uniform layer over the entire surface and thus uniform protection.

Coatings
If you're using a paint coating instead of a traditional car wax or paint sealant, after the polishing step you would clean and prep the paint per manufacturer's directions and apply the coating.

How To Buff Your Car Section By Section

Another option is to tackle a detailing project by dividing the car up into sections. Complete one section at a time with all of the steps in the correction process.

A few reasons why to break a car up into sections:

1. **Limited time** - Instead of spending an entire day buffing out an entire car from start to beginning, divide the car up into smaller, manageable sections. Perform all the steps to just these sections until you finish with the last step, wiping off the last coat of wax. By doing this, you don't tie up your entire day in the garage working on your car. The next day, or the next weekend, move to a new section and repeat the process.

2. **Avoid injury** - In other words, don't over-do it. Detailing a car from start to finish whether you work by hand or machine will tax all the muscles in your body, especially if you don't detail cars on a regular basis.

3. **Physical limitations** - If you have any type of physical limitations, instead of tackling an entire car in one day, divide it into sections. By limiting how much time you invest into detailing your car, you'll also limit your exposure to muscle strain.

Here are some common ways to divide a car into sections:

- **Roof**
  If the car is a convertible, put the top up and cover it using a plastic drop cloth. With the top up, the interior is protected from splatter and if you cover the top with a drop cloth, you won't get residue into the grain or weave of the convertible top material.

- **Hood or front clip**
  The front clip includes the hood, front fenders and any paint around the grill or bumpers.

- **Trunk lid or rear clip**
  The rear clip includes the trunk lid and rear two fenders, plus any paint at the rear of the car.

- **Doors/sides**
  This includes the sides of the vehicle, including the doors and any other panels.

☞ Mike's Method

When I detail a vehicle, I use a combination of both approaches. Normally, I detail the entire vehicle in one day, starting by completing to entire process to the roof. After the roof is completed, I will then cover it with something soft like a soft flannel bed sheet.

Here's why I do this and this approach works for me.

1. **Save wiping time**
   When you machine polish the roof of a car, you can't help but throw product splatter onto the paint below. Each time you throw splatter, before you can work on the lower panel, you have to wipe off the splatter. This takes time. In a three step process, you would have to wipe the hood, trunk lid, and anywhere else the splatter lands three times. If you cover the hood and trunk lid with some something and then do the entire multiple-step process to the roof, then you don't waste any time wiping splatter off lower panels.

2. **Marketing**
   If you're detailing cars for money, you know that doing a multiple

step process to any car requires a lot of time. This could be anywhere from 10 to 12 hours to a couple of days, depending upon the project.

Now follow me on this
If while working on the car, you don't have a "finished section", then you have no way to showcase your work and talent to anyone that happens to walk by. This could be the owner or a potential customer. If all they can see is a work in progress, or a car covered in compounding or polishing residue, then there's nothing to get too excited about. If you put the roof through the entire process all the way to wiping off the first application of wax or paint sealant, now anytime someone walks by and comments or asks questions about your work, you can make a "sales presentation" by showcasing your skill and ability.

In my experience, anyone looking at the finished results can usually imagine how the rest of the car is going to look. That puts the "big picture" together, allowing them to appreciate the work you're doing.

The flannel bed sheet is covering the roof, because at the point in time at which this picture was taken, it had been:

- Dampsanded
- Compounded
- Machine polished twice
- Machine waxed

The reason we covered the finished roof with a soft, flannel bed sheet was so that as we continued to work the lower panels, the bed sheet prevented any airborne dirt, dust or splatter from getting on it.

Personal preference
Of course, it goes without saying that this style of process is personal preference. Each person can find a way that works best for them.

How To Remove Swirls And Scratches: The Major Correction Step

Before you dive in and start the major correction step, you should have already done these things:

- Washed and dried the car
- Inspected the paint visually for swirls, scratches, water spots and oxidation.
- Inspected the paint physically with your sense of touch and the baggie test.
- Performed a test spot and dialed-in a process.
- Decided on an approach to complete the entire vehicle.
- In your mind's eye, divided the car's panels into smaller sections.

If all of the above has been done, you're ready to start the major correction step.

🔴 The Major Correction Step - One Section At A Time

Performing the major correction step is just a matter of dividing each panel of a car into smaller sections and buffing one section at a time. After you finish buffing a section, carefully wipe any residue from the paint and move onto a new section. Be sure to overlap a little into the previous section.

Step by step directions

- **Prime your pad**
  If you're starting with a clean, dry pad, the first thing you want to do is prime it.

- **Apply working product to face of pad**

- **Spread product**
  Next, set the speed setting to around 3 to 4. Place the pad against the paint. Turn the polisher on and spread the product over the area you're going to work.

- **Increase speed setting**
  After you have the product spread over the working area, you need to turn the speed setting up to 5 or 6. You can do this by turning the polisher off and adjusting the variable speed dial, or you can do it on the fly with the polisher running.

Caution - Pad always needs to be in contact with paint when the polisher is on. You don't want to lift the face of the buffing pad off the surface of the paint because you'll throw splatter dots everywhere!

Wrong technique
Don't place the pad against the paint, turn the polisher on and start making your section passes right away. Start by spreading the product over the area you're going to work. Then, start making your section passes. Spreading your product distributes an even layer of abrasives over the section for even abrading action and thus more uniform swirl removal results.

Start making section passes
- Speed should be on the 5 to 6 setting.
- Place pad against paint
- Turn polisher on and start making slow, overlapping passes. Overlap by 50%.
- Use a slow arm speed.
- Keep pad flat to the surface whenever possible.
- Make 6 to 8 section passes, then turn the polisher off. Make sure the pad stops spinning before you lift it off the paint.
- Remove polish residue and inspect results. If defects are gone, clean your pad and move on to next section and overlap a little into the previous section.

Mike Phillips' - The Art of Detailing

There are two instances when you will use the polishing or minor correction step:

1. After the major correction step

If you've polished the paint using an aggressive compound or polish with a foam cutting, fiber, or even a polishing pad to remove swirls, scratches, water spots and/or oxidation, the next step towards your goal will be to re-polish each square inch of paint using a less aggressive pad and product. The goal now is to refine the results created during the major correction step to maximize the clarity, gloss and smoothness of the paint.

2. As the only correction step for paint with minor defects

If the paint you're working on is in good to excellent condition, then your test spot would have shown that you could remove these defects using the least aggressive product approach. This would include either a medium to fine finishing polish with either a polishing pad or a finishing pad. Neither an aggressive compound or polish nor an aggressive buffing pad are needed.

For either instance, the procedures are the same. Repeat the same process explained in the major correction step with a less aggressive pad and product and usually a speed setting around the 4 to 5 range.

The Polishing Or Minor Correction Step - One Section At A Time

Step by step directions

- **Prime your pad**
  If you're starting with a clean, dry pad, the first thing you want to do is prime it.

- **Apply working product to face of pad**

- **Spread product**
  Next, set the speed setting to around 3 to 4. Place the pad against the paint. Turn the polisher on and spread the product over the area you're going to work.

- **Increase speed setting**
  After you have the product spread over the working area, you need to turn the speed setting up to 4 or 5. You can do this by turning the polisher off and adjusting the variable speed dial, or you can do it on the fly with the polisher running.

Caution - Pad always needs to be in contact with paint when the polisher is on. You don't want to lift the face of the buffing pad off the surface of the paint because you'll throw splatter dots everywhere!

Wrong technique

Don't place the pad against the paint, turn the polisher on and start making your section passes right away. Start by spreading the product over the area you're going to work. Then, start making your section passes. Spreading your product distributes an even layer of abrasives over the section for even abrading action and thus more uniform swirl removal results.

Start making section passes

- Speed should be on the 4 to 5 setting.
- Place pad against paint
- Turn polisher on and start making slow, overlapping passes. Overlap by 50%.
- Use a slow arm speed.
- Make 4 to 5 section passes with firm downward pressure, then reduce pressure and make 2 to 4 more section passes.
- After your last section pass, turn the polisher off. Make sure the pad stops spinning before you lift it off the paint to avoid slinging splatter dots.
- Carefully wipe off any polish residue and inspect the results. At this point, the paint should look clear and glossy as proven by your test spot.
- Clean your pad and apply fresh product. Move onto a new section and be sure to overlap a little into the previous section.
- Continue this process until you've completed the entire vehicle or the panel or section of the vehicle that you're working on.

Seal or Jewel

After this step, you are ready to seal the paint using a wax, paint sealant or a coating. Or, if you choose, you can do a second ultra fine polishing step, commonly referred to as "jewelling the paint".

How To Jewel Paint Using A DA Polisher - Optional Step

Note: The jewelling step is optional. If you are satisfied with the results from your correction steps, you can skip the jewelling step and apply a wax, paint sealant or coating.

Jewelling is another term for final polishing. This means to bring the paint to the highest degree of gloss, shine, depth, and reflectivity. To do this, the paint must be as flat as possible at the microscopic level.

Jewelling - definition

The final machine polishing step in which a soft to ultra soft foam finishing pad with no mechanical abrading ability is used with a high lubricity, ultra fine finishing polish to remove any remaining microscopic surface imperfections. This is performed after the paint has been previously put through a series of machine compounding and polishing procedures to create a near-perfect finish.

Time consuming

Jewelling is time consuming. It would defeat the purpose to rush any part of the jewelling process, including paint preparation.

Work surgically clean

Jewelling paint starts with a surgically clean finish. All residues from previous machine polishing steps must be meticulously removed from all the major panels so there's no risk of any leftover residue entering into the jewelling process.

Pads

Jewelling with a DA polisher requires you to use the softest foam pads you can obtain. Ideally, you want to use a foam pad that offers no mechanical abrading ability. Aggressiveness of a foam pad is relative to the hardness of the paint system you're working on.

Below is a list of pads recognized as being very soft and suitable for jewelling for most paint systems.

🖥 *Lake Country*
- 5 1/2" and 6 1/2" CCS Pads Black, Blue, Red, Gold
- 5 1/2" and 6 1/2" Flat Pads Black, Blue
- 5 1/2" and 6 1/2" Hydro-Tech Crimson
- 5 1/2" and 6 1/2" Constant Pressure Black

🖥 *Griot's Garage*
- 6" Red Finishing pad

🖥 *Meguiar's*
- 6 1/2" Soft Buff Pads Tan Finishing Pad
- 7" Soft Buff Pads Black Finishing Pad

🖥 *The Edge Company*
- White Ultrafine Polishing DuraFoam Pad

Products

Here's a list of fine and ultra fine finishing polishes:

Pinnacle
🖥 *Advanced Finishing Polish*
🖥 *XMT Ultra Fine Swirl Remover #1*

Wolfgang
🖥 *Finishing Glaze 3.0*

Menzerna
🖥 *FF 3000 – Final Finish Polish (PO85U)*
🖥 *SF 4000 – Super Finish Polish (PO106FA)*
🖥 *PO87MC Micro Polish (To be discontinued and replaced by FF3000)*
🖥 *SF 4500 – Super Finish Polish (PO85RD)*

Meguiar's
🖥 *Ultimate Polish*
🖥 *SwirlX*
🖥 *M09 Swirl Remover 2.0*
🖥 *M82 Swirl Free Polish*
🖥 *M205 Ultra Finishing Polish*

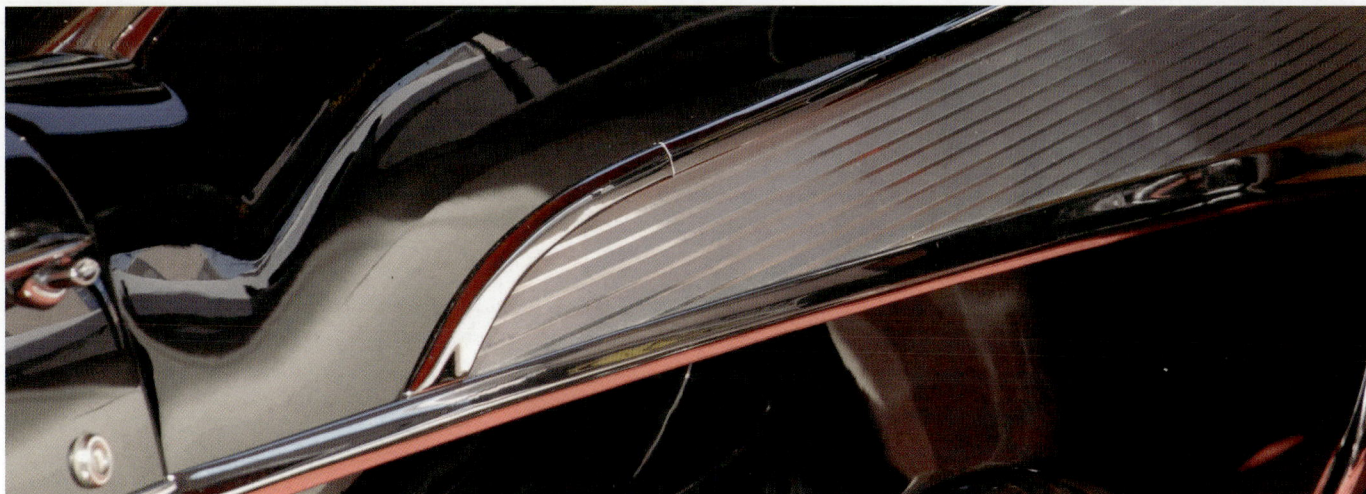

Optimum
- *Optimum Polish II*
- *Optimum Finish Polish*

Prima
- *Prima Finish*

Mothers
- *Foam Pad Polish*
- *PowerPolish*

Poorboy's World
- *SSR1 Light Abrasive Swirl Remover*

Finish Kare
- *303 Foam Pad Glaze*

3M
- *Perfect-It 3000 Ultrafine Machine Polish*

👓 Jeweling How-To

Step by step directions

- **Prime your pad**
  If you're starting with a clean, dry pad, the first thing you want to do is prime it.

- **Apply working product to face of pad**

- **Spread product**
  Next, set the speed setting to around 3 to 4. Place the pad against the paint. Turn the polisher

on and spread the product over the area you're going to work.

- **Increase speed setting**
  After you have the product spread over the working area, you need to turn the speed setting up to 4 or 5. You can do this by turning the polisher off and adjusting the variable speed dial, or you can do it on the fly with the polisher running.

Caution - Pad always needs to be in contact with paint when the polisher is on. You don't want to lift the face of the buffing pad off the surface of the paint because you'll throw splatter dots everywhere!

Wrong technique
Don't place the pad against the paint, turn the polisher on and start making your section passes right away. Start by spreading the product over the area you're going to work. Then, start making your section passes. Spreading your product distributes an even layer of abrasives over the section for even abrading action and thus more uniform swirl removal results.

Start making section passes
- Speed should be on the 4 to 5 setting.
- Place pad against paint
- Turn polisher on and start making

slow, overlapping passes. Overlap by 50%.
- Use a slow arm speed.
- Make 4 to 5 section passes with firm downward pressure, then reduce pressure and make 2 to 4 more section passes.
- After your last section pass, turn the polisher off. Make sure the pad stops spinning before you lift it off the paint to avoid slinging splatter dots.
- Carefully wipe off any polish residue and inspect the results. At this point, the paint should look clear and glossy as proven by your test spot.
- Clean your pad and apply fresh product. Move onto a new section and be sure to overlap a little into the previous section.
- Continue this process until you've completed the entire vehicle or the panel or section of the vehicle that you're working on.

Vitally Important
At this stage of the game, you REALLY need to be wiping any and all residues off incredibly carefully. If you've done everything right, then even the slightest, lightest imperfection will show up including wiping or toweling marks.

For more information:
- *How To Remove Dried Wax Using A DA Polisher*

How To Wax And Seal The Paint

After you've performed any necessary machine polishing steps, it's time to protect the paint by sealing with your choice of a wax, synthetic sealant or coating.

Most people wax their cars for one of two reasons (and usually both).

1. Add a layer of protection
2. Make the paint look good

A quality wax, sealant or coating will do both. Let's take a look at both of these reasons for waxing your car.

1. Add a layer of protection
Modern paint technology is actually very durable and resistant to corrosion and degradation under normal conditions. That said, most people like the idea of applying an additional coating over the paint to provide an extra measure of protection. This coating is considered a sacrificial barrier coating.

• **Sacrificial Barrier Coating**
The primary purpose of a wax or sealant is to act as a sacrificial barrier coating over the surface of your car's paint. Any time anything comes into contact with your car's paint, before it can cause any damage to the paint it first has to get past the layer of wax or paint sealant. When your car's paint is under attack, the layer of wax or paint sealant sacrifices itself.

The cost of a new paint job can run into the thousands of dollars, so most people agree that regularly applying a coat of wax is cost-effective preventative maintenance.

2. Make the paint look good
Besides adding a layer of protection to the paint, most people like to wax or seal their car's paint to make it look good. Nothing makes your car look better than a fresh coat of wax, especially if the paint is in good to excellent condition to start with. Besides restoring that glossy, factory new look, many people find spending an afternoon washing and waxing their pride and joy a relaxing escape from our hectic, fast-paced world.

How To Apply Paste Waxes

In the same way that the DA polisher does a better job of removing swirls and scratches as compared to working by hand, it also does a better job of applying a well-worked, thin uniform layer of paste wax.

The tricky part
The trick is getting the paste wax onto the pad. Here are three ways you can do this:

1. **Physically remove the entire block of paste wax out of the can or jar**
This works best with paste waxes that come in plastic jars around 4" in diameter. The wax will stay together and you can easily grip it in your palm.

Microfiber glove
This really works best if you have a clean, microfiber glove on one of your

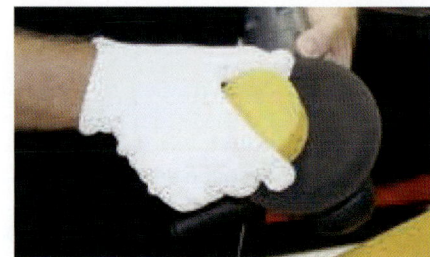

hands. This will enable you to grip the slippery block of wax that slides out of the jar. It will also prevent you from dropping it on the floor, contaminating it or getting wax on your skin.

Knock knock

To get the wax out of the jar, you need to carefully knock it out. Hold the jar upside down and knock it firmly against your hand with the microfiber glove on it. Sometimes, it helps to lightly heat the outside of the plastic jar with something like a blow dryer as this will loosen the bond and grip created by surface tension when the wax was originally poured into the jar. After you get the wax out of the jar, you can apply it to the face of your foam finishing pad in two ways:

- **Using your hand.** Simply swipe the wax a few times across the face of a foam finishing pad.

- **Use the power of the polisher.** While holding the block of wax against the face of the pad, blip the on/off button of the polisher for a couple of short bursts. The oscillating/rotating action will quickly transfer wax onto the face of the pad.

After you distribute some wax onto the face of the pad using one of the above techniques, you then want to carefully place the block of wax aside. Either place it back into the jar, or with the lid upside down, rest it inside the lid.

Applying wax using either of the

above methods also primes the face of the foam pad so that it is lubricated with wax when you turn on the polisher.

When starting with a clean, dry pad, you'll initially use a little more product. After that, you'll find it takes very little to re-dampen your foam finishing pad with wax to continue working around the car.

Place the face of the pad into the can or jar

If you're using a paste wax in a wide mouth can, you can use a foam finishing pad that's small enough to place inside the can. Simply blip the on/off switch for a couple of short bursts and this will quickly transfer wax onto the face of the foam pad. The benefit to this method is you don't have to remove the wax from the can and it's very fast and easy to do.

Scoop some wax out of the can or jar

This is another option that works just as well. Simply scoop some wax out of the jar or can and then spread it onto the face of the pad as you would use a knife to spread peanut butter over bread. With soft paste waxes this is pretty easy, but it is a little more difficult to do with a hard paste wax.

A lot of people use a handy little tool that's already nearby and that's the flat handle of the backing plate wrench that came with your polisher. It's flat like a butter knife and actually works really well. Just make sure to clean it before sticking it into the can of wax.

✦ Step By Step Directions

After you get wax onto the face of the foam finishing pad, simply apply the wax in the same manner as explained in the chapter for using a liquid wax.

For more information:
   📖 liquid wax section

▶ How To Apply Liquid Waxes With A DA Polisher - Kissing The Finish

"Kissing the finish" is a technique you can use to apply a liquid wax which helps keep the wax spreading out over the paint instead of loading up inside your pad.

I use this technique when applying any liquid wax or paint sealant. To kiss the finish, touch the face of the foam pad (with wax on it) onto your panel at an angle, thus depositing only a portion of the wax from the pad to one area of the paint.

The effect is to have a bunch of dabs of wax on the paint deposited from the face of the pad. Your car's panel will look like it has spots or arcs or lines of product on it.

How To Wax And Seal The Paint

Step By Step Directions

First, shake shake shake

Always shake liquid car care products thoroughly before applying.

Prime your pad

Next, apply some product onto the face of the pad. Then, using your clean finger, spread the product so the entire face of the pad is dampened with product.

Apply working product

Apply more product to the face of the pad. For this, I place a circle of product around the outside edge of the buffing pad.

Kiss the finish

Next, touch the edge of the face of the foam pad and deposit some wax to a portion of the panel you're working on. Continue doing this over an entire panel until you've deposited what looks like little arcs or smiles of product onto the paint.

After you've kissed the finish in a few places, take what's left and place the face of the foam pad against the paint. Then, turn the polisher on, making passes overlapping by about 50%.

On this El Camino, I can easily reach and work on half of the hood at one time. I used enough wax to coat over half of it and moved the pad over each square inch at least 2 to 3 times to sufficiently work the wax over and into the paint.

As I came up to a dab of wax where I kissed the finish with my pad, I tilted the polisher, lifting the leading edge of the pad but maintaining constant contact with the trailing edge. I then ran the pad over the dab of wax and then immediately laid the pad flat again to work new territory with this new dab of wax.

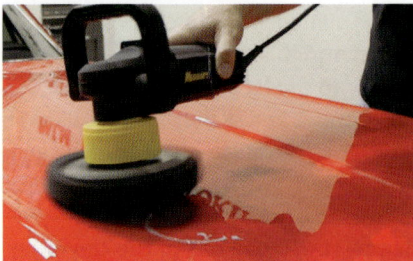

Tilt the polisher a little to lift the leading edge of the pad.

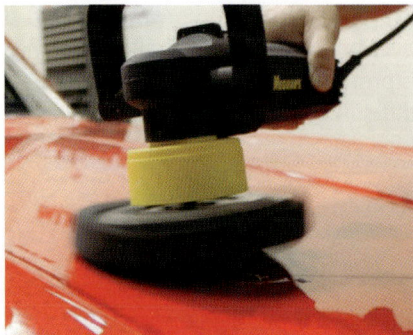

Move the tilted leading edge over the wax to draw and trap the wax between the paint and the pad.

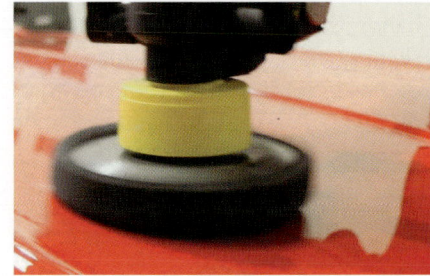

Lay the pad flat and begin working the wax over the paint.

Keep one edge (the trailing edge of the pad) in contact with the paint so it doesn't quickly speed up and throw splatter or fling the pad off the backing plate.

Then, move the raised side of the pad quickly over the dab of wax or sealant and quickly lay the pad down flat and continue spreading the product. This should be one seamless, flowing motion.

- **Use a slow to medium arm speed**
  When applying a wax, your goal is to spread out a thin layer of product and also to work the wax over and into the paint. This is best done using a slow to medium arm speed using overlapping motions. Overlap your passes by about 50% and go over each square inch of each panel 2 to 3 times.

- **No limits for work size area**
  Unlike removing swirls, you can work a section as far as you can reach as long as you have ample product to spread out.

- **Apply a thin layer**
  No matter how you apply your waxes, paint sealants, or coatings, the goal is to always apply a thin layer over the paint. Thick layers of product simply waste money and make wipe-off more difficult.

- **How thin is thin?**
  It's common for someone to ask, "how thin is thin?" Or, "what does

a thin coating look like?" Both of these are great questions! A thin coating should look like a thin film covering the surface. Because a thin layer is hard to see with your eyes, it's also hard to capture with a camera. But, here are a few pictures to hopefully give you an idea of what a thin coating looks like.

Apply to the entire car at once

Assuming you have already prepped the paint for application of wax, go ahead and apply your choice of wax or paint sealant to the entire car at one time.

Follow the manufacturer's directions

Manufacturers know their product formulas best, so take a moment to read the directions for application and removal on the label and then follow them as recommended.

How To Apply Cleaner Waxes

First, choose the best foam pad for the condition of the paint

A polishing pad, together with the cleaners and abrasives, will offer the right balance of cleaning ability while finishing out to a clear, high gloss. If the paint you're working on is in severely neglected condition, you'll have more correction ability using a foam cutting pad, but you do risk leaving some micromarring. Test first and match the right pad to the condition of the paint and the cleaner wax you choose to use.

Step By Step Directions

The key to getting great results to a neglected finish using only a one-step cleaner wax comes down to five techniques or steps:

» **Speed setting = 5 to 6 on all DA polishers**
Be sure to mark your backing plates - you want to see the pad rotating at all times.

Machine applied thin coat of wax

1. **Use the product heavy or wet**
It's only when you're applying finishing waxes and paint sealants that you only use a small amount of wax in order to lay down a thin, uniform coating. When using a cleaner wax by machine, it's just the opposite - you want plenty of cleaning agents and lubrication.

2. **Use the section pass technique - only work small sections at a time**
Just like doing any correction work with a compound or medium polish, the worse the condition of the paint, the smaller the area you want to work. The better the condition of the paint, the larger the area you can work. However, you normally don't want to go any larger than 2' x 2'. Smaller sections tend to be better as you're focusing more cleaning ability to a smaller section of paint.

3. **Overlap your section passes**
When starting a new section, be sure to overlap into the previous section for a uniform appearance after final wipe off of the wax residue.

4. **Clean your pad on the fly often or switch to a clean, dry pad**
If you don't clean your pad often or switch to a clean, dry pad, the residue build-up will interfere with

the cleaning agents. So, clean your pad often or after working a panel or two, switch to a clean, dry pad.

5. **Allow the wax to dry before removing**
Most cleaner waxes are also drying waxes, which means you want to use the wet buffing technique. Leave a uniform layer of product on each section you buff so that you end up with an even coating of wax over the entire vehicle. Be sure to read the label for specific instructions from the manufacturer.

How To Do The Swipe Test

To perform the swipe test, take your clean finger and swipe it briskly across a waxed finish. If the paint where you swipe is clear, without any smeary wax left behind, then this is an accurate indicator that the wax is dry and ready to wipe off. If the residue

How To Wax And Seal The Paint

smears and streaks, it has not fully cured and needs more time to set up. If the swipe test shows the wax is still wet, wait a little longer until the paint swipes clear.

👀 How To Remove Dried Wax

There are two ways to remove wax from your car's paint - the normal way (by hand) and by machine.

Benefits to machine removal of wax
Removing wax by machine is personal preference; some people like this technique while others prefer to simply wipe waxes and paint sealants by hand.

Equal pressure
The technique of using a microfiber bonnet over a foam cutting pad provides equal pressure over the entire face of the pad. This removes any pressure points created by your fingertips when wiping off by hand.

Physical advantage
For some people, letting the machine do the work might be a physical advantage versus using their hands, arms and shoulders to wipe the wax off.

- **Waxes that dry**
  Removing wax by machine works best if you're using a wax that is supposed to dry first before removing. Be aware that some are formulated to be wipe-on, wipe-off waxes and these are best removed by hand.

- **Thin coats**
  Removing dried wax by machine works best when a thin coat is applied.

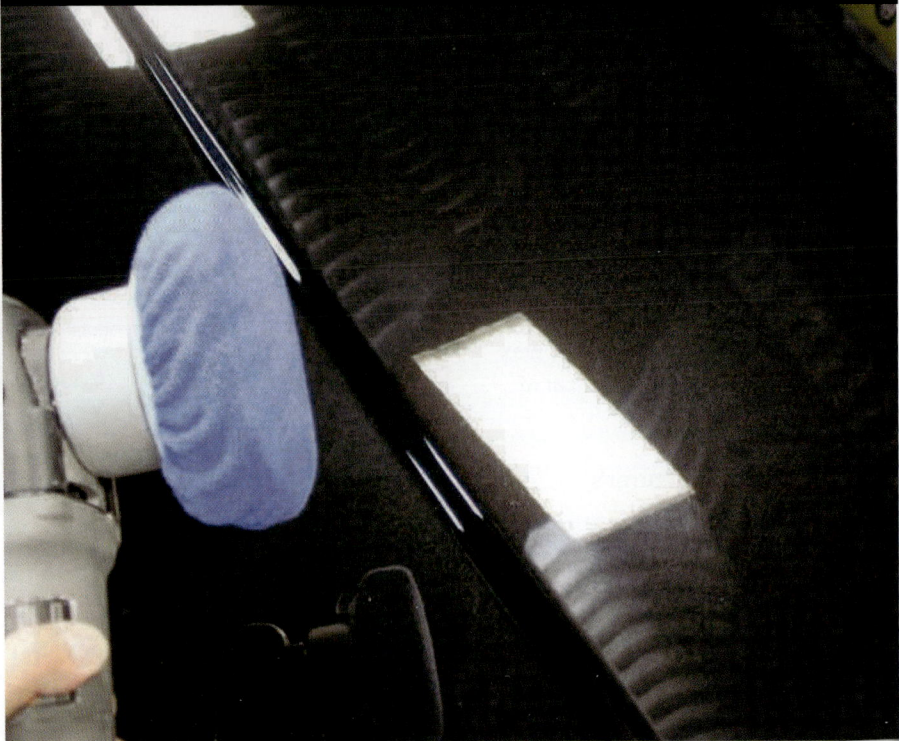

If you look at the paint you can see where I made a single pass with the bonnet on the DA Polisher and left a crystal clear finish

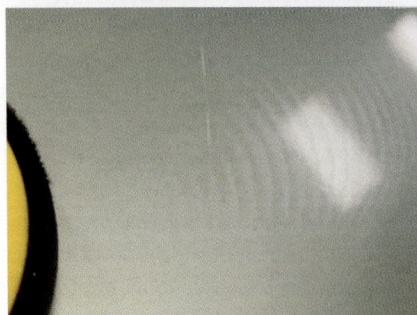

🚶 Step By Step Directions

Products Needed

- **Reversible microfiber bonnets**
  Microfiber bonnets are almost always reversible. You can use one side until it loads up with dried wax and then remove it, turn it inside out, give it a shake and put back onto your buffing pad. I'll show you my technique for cleaning your bonnet on the fly. Often times, using this technique, you can remove all the wax from an average sized vehicle with just one bonnet.

- **Clean, dry pads for use under the bonnet**
  My personal preference has always been to use a firm foam pad because it provides a level of cushion due to the nature of the foam cell wall structure. The cushion offered by foam enables the pad to conform to curves and body lines better than a lambswool pad with a microfiber bonnet over it.

Removing the wax
It doesn't matter where you start, but the normal protocol is to start where you first applied wax and then follow your path of travel.

Another way is to start at the top and work your way down. As long as the wax is dry, it's not a huge issue where you start or tackle the various body panels.

Speed setting
Use the high speed setting to remove dried wax. I tend to use the 6 speed setting because you really want all the power the tool has to offer when trying to convince dried wax to give up its grip on the paint.

Downward pressure
You want to use firm, downward pressure when removing the wax. You want the nap of the microfiber slicing into the coating of wax and breaking it up, which cannot be accomplished with light pressure.

A technique for moving from one panel to another panel without turning the polisher off
At the same time you lift the pad off the surface, quickly place your clean hand against the face of the bonnet and keep it there until you're ready to place it against the next panel.

This is safe to do and having the firm pressure of your hand against the pad will keep it from flying off the polisher.

A technique for cleaning your bonnet on the fly
As you work your way around the car removing dried wax or paint sealant, you will get a build-up of dried wax residue on the face of the microfiber bonnet.

While you have the option to remove the bonnet and reverse it, I prefer cleaning on the fly. To do this, lift the pad from the paint while holding your fingernails against the bonnet. Apply enough pressure to keep the pad from flying off the polisher but not so much that it stops rotating. This is usually effective enough to remove any dried wax residue from the working face of the microfiber bonnet.

Variation of the bonnet - Just use a microfiber towel
Some people will simply place a clean, dry microfiber towel flat onto the paint and then place a clean, dry buffing pad against the microfiber to remove wax. I'm not a big fan of this method because the microfiber towel can easily work its way out from under the pad, especially if you try this on a vertical panel.

Products for removing wax by machine

- **Bonnets**

  - *Cobra Indigo 6 Inch Microfiber Bonnets 2 pack*
  - *All Bonnets on Autogeek.net*

- **Small, firm dense foam buffing pads**

  - *Lake Country Hydro-Tech 5 1/2" Cyan Cutting Pad*
  - *5 1/2" Lake Country Flat Yellow Cutting Pad*
  - *5 1/2" Lake country Flat Orange Light Cutting Pad*
  - *5 1/2" Lake Country CCS Yellow Cutting Pad*
  - *5 1/2" Lake country CCS Orange Light Cutting Pad*
  - *6" Lake Country Purple Kompressor Pad*
  - *6" Lake Country Orange Kompressor Pad*

- **Small, firm lambswool pads**

  - *6" Lake Country Lambswool Polishing Pad*

The Final Wipe Technique

Note: The final wiping technique is not for the initial wiping off of a glaze, wax or paint sealant, but instead is to be used after the majority of product has already been removed and now all you're doing is giving the finish a final wipe.

The Final Wipe
After all the work is done, you usually want and need to give the paint a final wipe-down. This final wipe is to ensure you didn't miss any spots and to remove any trace residues from the paint.

The technique - slow down
The technique is to wipe the paint down s-l-o-w-l-y using your best, premium quality microfiber polishing towel using gentle, even pressure.

Show car quality work demands focusing on the task at hand and using your best skills and tools to reach the goal of a flawless show car finish.

Rushing at the very end doesn't make sense and if you instill swirls and scratches, you're working backwards in the process.

Simply put, sometimes you have to slow down to speed up. Using a slow wiping motion will be more effective at removing all microscopic trace residues from the paint. This enables you to reach your goal safely and effectively.

Maintenance

How To Use A Spray Detailer To Maintain Your Car

Spray detailers are for removing:
- Light dust
- Fingerprints
- Smudges

Spray detailers are wonderful, time-saving products if used correctly on the correct condition of finish. They enable you to restore that "just detailed" look quickly and easily without having to wash and wax your car.

The key is evaluating the condition of your car's paint and making the right judgment as to whether it's safe to use a spray detailer or if the vehicle is too dirty.

How dirty can a car be to safely use a spray detailer without inflicting swirls and scratches in the process?

If the car is only lightly dusty and you use a premium quality spray detailer, microfiber towel and good technique, you can successfully wipe the surface clean and not instill any swirls and scratches.

How a spray detailer works
A quality spray detailer is supposed to hyper-lubricate the surface to help prevent scratching. A quality spray detailer will encapsulate dirt and dust particulates to help prevent scratching the paint.

Tools needed
- A premium quality spray detailer
- A collection of premium quality microfiber polishing cloths, each folded 4-ways.

How To Use A Spray Detailer

First, mist the spray detailer over a small section of a panel.

Next, spread the spray detailer around gently with one side of a microfiber polishing cloth (folded 4-ways).

Then, quickly turn to the dry side and gently remove the spray detailer and buff the paint in this section to a dry, high shine. You are now finished with this section.

Before moving onto a new section, re-fold your microfiber polishing towel to expose a clean, dry side.

When starting a new section, remember to overlap a little into the previous section.

After you've used all eight sides of a single microfiber polishing towel, switch to a fresh, clean microfiber polishing towel.

Two Things That Help A Spray Detailer Do Its Job

1. Use PLENTY of premium quality microfiber polishing towels
Don't try to wipe your entire car down using one or two towels if the goal is to maintain a flawless finish. Use 10 to 12 microfibers for an average sized car. This is not a hard rule, but an average based upon what it takes to do a safe job of wiping the exterior of a car clean while avoiding cross-contamination.

2. Use good technique
Always fold your microfiber polishing towels 4-ways. This will give you eight wiping sides and helps to spread out the pressure from your hand.

How To Use A Spray Wax

There are two general groups of spray-on waxes.

- **Standalone or dedicated wax**
  This type of product is an actual replacement or substitute for a normal paste or liquid wax. A spray-on wax in this category can be used as the primary protection product after the paint has been put through a series of compounding and polishing procedures.

- **Booster wax or maintenance wax**
  This is a product that's more like a spray detailer with the

added bonus of some type of protection ingredients. Products in this category are best used as maintenance products that you use in between normal washing and applications of an actual paste or liquid wax. They are not a substitute for a normal coat of wax.

How To Apply

There are two ways to apply a spray-on wax. First consideration should go to the manufacturer's recommendations.

1. **Wipe off wet** - Mist on, spread around and wipe off
2. **Wipe off dry** - Mist on, spread around, allow to haze, wipe off

There are different techniques for the two ways to apply these products, which I'll go over below. To start, here's a few guidelines for using spray on waxes.

Always apply to clean vehicle
First, you need to start with a clean car. You can either wash and dry the car, or use one of the other methods mentioned in the washing chapter.

For more information:
📖 **Washing Chapter link**

Start at the top and work your way down
When spraying a spray-on wax directly onto the panel, be mindful of overspray, especially around the glass. Most companies don't recommend their waxes for use on glass and especially windshields, but check each company's official recommendations.

Work on a cool surface in the shade
Hot surfaces will make a thin liquid spray-on wax more difficult to spread out and wipe off as the carrying agents will evaporate quickly. If you do work on a warm surface in direct sun, shrink the size of your work area. This will make it easier to spread and wipe off the product.

Do a test spot
While most people think doing a test spot is only for testing pad and polish combinations, there's nothing wrong with testing out any paint care product to a small area. Make sure you're getting the results you expect and familiarize yourself with the application and removal characteristics of the product.

Tips And Techniques
Mist-On & Wipe-Off Spray Waxes

- Shake product well before and during use.
- Have plenty of clean, soft microfiber towels on hand.
- Wear a microfiber glove on your towel hand.
- Fold your microfiber towels 4-ways to provide eight sides to wipe with and spread out the pressure from your hand.
- Hold sprayer about a foot away from the surface and squeeze trigger firmly. Most quality spray waxes use a nozzle that will atomize the product but require a firm squeeze to work.
- Spread product over the surface using an overlapping circular motion for large panels, back and forth for long, thin or narrow panels.
- After spreading product, turn or fold your microfiber towel to a dry side or portion and wipe residue off until you see a dry, hard shine.
- Move to new section and overlap a little into previous section.

Tips And Techniques
Mist-On, Allow To Dry To A Haze & Wipe-Off Spray Waxes

Trickier to use successfully without the secret technique
Using a spray-on wax that is recommended to be allowed to dry to a haze before removal is a little trickier than using a product that you wipe off immediately.

First, dampen one side of a microfiber towel with the spray-on wax. Then, mist a little wax onto the paint and use the dampened side of your microfiber towel to spread the product. A dampened microfiber towel works best because it's easier to spread out a thin liquid film if your applicator cloth is already wet or dampened with the product you're trying to spread out. If you try to use a dry microfiber towel to try to spread out a thin, liquid film, at the same time you're trying to spread the product onto the surface, the dry cloth will absorb the product from the paint at the same time you're trying to leave it behind.

Tips

Apply to entire vehicle
Start at the top and continue applying to the rest of the vehicle using your dampened microfiber towel until the entire car is covered with a thin coating of wax.

With a wipe-on, wipe-off spray wax, there's no waiting for the product to dry. A wax that needs to dry to a haze will take about 10 to 20 minutes depending upon temperature, humidity, and wind currents. If you just apply to one section or panel before moving on, you'll be waiting there until the wax dries before you can remove it and move on.

Follow your path of travel
Wipe off the dried wax by starting where you first applied the product. Follow your path of travel, gently and carefully wiping the dried residue off the paint. Be sure to switch to a clean, dry microfiber polishing cloth folded 4 ways to remove the dried film of wax.

- **Spray Detailers**
- Pinnacle Crystal Mist Detail Spray
- Wolfgang Instant Detail Spritz
- Pinnacle XMT Final Finish Instant Detailer
- Detailer's Pro Series Final Gloss Quick Detailer
- Dodo Juice Red Mist Tropical Protection Detailer
- Dodo Juice Time To Dry Drying Detailer
- Muc-Off Split Second Detailer

- Griot's Garage Speed Shine Detailer
- Prima Slick Quick Detail Spray
- Finish Kare 425 Extra Slick Final Body Shine
- Finish Kare Anti Static Poly wipe Finish Restorer Spray Detailer
- Sonus Acrylic Spritz Quick Detail Spray
- Meguiar's NXT Speed Detailer
- Mothers California Gold Showtime Instant Detailer
- Meguiar's #135 Synthetic Spray Detailer
- Meguiar's NXT Generation Speed Detailer
- Meguiar's #34 Final Inspection
- Meguiars Ultimate Quik Detailer
- Optimum Instant Detailer & Gloss Enhancer
- Ultima Detail Spray Plus
- Optima Opti-Clean Cleaner & Protectant
- Poorboy's World Quick Detailer PLUS QD+
- Poorboy's World Spray & Gloss

- **Spray Waxes**
- 1Z Einszett Spray Wax
- Prima Hydro Wax As You Dry Spray
- Sonus Carnauba Spritz Quick Detailer
- Mothers California Gold Spray Wax
- Mothers FX Engineered Spray Wax
- Mothers Reflections Advanced Spray Wax
- 3M Quick Wax
- Stoner SpeedBead One-Step Quick Wax
- Meguiar's NXT Spray Wax
- Meguiars Ultimate Quik Wax
- Optimum Car Wax
- Poorboy's World QW+ Quick Wax Plus

How to Mix IPA for Inspecting Correction Results

Most compounds and polishes are made using some type of abrasives, embodied in some type of lubricating carrying agent or base. The lubricating base normally has a lotion-like consistency and can contain some type of oil which reduces scouring of the paint by the abrasives.

The lubricating base is extremely important as it cushions or buffers the abrading action of the abrasives. Too many people discount the lubricating agents as simply fillers and don't understand that without them, they won't be able to remove things like swirls and scratches and leave a better looking finish at the same time.

The problem with lubricating agents is that they can mask or hide any defects in the finish, making it appear as though they've been removed, even though they are still present in the paint.

After these lubricating agents or polishing oils wear off, the swirls and scratches show up again, bringing you back to the correction step.

One way to make sure you've removed all the defects is to remove the polishing oils and then inspect the paint.

You can remove these polishing oils a number of ways:
- Wipe the paint with a diluted mixture of isopropyl alcohol and water
- Wipe the paint with a product specifically designed to wipe and strip the paint
- Wash the car using a detergent soap
- Wipe the paint using mineral spirits

My recommendation is to read through this section and then test out

Common, easily found options for Isopropyl Alcohol also called IPA - 50%, 70%, 91%

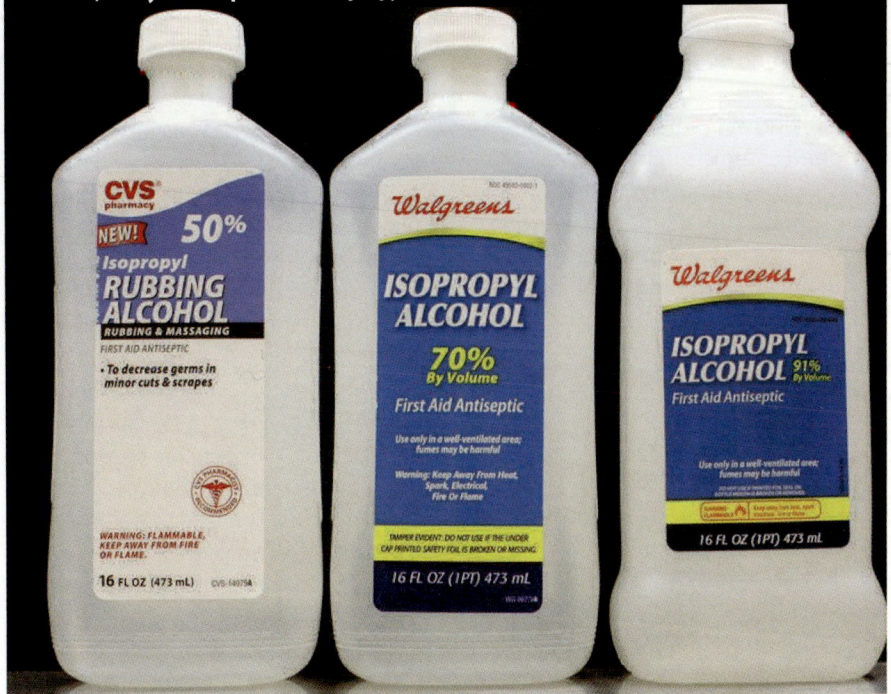

and decide which approach works best for you.

WARNING - Do not chemically strip FRESH PAINT. This means paint that is less than 30 days old. Fresh paint has not fully cross-linked, dried and hardened. Introducing any type of solvent to the surface and allowing it to dwell could have a negative effect on the paint. This does not affect a new car because the paint on a new car was baked on at the factory before the car rolled off the assembly line.

Note: This is NOT an official recommendation by Mike Phillips or Autogeek. It is an attempt to clear up any confusion on the topic of chemically stripping paint with the common products used for this procedure. If you choose to chemically strip paint, all the risk is yours. Any time you use a new product or procedure, it's a great idea to first test in an inconspicuous area and check the results before moving forward.

What NOT to do
Most recommendations I've heard can

be one of two options:

- Dilute IPA 1:1 (50%) with water
- Use it straight out of the bottle

Dilute IPA 1:1 (50%) with water
If you simply dilute the commonly found bottles if IPA by 50%, here's what you'll get:

- Diluting 91% IPA 1:1 (50%) = a 45% dilution of IPA to water solution.
- Diluting 70% IPA 1:1 (50%) = a 35% dilution of IPA to water solution.
- Diluting 50% IPA 1:1 (50%) = a 25% dilution of IPA to water solution.

TOO STRONG!
After talking to chemists in this industry, they all felt that these dilution levels were overkill and too strong for removing residues after compounding and/or polishing paint.

Most quality name brand compounds and polishes are water soluble and don't need a strong solution of isopropyl alcohol to dissolve, emulsify and loosen any leftover residues on the surface.

Miscellaneous Topics

The most common dilution levels you can purchase over the counter are 50%, 70% and 91% isopropyl alcohol.

After talking at length with 3 seasoned chemists in the car wax industry, they all agreed that an approximate 10% dilution of IPA to water solution was a good range for chemically stripping paint for inspection.

High-solid clear coat paints are "alcohol friendly", meaning products like isopropyl alcohol can and will penetrate, soften, wrinkle and/or stain the paint. To avoid any of these problems, a 10% dilution of IPA to water solution is recommended and adequate to remove any compounding and polishing residues without risking any danger to your car's paint.

How to Mix IPA for Inspecting Correction Results

Here are the easiest ways to mix an approximate 10% solution for the most popular concentrations of isopropyl alcohol available at the retail level.

- **91% IPA**
  To mix a 32 ounce spray bottle
  Pour 4 ounces of 91% IPA into a 32 ounce spray bottle and top the rest of the bottle off with water. This will make 32 ounces of 11.375% IPA to water solution.

- **70% IPA**
  To mix a 32 ounce spray bottle
  Pour 8 ounces of 70% IPA into a 32 ounce spray bottle and top the rest of the bottle off with water. This will make 32 ounces of 17.5% IPA to water solution.

- **50% IPA**
  To mix a 32 ounce spray bottle
  Pour 8 ounces of 50% IPA into a 32 ounce spray bottle and top the rest of the bottle off with water. This will make 32 ounces of 12.5%

IPA to water solution.

For what it's worth...
Common household glass cleaners have been used for years as a convenient way to strip the finish to inspect correction results, often times because it's a commonly found product in a detailing environment. Most glass cleaners that use alcohol are around the 10% range or lower.

💬 My personal recommendation for IPA - If you want to chemically strip paint to remove any compound or polish residues so that you can accurately see the true condition of the paint after any correction steps, then I recommend using a 10% dilution of IPA to water solution. This is a safe approach to remove any residues masking the true results of your process to the paint without the risk of causing any harm.

Checking your test spot vs checking the entire car
Theoretically, if you use IPA to chemically strip your test spot and the results look good, duplicating the same correction process over the rest of the panels should yield the same results as seen in your test spot.

Assuming all the panels have the same type of paint, then you shouldn't have to continue stripping all the paint on each panel. Keep doing the same work you did for your test spot and trust your skills and abilities - consistent work yields consistent results.

Chemically removing waxes and/or paint sealants
💬 **Note** this article addresses IPA dilution strength for removing compounding and/or polishing lubricating oils (sometimes called "fillers") during the paint correction process. You can also use this to try to remove any previously applied wax or paint sealant, but isopropyl alcohol may not effectively remove some

polymer products.

To remove any previously applied wax or paint sealant, I recommend using a light paint cleaner or a fine polish applied by hand or machine. A light paint cleaner or abrasive polish will effectively remove any previously applied wax or paint sealant AND leave the paint looking clear and glossy.

If you're dead set on chemically stripping the paint, then a combination of using both a 10% solution of IPA to water followed by wiping with mineral spirits should remove any previously applied wax or paint sealant.

How to check your work with IPA

Removing compound and polish residue
Now that you have a safely diluted mixture of IPA and water, if you want to check your work during any of the correction steps, the first thing you want to do is to wipe off any visible residue. After you've wiped a panel clean, you're ready to chemically strip the paint for inspection.

Simply mist some of the IPA mixture onto the area and spread it using a clean microfiber towel folded 4-ways. Work the product gently over the paint, turn the towel to a dry side and wipe until the surface is dry and clear.

Safety precautions
Always wear the appropriate safety gear when working with chemicals. This includes safety glasses, protective gloves and a shop apron.

💬 **My comments...** In the last year, I used some 70% IPA to chemically strip paint while doing some polish comparisons. I had used painter's tape to tape off specific sections for the test. After wiping the area with straight 70% IPA, some of the IPA penetrated between the tape and the paint, allowing it to dwell while I continued testing. When I removed the tape, there was a visible spot where the clear coat paint wrinkled from too long of exposure to the high concentration of IPA.

Removing previously-applied wax or paint sealant

To remove previously-applied wax or paint sealant, simply mist some of the IPA mixture onto the area and spread it around using a clean microfiber towel folded 4-ways. Work the product gently over the paint, turn to a dry side and wipe until the surface is dry and clear.

Options besides IPA

🖥 *Menzerna Top Inspection*
Formulated specifically for removing compound and polish residues for inspecting correction results.

🖥 *Griot's Garage Pre-Wax Cleaner*
Formulated to be used after compounding and polishing to prepare the surface for wax or paint sealant.

🖥 *Griot's Garage Paint Prep*
Formulated to remove previously applied waxes, silicones and oils either before doing any correction work with compounds and polishes, or before application of wax or paint sealant.

🖥 *Optimum Power Clean All Purpose Cleaner*
A good all-around all purpose cleaner that can be used for a variety of cleaning purposes, including stripping paint.

While these products are sometimes recommended for stripping paint, the manufacturers recommend that after applying these products, the

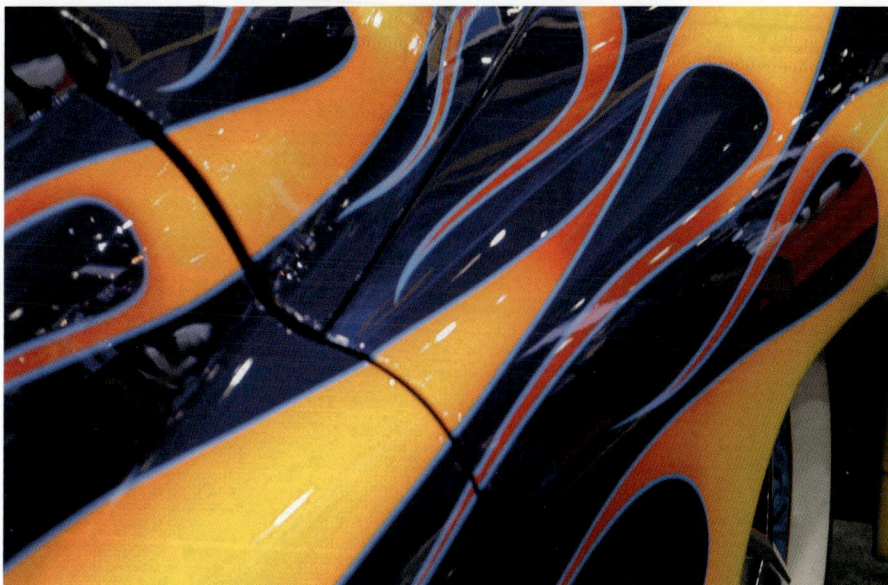

paint should be rinsed with water to remove any residues. As such, they are not spray-on / wipe-off products.

Odorless mineral spirits

Mineral spirits are another option for chemically stripping an automotive finish. Odorless mineral spirits should be chosen as the process for removing the odors is actually removing a lot of nastier substances through further refining of the product. Mineral spirits will tend to wipe easier than most other options and leave a more clear finish.

Percent volatile

When discussing mineral spirits, the idea has been brought up that they may leave behind a film that could, like compound or polish residues, mask defects and thus defeat the purpose of stripping the finish after correction work. I brought this up with two of my chemist friends and they both said that it's not an issue, but if you want to be sure, choose a brand of mineral spirits that states the "percent volatile" is 100%.

All purpose cleaners and/or degreasers

All purpose cleaners and degreasers are more complex in their formulas in that they contain more ingredients to give them the ability to clean

or dissolve a wide spectrum of substances like grease, oil, road grime, etc. It's this expanded ability that make all purpose cleaners and degreasers excellent for cleaning things like engine compartments, but this same ability makes them riskier to use on a delicate, clear coat finish on which they can stain or dull paint.

💬 Personal thoughts on inspecting correction work

I tend to use a combination of all of the above. I don't have an allegiance to just a specific product or process, but instead which product I will use may depend upon what I'm trying to accomplish, or even simpler, what's closest to my hand at the time I'm working on a project.

On the Autogeek.net Store:

🖥 *Menzerna Top Inspection*
🖥 *Griot's Garage Paint Prep*
🖥 *Griot's Garage Pre-Wax Cleaner*
🖥 *Optimum Power Clean All Purpose Cleaner*
🖥 *Black Nitrile Gloves*
   Show Car Garage Apron
🖥 *Autogeek 32 ounce Heavy Duty PVC Clear Spray Bottle*
🖥 *Spraymaster Trigger Sprayer - Chemical Resistant Spray Head*

Conclusion

Time to put what you've learned into practice! Just go through the steps:

- Wash and dry the car
- Inspect and evaluate the condition of the finish
- Determine your goal - this tells you which pads and products you'll need
- Clay the paint if you discovered above-surface bonded contaminants
- Remove the swirls and scratches or use a one-step cleaner wax
- Polish the paint to a high gloss if you choose to do a multiple-step procedure
- Seal the paint with a coat or two of your favorite wax, paint sealant or coating
- Maintain your car's finish and all your hard work using spray detailers and spray-on waxes.

Feel free to share your before and after pictures in the Show and Shine section of AutogeekOnline.net.

◉◉ Conclusion

There's a lifetime of tips and techniques jammed into this how-to book, with the intended goal of sharing knowledge that I have gained over years of experience.

Creating a show car finish starts with knowledge

The information in this book is real and based upon a lifetime of polishing paint and teaching others. Your job is to absorb this information and save years of time learning everything through testing and practice via trial and error.

The best news of all is, after reading this how-to book, if you should have any questions, you'll find answers on our AutogeekOnline.net discussion forum. Feel free to start a thread and ask any questions that you may have. A host of incredibly sharp, friendly

and helpful forum members and I will go out of our way to see you through to success.

I can also be reached via phone at Autogeek's headquarters, but prefer to answer questions on the public forum. This is simply because if you have a question, odds are that others have the same question and by using the forum to interact, more people benefit.

So read through this how-to book, take what you've learned out into your garage, and start doing some testing to dial in a successful system that creates the results you wish to achieve.

See you in the garage!
Mike Phillips
www.AutogeekOnline.net
1-800-869-3011 x206

A

Abrasive Particulate
Any small, hard, sharp particle, normally referred to as it relates with the potential and ability to instill swirls and scratches into clearcoat paints.

Aggressive Cut Compound
A very aggressive liquid or paste that uses some type of abrasive technology to cut or abrade paint quickly. In the body shop world, compounds are used to remove sanding marks. In the detailing world, compounds are used to remove deep below-surface defects like swirls, scratches and water spot etchings. Depending upon the abrasive technology and the application method and material, some automotive compounds can remove down to #1000 grit sanding marks. Of course, topcoat hardness is an important factor that affects a compound's effectiveness.

AIO *see Cleaner Wax*

Air Currents
Spinning buffing pads create air-currents on the surface. It's possible for this air current to draw any loose dirt particles into the buffing process, trapping them between the paint and the pad, potentially inflicting swirls and scratches throughout the entire finish.

Ample
An amount of product that is fully sufficient to meet the needs of the buffing process.

Arm Speed
How fast or slow you move the polisher over the paint.

B

Backing Plate
An interface that attaches to the free floating spindle bearing assembly by using a 5/16" arbor. The other side has hook material for attaching buffing pads as a part of a hook and loop pad attachment system.

Basecoat/Clearcoat
A two part paint system in which the color coat is sprayed over the body panels and the clear layer is sprayed on top. In most cases, the color coat offers no gloss or shine and is matte in appearance. The clearcoat layer of paint creates the gloss and brings out the full richness of color.

Bodyshop Safe
Products that are bodyshop safe contain no ingredients that could contaminate a fresh paint environment by introducing substances that would cause surface adhesion problems on body panels to be sprayed with fresh paint.

Buffing Cycle
The buffing cycle is the amount of time you are able to work a product before the abrasives have broken down.

Burning-through
To buff so long on a section that enough paint is removed to abrade through the clear layer of paint, exposing the colored layer. When working on a single stage paint, if you burn through the colored coat, you'll expose the primer.

C

Carnauba Car Wax
A product that contains some type of naturally occurring waxy substance intended to protect the paint while creating a clear, glossy finish. Carnauba wax is the most commonly used naturally occurring wax found in car wax formulations. This category of traditional waxes will wear off under normal wear and tear, repeated washings and exposure to the environment. It should be reapplied on a regular basis to maintain a protective coating on the surface of the paint.

Circle Pattern
An alternative way to add working product to the face of the pad. When using the circle pattern, apply your product to the outside edge to help prevent your pad from becoming saturated in the center.

Clay Haze
Marring or scratching left in the paint, typically from the use of an aggressive clay.

Cleaner Wax *also called an AIO*
A cleaner wax or All-In-One (AIO) is a one-step step product formulated using a blend of chemical cleaners and often some type of abrasives, with some type of protection ingredients that will remain on the surface after the cleaning action is finished and the residue is wiped from the paint.

Clear Coat Failure
Clear coat failure is when the clear layer of paint either delaminates from the basecoat and peels off or when it deteriorates by first turning an opaque whitish color. Clear coat failure cannot be fixed by applying any type of compound or polish. The only remedy is to repaint the affected area or the entire car.

Cobweb Swirls *also called Spiderweb*
This term comes from the appearance of swirls in the paint which can look like a spider's cobweb. These swirls have a circular or radial pattern to them when the paint is highlighted with a strong focused point of bright light.

Correction
The process of removing below-surface defects like swirls and scratches, normally using an abrasive medium polish or true compound with a cutting or polishing pad. For shallow defects, a fine polish can also be used.

Glossary

Crater Etching
Usually a round or irregular shaped depression in the paint where some type of liquid or other substance has dwelled long enough to eat into or dissolve enough of the paint coating to leave a void.

Creeping Out
Using a folded microfiber towel, gently begin moving outward from a shiny spot, taking wax off in little bites using small, overlapping circular motions.

◉ D

Dampsander
Any tool that can be used with sanding and finishing discs to dampsand paint to remove orange peel and other surface defects.

DA Polishers (Dual Action)
A generic term for polishers that offer both rotating and oscillating action.

Dampsanding
Dampsanding is simply a variation of wetsanding that uses less water with sanding discs that are designed specifically for this process.

Dry Buffing
There are some products on the market whose manufacturers recommend buffing the product until it dries. As the product dries, you'll tend to see some dusting as the product residue becomes a powder and the paint will have a hard, dry shine to it.

◉ E

Edging
Buffing along an edge before buffing out the rest of the major portions of the panel. By edging a panel first, you don't have to buff near the edges as closely when you switch over to a larger pad to buff out the panel.

◉ F

Fine Cut Polish
A liquid or paste that uses some type of abrasive technology to cut or abrade the paint, but is less aggressive than a true medium polish. Depending upon the abrasive technology and the application method and material, some fine polishes can remove down to #2500 grit sanding marks while still finishing LSP ready. Topcoat hardness is an important factor that affects a fine polish's effectiveness.

Fingermarks
A type of scratch pattern left in the paint by the pressure from your fingertips. Usually caused by pressing down on some type of applicator pad when using a product that's either too aggressive to be used by hand or not safe for clear coat paints.

Forced Rotation Dual Action Polishers
A tool that uses a direct drive gear mechanism to both rotate and oscillate a buffing pad at the same time. There is no slippage with this type of drive mechanism as there is with a free floating spindle bearing assembly.

Free Floating Spindle Bearing Assembly
A unique drive mechanism that will simultaneously rotate and oscillate a buffing pad, enabling the user to safely remove swirls, scratches, oxidation and water spots. If too much downward pressure is applied, or if the tool is held so that more pressure is applied to an edge of the buffing pad, the pad will simply stop spinning, preventing you from burning through the paint or instilling swirls.

◉ G

Glaze or Pure Polish - Non-Abrasive Products
Historically, the term glaze is used to describe a bodyshop safe, hand-applied liquid used to fill-in and mask fine swirls while creating a deep, wet shine on fresh paint.

Grit Guard Inserts
A plastic insert that fits into the bottom of a 5-gallon bucket that traps dirt that comes off your wash mitt. The design includes a plastic grill that dirt and other abrasive particles can fall past to the bottom of the bucket. The grill is suspended about two inches off the bottom by four vanes. These vanes help to trap dirt particles by preventing the water at the bottom from swirling around, thus preventing dirt particles from rising back above the grill where they could potentially get onto your wash mitt.

◉ H

Hard Water Spots
Hard water spots are mineral deposits left behind on the paint surface. These minerals are either dissolved or embodied in water, and when the water evaporates, it leaves the physical minerals behind on the surface.

◉ I

Impermeable
A material that will not allow substances such as fluids or gasses to pass through it.

IPA
Isopropyl alcohol, also called rubbing alcohol. Easily found in most drug stores in varying dilution strengths. Mixed with water to chemically strip paint to remove any fillers or polishing oils so you can more accurately inspect the true results of an abrading process.

◉ J

Jewelling - Definition
The final machine polishing step in which a soft to ultra soft foam finishing pad with no mechanical abrading ability is used with a high

lubricity, ultra fine finishing polish to remove any remaining microscopic surface imperfections. This is performed after the paint has been previously put through a series of machine compounding and polishing procedures to create a near-perfect finish.

K

Kissing the Finish

To kiss the finish, touch the face of the foam pad (with wax on it) onto your panel at an angle, thus depositing only a portion of the wax on the pad to one area of the paint. This technique helps keep the wax spreading out over the paint instead of loading up inside your pad.

L

LSP = Last Step Product

The last product to be applied to and removed from the paint before the final wipe.

LSP Ready

Paint that is ready to be sealed with a car wax, a paint sealant or a coating. This means that all above-surface bonded contaminants and the majority of below-surface defects have been removed, leaving behind a predominantly defect-free surface.

M

Medium Cut Polish

A liquid or paste that uses some type of abrasive technology to cut or abrade the paint, but is less aggressive than a true cutting compound. Depending upon the abrasive technology and the application method and material, some medium polishes can remove down to #2000 grit sanding marks and finish LSP ready. Topcoat hardness is an important factor that affects a medium polish's effectiveness.

Mil

Metric unit of measurement that equals one ten thousandth of a millimeter. When measuring paint coatings, mils or microns are the two most commonly used units.

N

Non-Reticulated Foam = Closed Cell Foam

Closed cell foam means the cell wall structure is closed. This makes the foam non-porous. While it's not impossible for air and liquids to flow through it, it is more difficult.

Normal Car Wash

A normal car wash is simply the more traditional method of using a hose and bucket to wash your car. This system works well, but it also uses a lot of water and in some geographical areas, this may not be allowed.

O

OEM = Original Equipment Manufacturer

While the word "equipment" can make you think of a part or component, it can also refer to the manufacturer of an entire vehicle.

Outgassing

The process in which solvents and other additives work their way out of the paint to the surface where they can evaporate.

Oxidation

Oxidation is the loss of at least one electron when two or more substances interact. When your car's paint is exposed to oxygen and moisture, the oxygen molecules interact with the paint resin, causing free radicals to be eliminated.

P

Paint Cleaner

A liquid, paste or cream that relies primarily on chemical cleaning

agents to remove any light topical contamination or surface impurities to restore a clean, smooth surface. Used as part of a process to prepare a painted finish for application of a wax, paint sealant or coating. Paint cleaners are for very light cleaning and are not normally intended to be used like an abrasive polish to remove below-surface defects.

Paint Coatings

Generally defined as any paint protection product that contains man-made or synthetic protection ingredients that are intended to permanently bond to the paint to provide a barrier-coating of protection and create a clear, high gloss finish. The products available in this category are considered permanent coatings, because like your car's paint, they cannot be removed unless you purposefully remove or neglect them.

Paint System

A paint system refers to both a brand and type of paint. There are different manufacturers for automotive paints, each with their own proprietary formulas for their paint lines.

Panel

Generally defined as a complete component of the car body.

Permeable

A material that can be penetrated, usually by liquids as it applies to car detailing.

pH

A measurement of the acidity or alkalinity of a solution in a range of 0 to 14, with the number 7 representing a neutral rating. The numbers 8 to 14 represent increasing alkalinity and numbers 0 to 6 represent decreasing acidity.

Pre-Wax Cleaner

Similar or the same as a paint cleaner. Most pre-wax cleaners are

Glossary

complimentary products in that they are part of a specific brand's system in which the pre-wax cleaner is matched to a wax or paint sealant. There's a chemical synergistic compatibility to ensure maximum performance between products that might not be achieved using products from outside the brand.

Priming A Pad

Applying, spreading and working product into the face of a buffing pad. Priming the pad ensures 100% of the face of the pad is loaded with abrasives and/or cleaning agents so that you maximize abrading and cleaning ability.

⊙⊙ R

Reticulated Foam = Open Cell Foam

Open cell foam means the cell wall structure is open, meaning the membranes are missing, leaving only the framework in place. This allows liquids and gasses to pass through easily.

RIDS = Random Isolated Deeper Scratches

This type of scratch comes from normal wear and tear. RIDS are like tracers in that they are deeper scratches that show up after the shallow scratches have been removed through a machine or hand buffing process, usually with a compound or paint cleaner. After the shallow swirls and scratches have been removed, any deeper scratches that remain will now show up like a sore thumb to your eyes because there are no longer thousands of lighter, more shallow scratches camouflaging them.

Road Grime

Usually a film on the outside of the car that is a mixture of oils and dirt.

Rotary Buffer

A tool that uses a direct drive gear mechanism to rotate a buffing pad in a single circular direction.

⊙⊙ S

Sacrificial Barrier Coating

The primary purpose of a wax or sealant is to act as a sacrificial barrier coating over the surface of your car's paint. Any time anything comes into contact with your car's paint, before it can cause any damage to the paint it first has to get past the layer of wax or paint sealant. When your car's paint is under attack, the layer of wax or paint sealant sacrifices itself.

Seal

To coat over a painted surface using a car wax, paint sealant or coating with the intended purpose of creating a uniform protective sacrificial barrier-coating.

Section

A section is a portion of a panel. For example, when using a DA Polisher to buff out the hood on a medium size passenger car, you'll usually slice the hood up into 4 to 6 sections.

Section Pass

A section pass is when you move the polisher back and forth with enough single overlapping passes to cover the entire section one time.

Single Pass

A single pass is when you move the polisher from one side of the section you're buffing to the other.

Single Stage Paint

Paint with pigment mixed into it that is used for a final top coat. Most single stage paints were used before the 1980s and were either a lacquer or an enamel type paint. They will tend to oxidize easily if not regularly maintained with polishing and waxing. They tend to be easier to remove swirls and scratches out of because they tend to be softer than basecoat/clearcoat paints.

Splatter Dots

Little dots of product sprayed

outward. Usually caused by accidently lifting a pad wet with product from the surface of a panel before allowing the pad to stop spinning.

Spray Detailer

A high lubricity spray and wipe product used for restoring shine and gloss while safely removing light dust, fingerprints and smudges.

Synergistic Chemical Compatibility = System Approach

Using all the polishing products from a single manufacturer to complete the entire buffing process.

Synthetic Paint Sealant

A product that contains some type of man-made or synthetic protection ingredients to protect the paint while creating a clear, glossy finish.

Swath

The width and length of a single wipe over the surface of paint with your hand on a folded microfiber towel, usually while you're wiping off a coat of wax or paint sealant.

Swirls

Scratches that appear to be circular when exposed or highlighted by a bright source of light.

⊙⊙ T

Tape Line

A tape line is used when inspecting the results of a buffing process. By only working on one side of the tape line, you make it easy to detect changes in before and after condition of the paint.

Terry Cloth

Cotton toweling that uses a nap or loop of cotton for the design of the weave.

Test Spot

Testing pads, products and tools to one small area to establish a proven buffing procedure before detailing

Mike Phillips' - The Art of Detailing

the entire vehicle.

Topcoat Hardness
A measure of how hard or soft the top layer of paint is as it relates to removing defects. Topcoat hardness is an unknown variable, and an important reason to do a test spot before buffing out any car.

Topping
The practice of applying a different type of wax or paint sealant over an initial application of a wax or paint sealant to either create a thicker and more durable layer of protection or to create a deep, wet-look shine.

Tracers
Tracers are deeper scratches left by the hand sanding process, usually in straight lines because most people move their hand in a back and forth motion when wet sanding. Tracers show up after the paint is compounded and all shallow scratches have been removed. Remaining in the paint are the deeper sanding marks and these are called tracers.

U

Ultra Fine Cut Polish
A liquid or paste that uses some type of abrasive technology to cut or abrade the paint, but is less aggressive than a true fine polish. Depending upon the abrasive technology and the application method and material, some ultra fine polishes can remove down to #2500 grit sanding marks while still finishing out LSP ready. Topcoat hardness is an important factor that affects an ultra fine polish's effectiveness.

UMR = Uniform Material Removal
Buffing a panel, section by section in a methodical and controlled manner, to remove a uniform amount of material equally from the surface.

W

Water Insoluble
Not able to be broken down or liquefied easily using water. Waxes and paint sealants, by their nature, are insoluble.

Water Soluble
Able to be broken down or liquefied using water. Most compounds and polishes are water soluble and are easy to wash from the car, microfiber towels and from buffing pads.

Water Spots - Type I
These are mineral deposits, or what people commonly call hard water spots. They can be the remains of minerals suspended in city water or well water that are left behind after the water evaporates from the finish. This can happen if hard water is allowed to dry on paint, whether it is from sprinkler water, acid rain, or other water sources.

Water Spots - Type II
These are actual etchings or craters in paint, caused by something corrosive in a water source landing on the finish without being removed before etching occured.

Water Spots - Type III
These are spots that look dull and faded and are found primarily on single stage paints. They are usually found after a water source pools on the paint and is allowed to dwell on the surface.

Waterless Car Wash
A waterless car wash is a high lubricity pre-mixed spray detailer used to heavily saturate a panel. The panel is then carefully wiped to remove any dirt or road grime.

Wet Buffing Technique
Maintaining a wet film of product on the surface while the pad is in contact with the paint.

Working Product
Product that is applied to the face of a foam buffing pad that has already been primed.

Glossary

Notes:

Glossary

Notes:

Glossary

Notes: